# OLD DOMINION UNIVERSITY MEN'S BASKETBALL

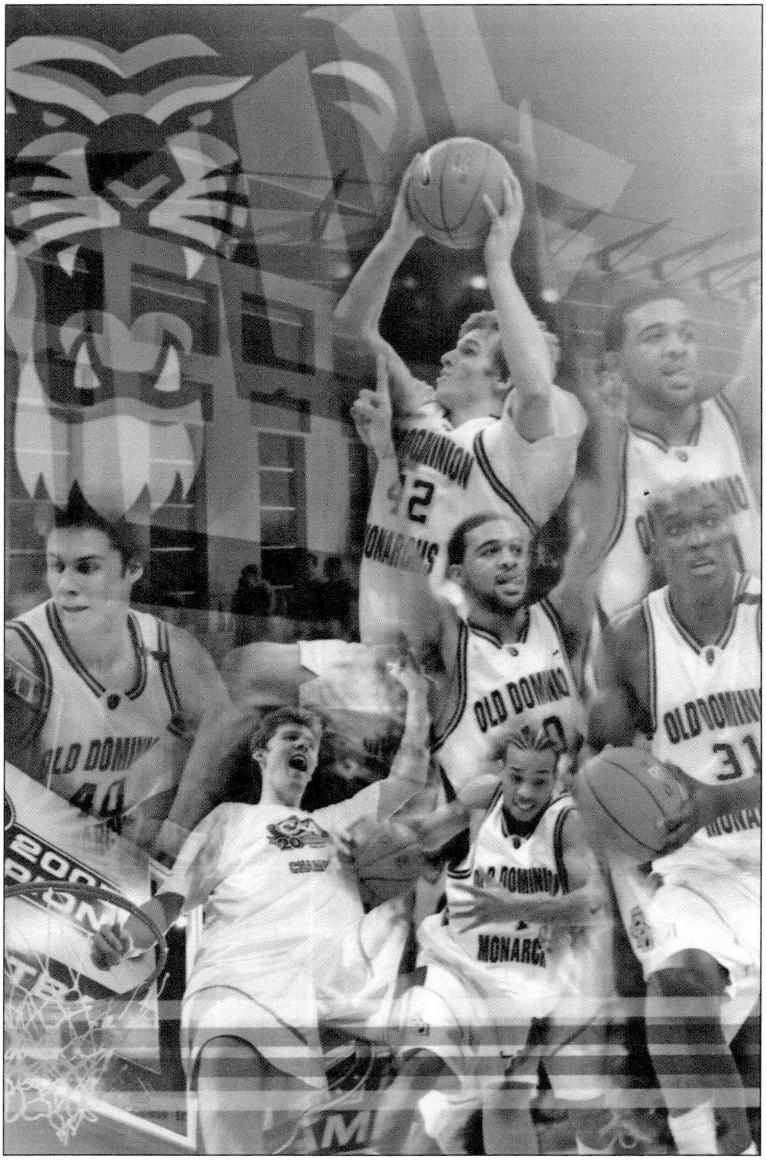

**MONARCH SENIORS 2006–2007:** This collage from the front of the *2006 Old Dominion University Men's Basketball Media Guide* shows Old Dominion Monarch seniors for the 2006–2007 season. Included in the image are Alex Loughton, 2006; Isaiah Hunter, 2006; Drew Williamson, 2007; Arnaud Dahi, 2007; and Valdas Vasylius, 2007. (ODU Archives.)

**FRONT COVER:** In this image, Monarch center Mark West, ODU All-American, dunks a ball with authority. From 1979–1983, this 6-foot-10-inch center scored 1,308 points, collected 1,113 rebounds, and had 446 blocks. (ODU Archives.)
**COVER BACKGROUND:** Pictured is the 1975 NCAA Division II National Championship team.
**BACK COVER:** Pictured is the Ted Constant Convocation Center at Old Dominion University. This multimillion dollar facility opened its doors in 2002. (ODU Archives.)

# OLD DOMINION UNIVERSITY MEN'S BASKETBALL

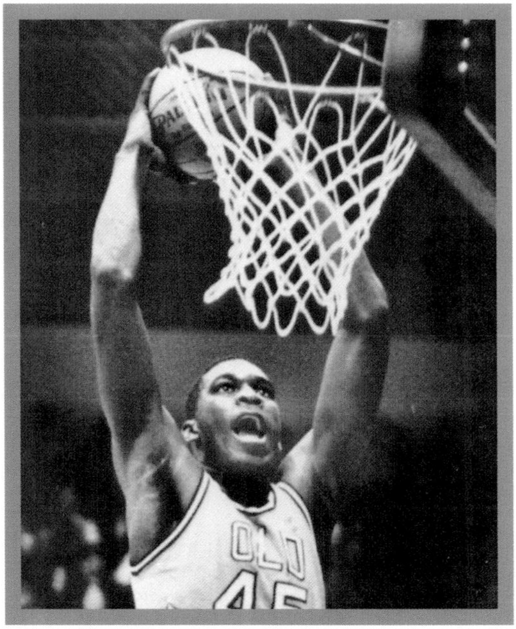

*Thomas R. Garrett and Clay Shampoe*
*With an introduction by Paul Webb*

ARCADIA
PUBLISHING

ISBN 978-0-7385-4292-X

Published by Arcadia Publishing
Charleston, South Carolina

Printed in the United States of America

Library of Congress Catalog Card Number: 2007923584

For all general information contact Arcadia Publishing at:
Telephone 843-853-2070
Fax 843-853-0044
E-mail sales@arcadiapublishing.com
For customer service and orders:
Toll-Free 1-888-313-2665

Visit us on the Internet at www.arcadiapublishing.com

**Photographs Legend**

**ODU Archives:** From the archives of Old Dominion University, Perry Library, and the Old Dominion University, Office of Athletic Public Relations.

**VP:** From the archives of the *Virginian-Pilot* Sports Department.

**CSTG:** From the personal collection of Clay Shampoe and Thomas R. Garrett.

All other photographs individually credited.

# CONTENTS

# ACKNOWLEDGMENTS

The authors of this book wish to thank the many individuals who provided the information and inspiration to make *Old Dominion University Men's Basketball* possible. If we overlooked anyone who was supportive during the writing of this book, we offer our thanks here and now.

The following university personnel went above and beyond in assisting with this book: Dr. Jim Jarrett, director of athletics; Debbie White, associate athletic director; Carol Hudson Jr., sports information director; Blaine Taylor, head basketball coach; Mark Benson, intercollegiate foundation; Ed Fraim, director of athletic development; Jeff Wilson, NCAA compliance coordinator; Dr. Peter Stewart, professor emeritus of history; Susan Catlett, former special collections coordinator; Harry "Mel" Frizzel III, special collections; and Mona Farrow, microforms services.

Tina Price, Old Dominion's director of athletic publications, deserves special thanks for always being available. Whenever we requested another image or fact, Tina always came through with a smile.

We were very fortunate to have a number of former Monarch greats to assist with images or their knowledge. From the "Division" years were Ed Kilgore, Bill Roughton, Joe Agee, Montgomery Knight, Leo Anthony, Harry Knickerbocker, and Marion Carroll. From the Monarch years were Jeff Fuhrmann, and coaches Marion Carroll and Eddie Webb. Members of the Monarch family, including Sugie Jarrett, daughter of Tommy Scott, the school's first coach, as well as former cheerleader Jerry Seelinger Knight also gave assistance. We want to express our sincere thanks to former Monarch coach Paul Webb for writing the foreword to this book. A true gentleman, coach Webb brought many memorable moments to Monarch fans during his 10 years and 196 wins.

As in our previous books about sports in the Hampton Roads area, we again relied on the assistance of Chic Riebel, sports editor of the *Virginian-Pilot* and Al Spradlin, who served as our photographic consultant for this project.

It's important to have someone who has an eye for editing and making critical suggestions. It's good when that person is close friend and longtime Monarchs fan Dr. Louis Martinette. We are also particularly grateful to have family and friends who have been extremely supportive during the writing of this book. Thanks to John James, Frank Borum, John Borum, Earl Chinn, Jim Winslow, John Hoofnagle, Larry Johnson, Ron Crevidi, Dale Ryder, Billy Hasty, and Ray Carson.

Finally we would like to thank our immediate families. Tom would like to give thanks to his wife, Carol; his father, Maynard; and son Andrew for their support and encouragement during this project. Clay wishes to thank his wife, Deborah, for her continued support in the completion of this project.

# FOREWORD

As fans sit in the Ted Constant Center watching Old Dominion battle opponents, it is a good bet that few know of the humble beginnings of basketball at the school. Authors Tom Garrett and Clay Shampoe have provided the readers of *Old Dominion University Men's Basketball* the unique opportunity to relive more than 75 years of Monarch basketball history.

My association and familiarity with the basketball program goes back to 1956. I was the head basketball coach at Randolph-Macon College, and each year we would play Bud Metheny's, Norfolk Division of William and Mary, cagers. Bud was a very knowledgeable coach, and from 1956 to 1965, we had some very spirited contests. I remember playing in Norfolk's gymnasium with fans sitting so close to the action that it seemed we played five on seven every time we took the court! I will never forget the shower in the locker room downstairs—one stall for the entire team to use. It took quite a while for our team to shower and dress.

When Sonny Allen came to Old Dominion in 1965, the program really began to take off. He ran a great fast break and wisely recruited speedy players to fit his game plan. Sonny culminated his career at Old Dominion by winning the Division II National Championship in 1975 and was named the Division II National Coach of the Year.

At the end of that season, Sonny left for Southern Methodist University. That is when I went from being foe to friend, taking over Sonny's reins in July 1975. In my inaugural season, we won the South Atlantic Regional and advanced to the Division II final four, only to lose to Puget Sound, the eventual national champions.

The following year we moved up to Division I, and as a member of the Eastern Collegiate Athletic Conference (ECAC), the Monarchs posted an impressive record of 25-4. We were fortunate to win 22 games in a row, still a Virginia state record. During the postseason, we defeated Georgetown in Washington to win the ECAC Southern Division Championship and narrowly lost to Syracuse for the ECAC Championship. Over the next nine seasons, ODU captured five conference championships with Ronnie Valentine, Ronnie McAdoo, Mark West, Kenny Gattison, and others contributing to the program's success.

After 34 years of prep and collegiate coaching, I decided that it was time to retire, which I did following the 1984–1985 season. Since my retirement, I am proud to see that ODU continues to develop top-notch student athletes, while fostering sportsmanship, integrity, and success on and off the court. My successors, Tom Young, Oliver Purnell, Jeff Capel, and Blaine Taylor, all have been outstanding leaders that have embraced the legacy developed over the years by such ODU legends as Tommy Scott, Bud Metheny, and Sonny Allen. I still enjoy going to the games at "The Ted" and seeing old friends, fans, and former players. It is without question that Old Dominion's basketball future looks brighter than ever. Go Monarchs!

—Coach Paul Webb
ODU, 1975–1985

# INTRODUCTION

Sitting in the new Ted Constant Center watching the Old Dominion University basketball team battle opponents, it is a good bet that few fans know of the humble beginnings of basketball at the school over 75 years ago. As a reader of Arcadia Publishing's Images of Sports: *Old Dominion University Men's Basketball*, you will get to see classic images of Monarch basketball from the archives of the special collections of Old Dominion University's Perry Library, as well as the Old Dominion University Athletic Department. Additional images came from the archives of the authors, the *Virginian-Pilot*, former players, and fans.

You will travel back to the early days of the basketball program of 1930, when 206 students enrolled in what then was known as the Norfolk Division of the College of William and Mary. You will view classic images that reflect the evolution of the basketball program over the past 75 years, from a school born during the Great Depression to today's vibrant university with more than 26,000 students and a multimillion-dollar facility for its basketball program.

Early images from 1930 to the early 1960s will include the players, teams, and games of longtime coaches Tommy Scott and Bud Metheny, as well as of some coaches who may not be as easily recognized, such as Stirnweiss, Chandler, Rubin, and Callahan. Special attention will be given to the career of Leo Anthony, the school's first All-American.

Through photographs, you will be taken through 42 years of a program that emerged from a school affiliated with William and Mary to an independent school known first as Old Dominion College and several years later as Old Dominion University. You will meet some of the Monarchs greatest teams under Coaches Sonny Allen, Paul Webb, Tom Young, Oliver Purnell, Jeff Capel, and Blaine Taylor. You will also meet ODU's 19 All-Americans, including Dave Twardzik, Joel Copeland, Wilson Washington, Mark West, Chris Gatling, and the school's newest All-American, Alex Loughton.

You will relive the Monarchs' most notable wins against teams such as DePaul, Virginia, Syracuse, Alabama-Birmingham, Western Kentucky, Alabama, Auburn, Baylor, Dayton, Georgetown, South Carolina, and Maryland, to name just a few.

Experience and learn of the lead-up to an NCAA National Division II Championship in 1975, a second-place finish in the 1971 NCAA Division II Championship, and 13 conference championships. Join the excitement of March Madness as the Monarchs and their fans are rewarded with bids to nine NCAA Division I Tournaments, including wins over West Virginia and a triple-overtime victory over third-seeded Villanova. Experience the enthusiasm of over 18 games in the National Invitation Tournament, including wins against Clemson, Seton Hall, Virginia Commonwealth, Colorado, Manhattan, and Hofstra. Travel to New York City as the Monarchs meet Michigan in the 2006–2007 final four of the NIT at Madison Square Garden.

We invite you to sit back and enjoy the rich narrative and photographic history of Old Dominion men's basketball.

# 1

# Humble Beginnings

## The Tommy Scott Years 1930–1940

On September 12, 1930, Norfolk relinquished its ignominious title of America's most populous city without an institute of higher education. On that late summer day, the doors to the abandoned Larchmont School opened, and 206 students registered for the first classes offered at the newly chartered Norfolk Division of the College of William and Mary. Midway through the first semester, notices appeared in the hallways announcing tryouts for the school's basketball squad under the leadership of Athletic Director Tommy Scott, a local sports legend at nearby Maury High and Virginia Military Institute. With only a limited number of qualified staff to lead the students in athletic competition, Scott had accepted the overwhelming task of coaching football, basketball, baseball, and track while teaching a number of math courses as well.

The Norfolk Division squad was christened the "Braves," and coach Scott hastily pieced together a schedule composed of willing local high-school squads and college-freshman teams for the 1930–1931 basketball season. As the first game of the season arrived with the team's uniforms still on order, the Norfolk cagers donned their rag-tag practice togs and defeated South Norfolk High on their home court at Blair Middle School. By the end of their inaugural campaign, the Braves posted a respectable 11-10 record as captain Harry Hamburger led the team in scoring with 141 points.

The following year found Scott's Braves competing against a higher caliber of opponents, including Campbell College and East Carolina. The high-scoring Harry Hamburger returned with Rufus Tonelson replacing him as team captain. The Braves struggled through the initial portion of the season but received a much needed boost when Roger Bowen transferred from Virginia Tech and took over the role of leading scorer for the team. Despite the addition of Bowen and steady play by Sam Phillips, Hack Brown, and Syd Sacks, the Braves ended the campaign with a losing record.

The following season, coach Scott had several of his veterans return, joined by newcomer Junie Mills. The schedule was considered light in that it included no college teams other than the parent school's freshman squad from Williamsburg. Mills developed into the team's most proficient scorer and led the Braves to a record of 8-6.

Coach Scott named returning veteran Junie Mills team captain for the 1933–1934 campaign. A handful of talented rookies including All-State prepster Vincent McCloud of Portlock High and Maury teammates Freddie Edmonds and Dick Dozier solidified Scott's squad. The Norfolk collegians were putting together their most impressive season to date when starter McCloud was unexpectedly lost to the squad due to academic ineligibility. Despite the setback, Scott filled the unexpected vacancy from his bench and went on to post a record of 10 wins against only 4 losses.

Over the next two seasons, the Braves continued to show an abundance of verve and talent on the hard court with changes taking place on campus as the school opened its new Administrative Building and gymnasium. With "Fast" Freddie Edmonds serving as captain, the cagers put together consecutive winning seasons in 1934–1935 and the following year. Coach Scott counted on the abilities of Woody Barnes, Dick Dozier, Bumpy Valentine, and Jimmy George to consistently put the ball in the basket and was not disappointed in their production.

The 1936–1937 season saw the elimination of high school teams from the schedule and the record at the end of the season, with eight wins and eight defeats, showed that the caliber of opponent had significantly improved. Barnes returned as captain and led the Braves to an exciting double-overtime victory in the season opener against the Norfolk Athletic Club.

Coach Scott looked optimistically toward the new campaign as six veterans formed the nucleus of 1937–1938 squad. Despite losing top-scorer Woody Barnes after the first contest of the season, Scott altered his strategy and crafted the offense around center Joe Wood. The 6-foot-4-inch pivot man would go on to captain the squad and lead the Braves in scoring. As the final buzzer sounded on the 1937–1938 season, coach Scott had guided the Braves to their best ever campaign by posting a record of 15-4.

For the final two seasons of the decade, the Braves continued to add more challenging opponents to their schedule. Scott's "quints" were again led by Joe Wood and a slew of gifted Maury grads, including Cecil Griffin, Jimmy Macon, Jack Callahan, and Pete Dozier. Despite its stable of talented players, the Braves posted back-to-back disappointing seasons with records of 8-14 and 4-16.

As the 1940s began, longtime coach Tommy Scott announced he was ready to step down after steering the Braves to a total of 92 victories during his tenure. Scott established himself as the founding father of athletics at the school and was responsible for initiating a number of sports programs that ignited the excitement and support of the student body and the surrounding Norfolk community. The talented cagers under his instruction set the standard and provided the groundwork for future success that was destined for the basketball program at the Norfolk school. When the roll call sounded for the Old Dominion University Sports Hall of Fame, coach Tommy Scott and several of his elite players, including Rufus Tonelson, Freddie Edmonds, Cecil Griffin, Woody Barnes, Dick Dozier, and Everett Tolson, accepted accolades with the humility, respect, and sportsmanship that continues to radiate throughout the ODU athletic program.

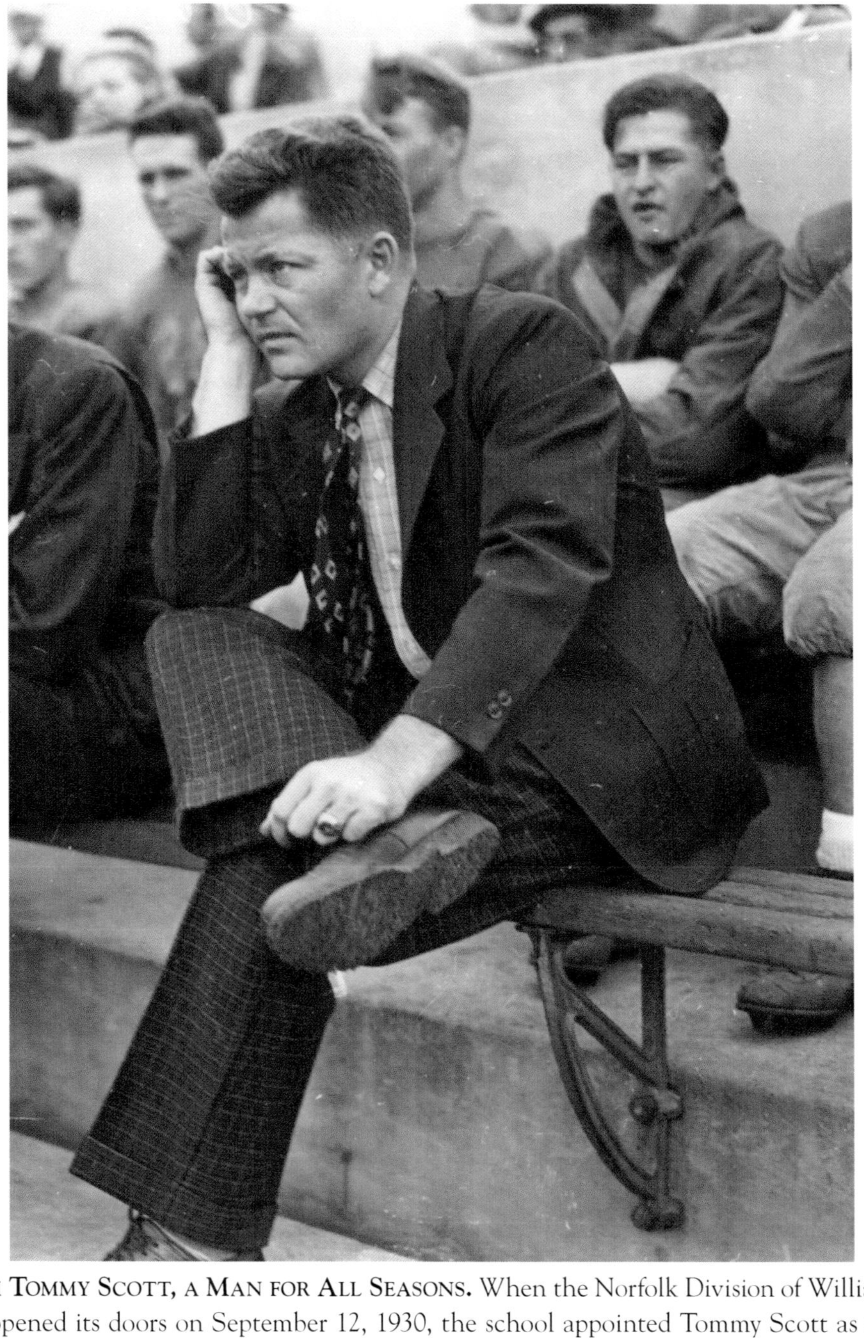

**COACH TOMMY SCOTT, A MAN FOR ALL SEASONS.** When the Norfolk Division of William and Mary opened its doors on September 12, 1930, the school appointed Tommy Scott as its first athletic director. Scott, a multitalented sports star at Maury High and later Virginia Military Institute, was responsible for coaching Norfolk's first football, basketball, baseball, and track teams. With little resources and no facilities to speak of, Scott led his young student-athletes by guidance and example and laid the groundwork for future Old Dominion University athletic programs. The Tommy Scott–era of athletics at the Norfolk school encompassed the entire decade of the 1930s. (CSTG.)

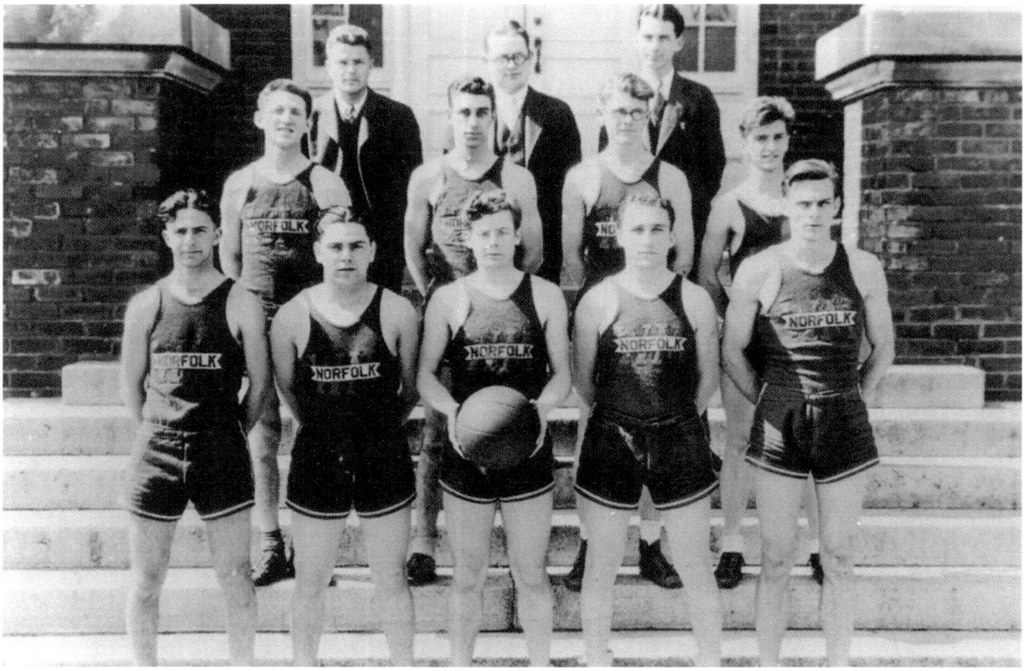


**First Cager Team for the Norfolk Division of William and Mary.** This classic image shows the inaugural basketball team under the leadership of coach Tommy Scott posing for the photographer on the steps of the new college, the former Larchmont School in Norfolk. The cagers were proudly displaying their new green uniforms trimmed in silver and orange with the Norfolk Division logo emblazoned on the front. (ODU Archives.)

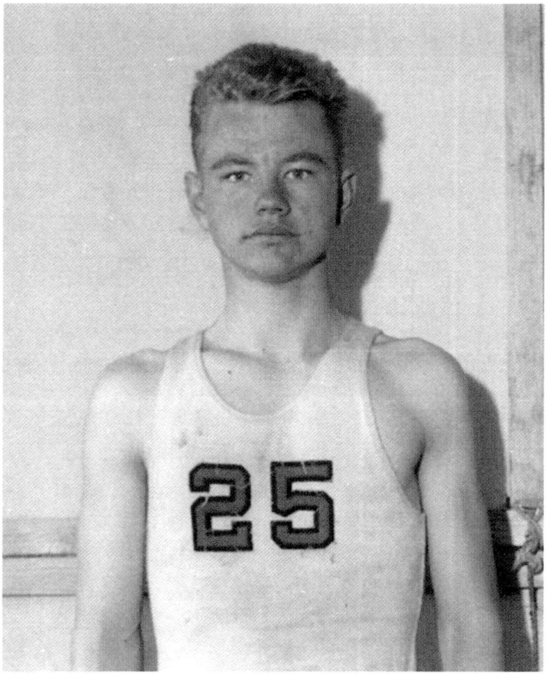


**Wilson "Dick" Dozier.** From 1933 to 1936, there were few athletes at the Norfolk Division of William and Mary more outstanding than Dick Dozier. The small-framed, energetic blonde quarterbacked the 1935 school football team and excelled on the diamond and the hard court for the Braves. Following his graduation from William and Mary, Dozier made the ultimate sacrifice when he was killed in action during World War II. (CSTG.)

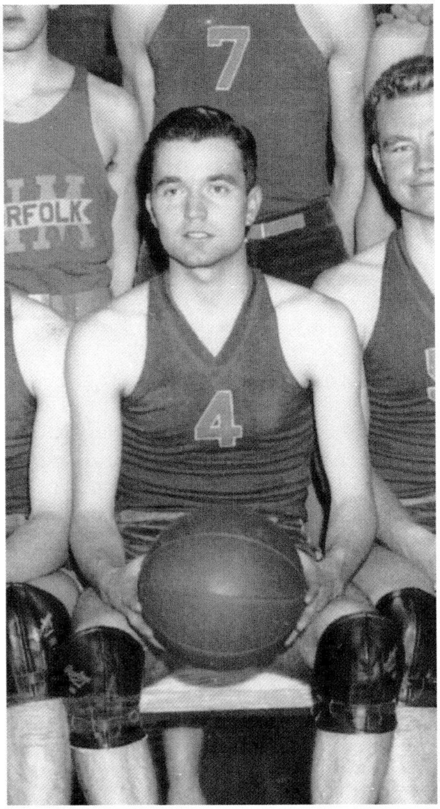


**"FAST" FREDDIE EDMONDS.** During the early 1930s, Freddie Edmonds ruled the hard court at the Norfolk Division of William and Mary. In 1932, the flashy guard was named leading scorer for the Maury High cagers and continued his offensive prowess in his first year with the Braves during the 1933–1934 campaign. An inspirational team leader, "Fast" Freddie led the Norfolk Division to back-to-back winning campaigns. (ODU Archives.)

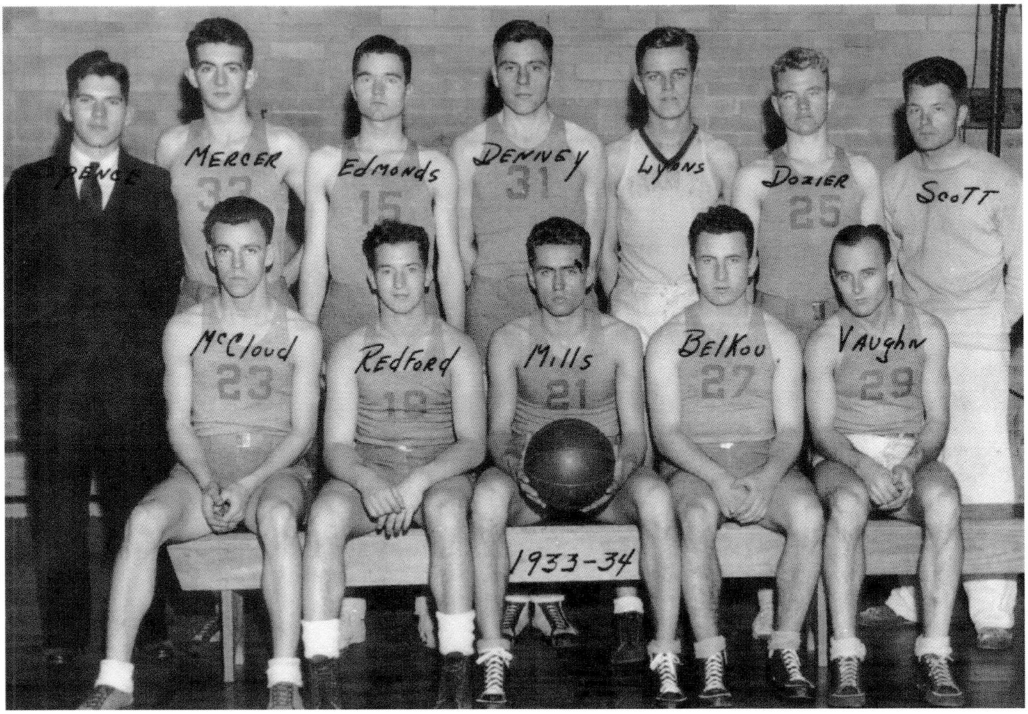


**NORFOLK DIVISION BASKETBALL TEAM, 1933–1934.** In coach Scott's fourth season at the school, his players put together their most successful campaign to date by posting an impressive 10-4 record. The season's highlights would include the team's first win over the William and Mary freshman squad from Williamsburg and a trouncing of local rival Maury High. Captain and scoring leader Junie Mills sits front and center. (ODU Archives.)

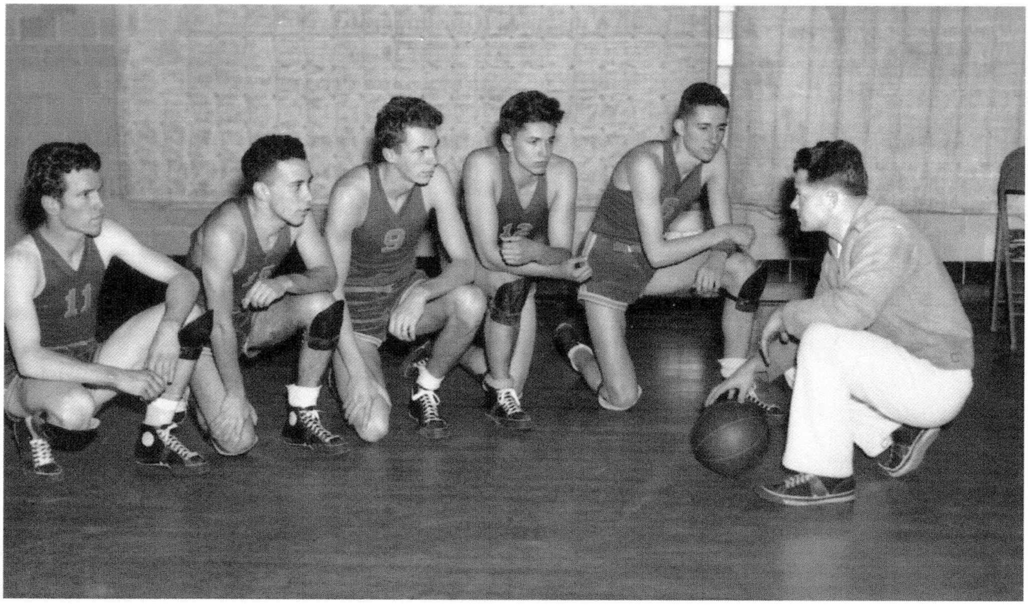

**Pre-Game Pep Talk from the Coach.** This photograph, which appeared in the December 14, 1937, edition of the *Norfolk Ledger-Dispatch*, shows coach Tommy Scott (far right) giving his starting five a word of encouragement before their contest against Bluefield College. From left to right are forward Woody Barnes, guard Sidney Popkin, center Joe Wood, guard Al Bondurant, and forward Larry Cohn. (CSTG.)

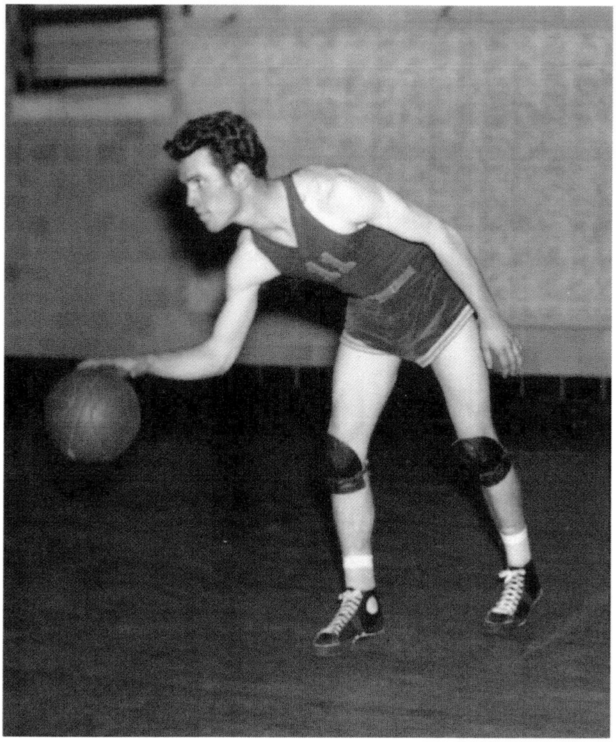

**Woody Barnes.** A talented athlete at South Norfolk High, Woody Barnes continued his athletic prowess as an integral part of Tommy Scott's Norfolk Division cagers. The 6-foot, 155-pound freshman excelled for the Braves and helped post an impressive 10-6 record for the 1935–1936 campaign. The following year, he was named team captain and led the squad in scoring with 153 points and a 9.6 average. (CSTG.)

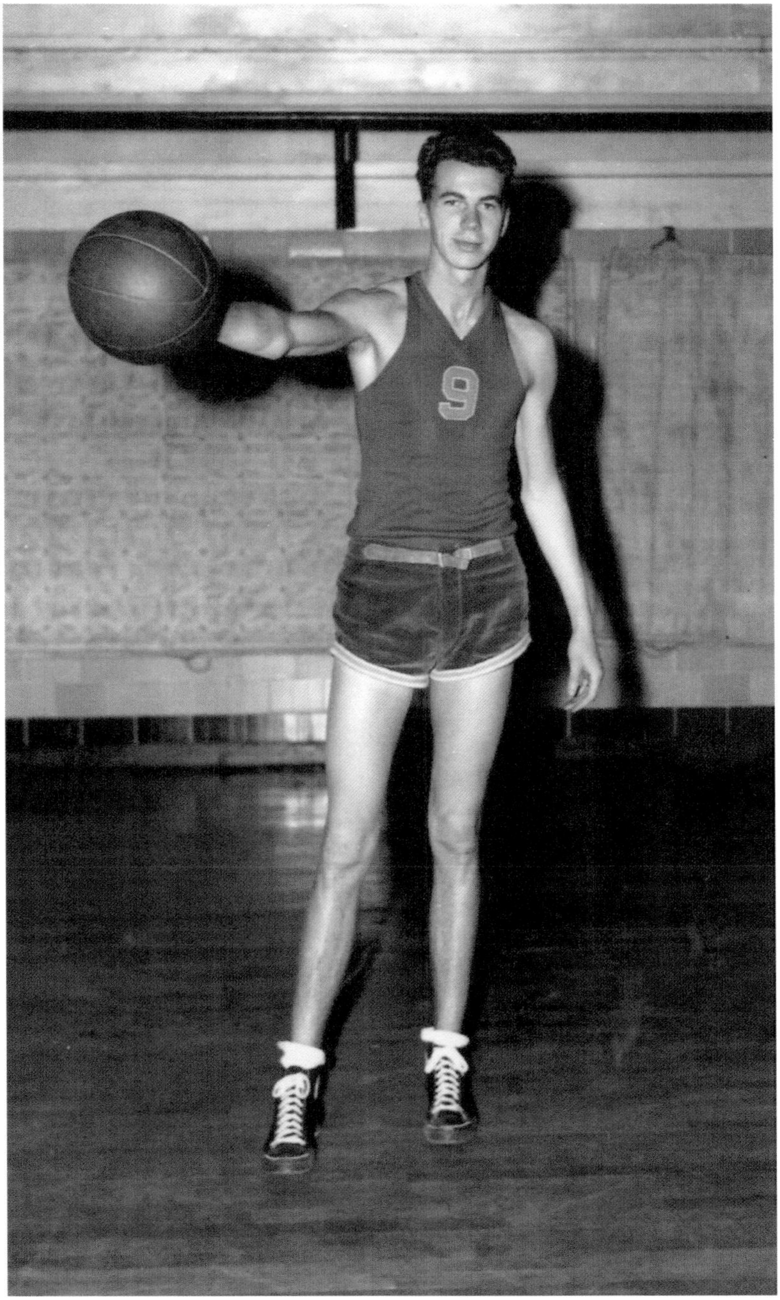

**Joe Wood, Big Man on Campus.** Considered small by today's hard court standards, 6-foot-4-inch Joe Wood was a tower of power for Tommy Scott's Norfolk Division Braves in the late 1930s. The talented center was named team captain for the 1937–1938 season and began the year with a bang by scoring 17 points in the home opener against Bluefield College on December 14, 1937. The following season, he turned in a career high of 22 points in a game and led the team in scoring at least 10 times over the campaign. The rangy cager was lost to the team in the final weeks of the 1938–1939 season due to a lingering illness. (CSTG.)

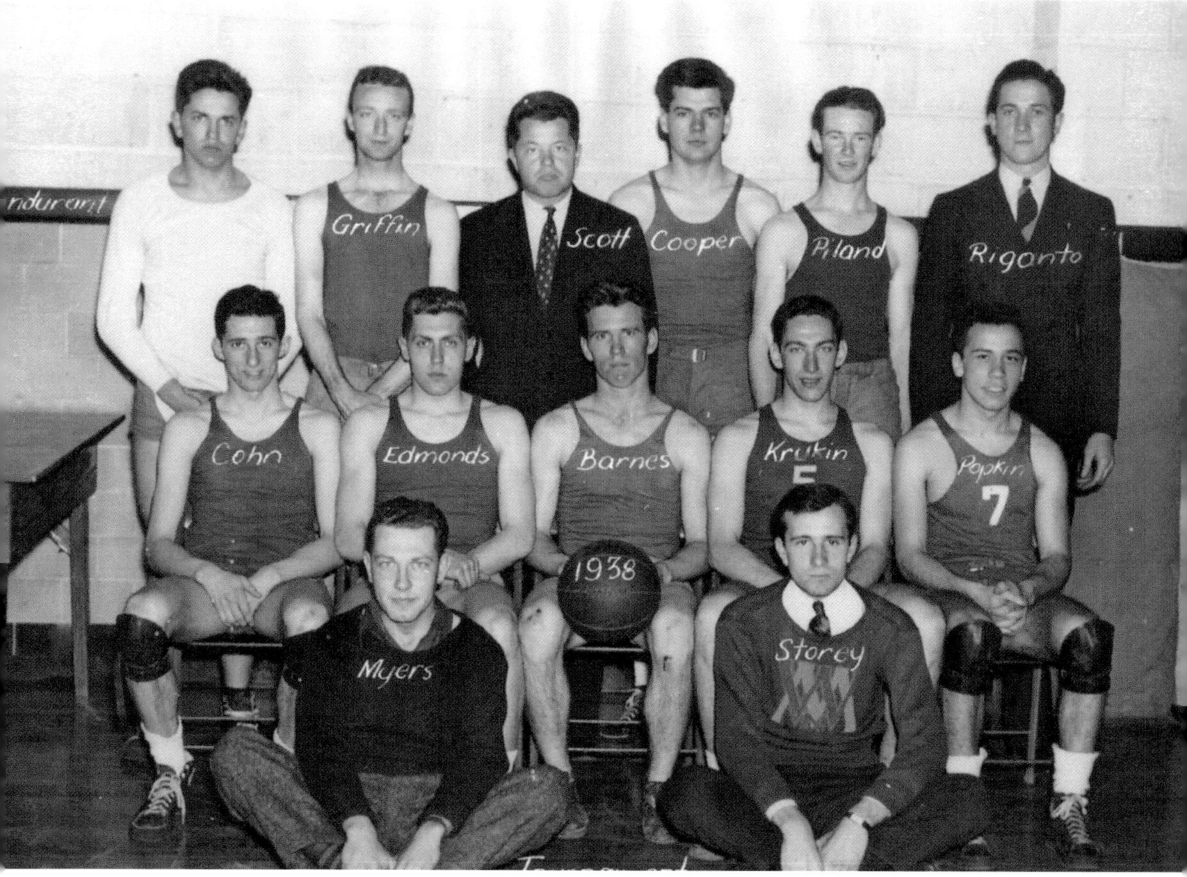


**THE 1938–1939 BRAVES.** Following their most impressive season, Tommy Scott's Braves tumbled to an 8-14 record against a group of tough opponents, including High Point, the defending National Junior College Champions. Newcomer Cecil Griffin, a Maury High alumnus, contributed immediately to the squad with scoring proficiency. This photograph was taken after the squad captured a local YMCA tournament. (ODU Archives.)

# 2

# The War Plays Havoc on the Hard Court 1941–1948

As legendary coach Tommy Scott reluctantly stepped away from his burgeoning plate of athletic responsibilities due to illness, the Norfolk Division of the College of William and Mary would soon find itself in a transition period beset by instability and disappointment on the hard court. During the school's first decade, the athletic department looked no further than the ubiquitous Scott to serve as leader and inspiration to the fledgling institution's sports programs. In 1930, the ever-resourceful coach spearheaded the division's football, basketball, baseball, and track programs with virtually no facilities, little resources, and limited support. By the end of the decade, Tommy Scott had laid the groundwork and foundation for all future major sports at what would become one of the Commonwealth's most successful and respected collegiate athletic programs. When the erstwhile coach packed his gym bag for the final time and cleaned out his desk, the "Scott Era" ended and a new tumultuous and challenging decade began, not only for the school but the community and nation itself.

The new basketball coach that would replace Scott came from an unlikely source. During the summer of 1940, a young All-American halfback known as the "Flying Dutchman" at the University of North Carolina declined an offer to play in the National Football League and instead signed a baseball contract with the New York Yankees. His name was George Stirnweiss and this multitalented athlete began his professional baseball career in Hampton Roads as a member of the Norfolk Tars, a minor league affiliate of the Yankees. As the Tars wrapped up their season, Stirnweiss remained in the area and served as player-coach for the Norfolk Shamrocks of the Dixie League. When the semi-pro gridiron season ended, Stirnweiss found himself idled in Norfolk until baseball beckoned in the spring. With the Norfolk Division still on the lookout to fill the coaching position vacated by Scott, the school offered the leadership role to Stirnweiss, who, despite a lack of experience on the hard court, took the job.

The new coach could count on only three returning lettermen to headline the Norfolk Division Braves for the 1940–1941 season. The Stirnweiss "Five" struggled all year and endured an embarrassing eight-game losing streak and a disappointing overall campaign resulting in a 4-15 record. Despite the scoring prowess of team captain Ed Kilgore, 1941–1942 proved to be even more disheartening for the Norfolk cagers, as they were unable to secure a single victory during the season.

With back-to-back disappointing seasons and baseball's spring training taking priority, Stirnweiss gave his resignation and donned Yankee pinstripes to begin a respectable 10-year major league career. His replacement was Joseph "Scrap" Chandler, an influential leader of William and Mary's athletic program, specializing in track and field. With a new coach at the helm, the 1942–1943 Braves turned it around and ended the season with a 12-10 record. Pompey Virgili, Crenshaw Reed, and team captain Dave Prosser were the most adept of Chandler's cagers in putting the ball through the hoop.

With the war in full swing, manpower to fill the school's athletic rosters was limited as enlistments took America's finest off to battle the Axis powers in Europe and the Pacific. Restrictions on travel and gas rationing limited the number of games scheduled as the majority of opponents were culled from local military establishments. As Chandler struggled to put a team on the court and keep the athletic program alive, the Braves posted three consecutive lackluster seasons, as they garnered a 1-7 record in 1943–1944, a 6-6 record the following year, and went 9-8 in 1945–1946. Key players during the war years proved to be Ted Bacalis, who had just completed his tour of duty, "Skeeter" Contrado, and Julius Rubin.

In 1946, Athletic Director Chandler relinquished his position as head basketball coach at the school to one of his most proficient former players, Julius Rubin. Despite the fact that Rubin had never coached a cager squad before, he became a well-liked leader for the players assembled to start the 1946–1947 season. Behind the scoring of veteran Bacalis, Charlie Kiley, Billy Roughton, and Hodges Viccellio, the Braves posted an impressive 14-8 record for the season and appeared to be shedding the dismal performances of the war years.

After coach Rubin's one-year run with the team, the school announced that another former player, Jack Callahan, would guide the Braves during the upcoming 1947–1948 season. With veteran and team captain Ted Bacalis leading the Braves on the floor, the Norfolk Division put together its best season to date with a 21-8 record, one that would go unequaled until the 1968–1969 campaign under coach Sonny Allen. The Norfolk cagers earned an invitation to play in the Eastern Regional Tournament of the National Small College Athletic Association and entered the postseason with an impressive 10-game winning streak but were eliminated by Bluefield College 81-65 in the tourney.

As the euphoria surrounding the Allied victory dissipated and the country prepared to embark into a new decade, the Norfolk Division of the College of William and Mary and its basketball program mended its wounds and emerged battered but intact. During this era, more than a few special individuals insured that the program's reputation would continue, among them were coach Joseph "Scrap" Chandler and cager star Ted Bacalis. Both of these legends deservedly grace the walls of Old Dominion University Sports Hall of Fame.

**FUTURE YANKEE TAKES THE HELM.** When Tommy Scott relinquished his role as basketball coach, his successor came from the gridiron rather than the hard court. George "Snuffy" Stirnweiss was a former All-American halfback at UNC and a promising ballplayer when he was named Norfolk's new coach in 1940. Following his two seasons with the Braves, Stirnweiss developed into an All-Star major leaguer with the New York Yankees. (CSTG.)

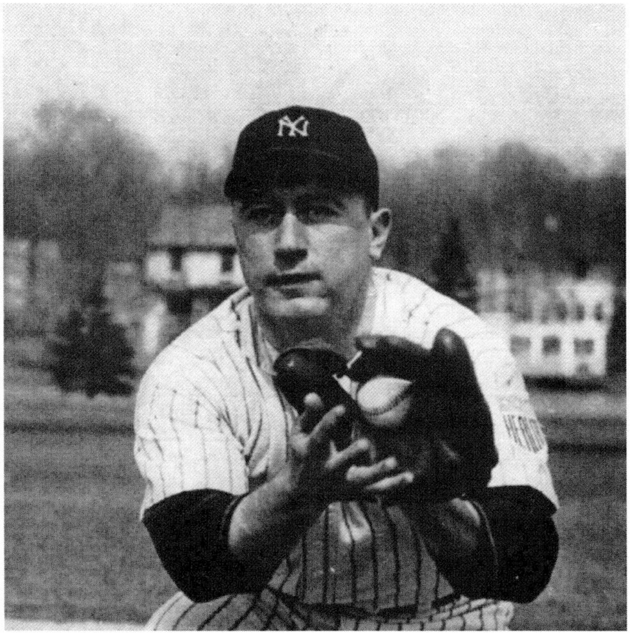

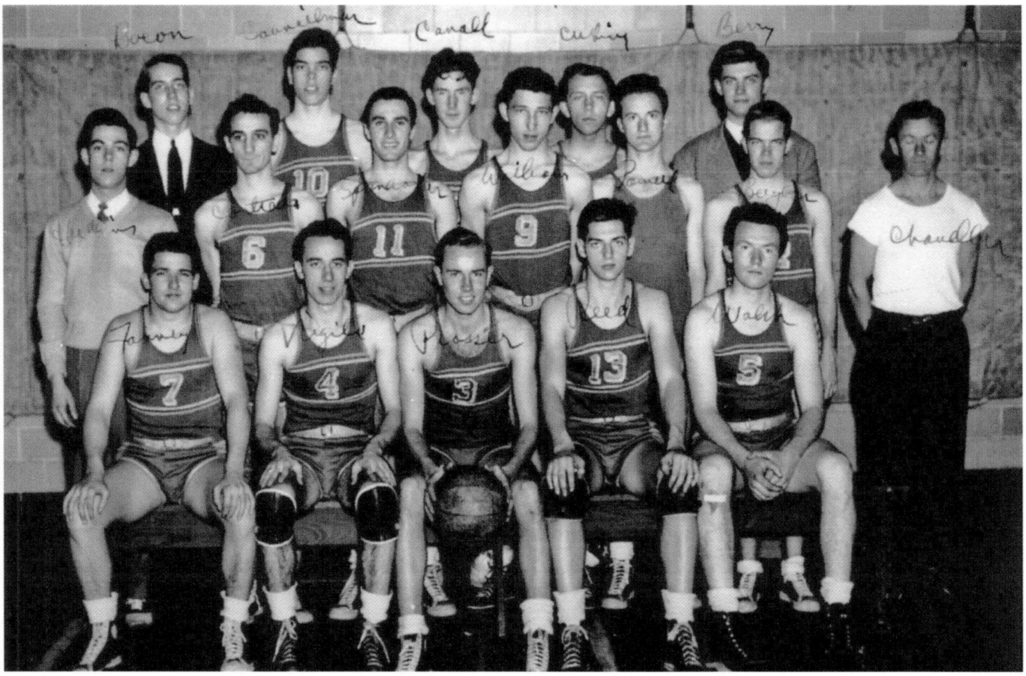

**"SCRAP" CHANDLER'S FIRST TEAM.** Newly appointed coach Joseph "Scrap" Chandler stands far right and strikes an unassuming pose in this photograph alongside his 1942–1943 Norfolk Division cagers. The Braves recovered from their previous winless season and were able to muster 12 victories with much of their success attributed to three talented veterans shown front and center: Pompey Virgili (4), captain Dave Prosser (3), and center Crenshaw Reed (13). (ODU Archives.)

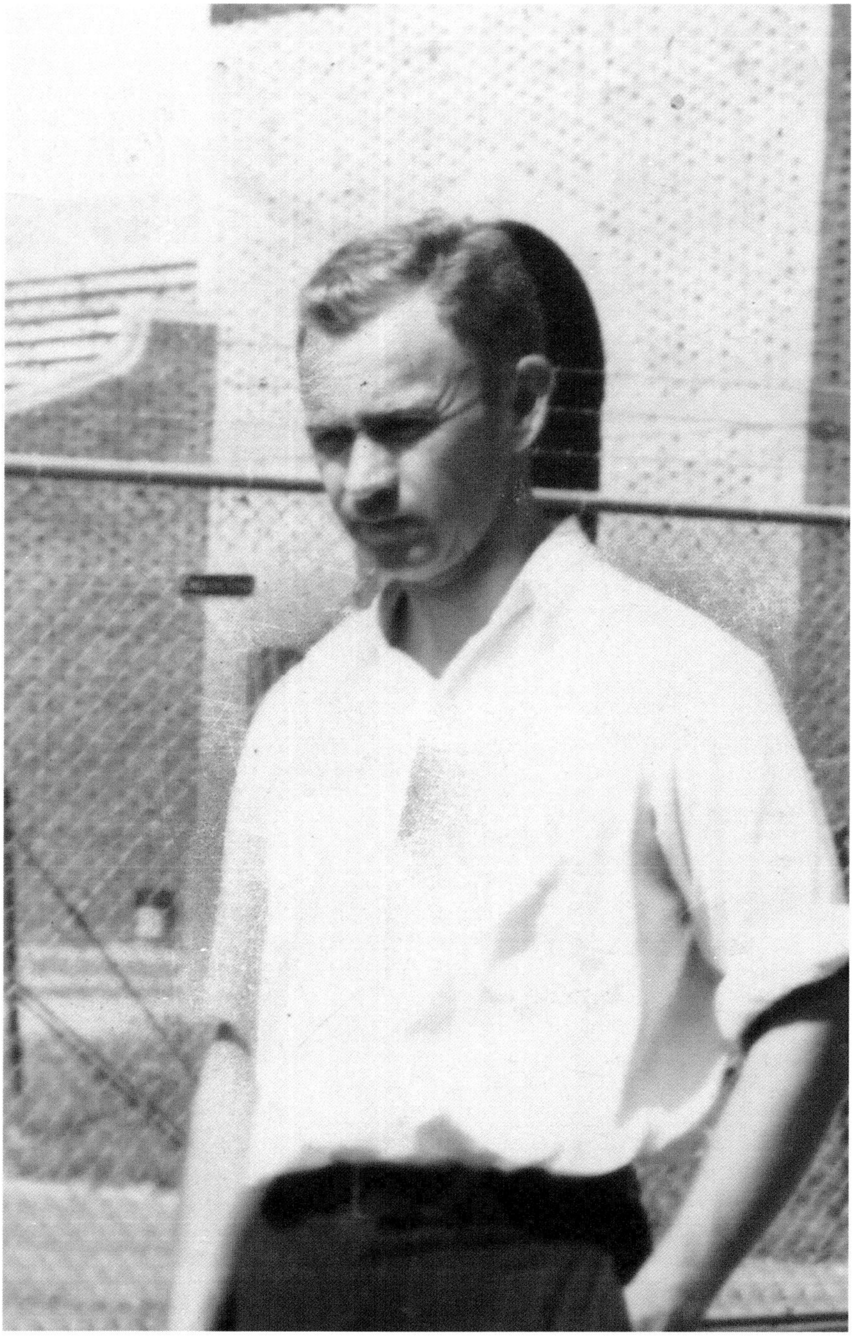

**JOSEPH "SCRAP" CHANDLER.** A brilliant athlete at William and Mary in the early 1920s, Joseph "Scrap" Chandler proved to be a big man on campus despite his small frame. In 1942, Chandler became the Norfolk Division's athletic director and head of the Health and Physical Education Program. He coached baseball, swimming, track, and basketball at various times until his retirement in 1968. Chandler was inducted into the ODU Sports Hall of Fame in 1980. (CSTG.)

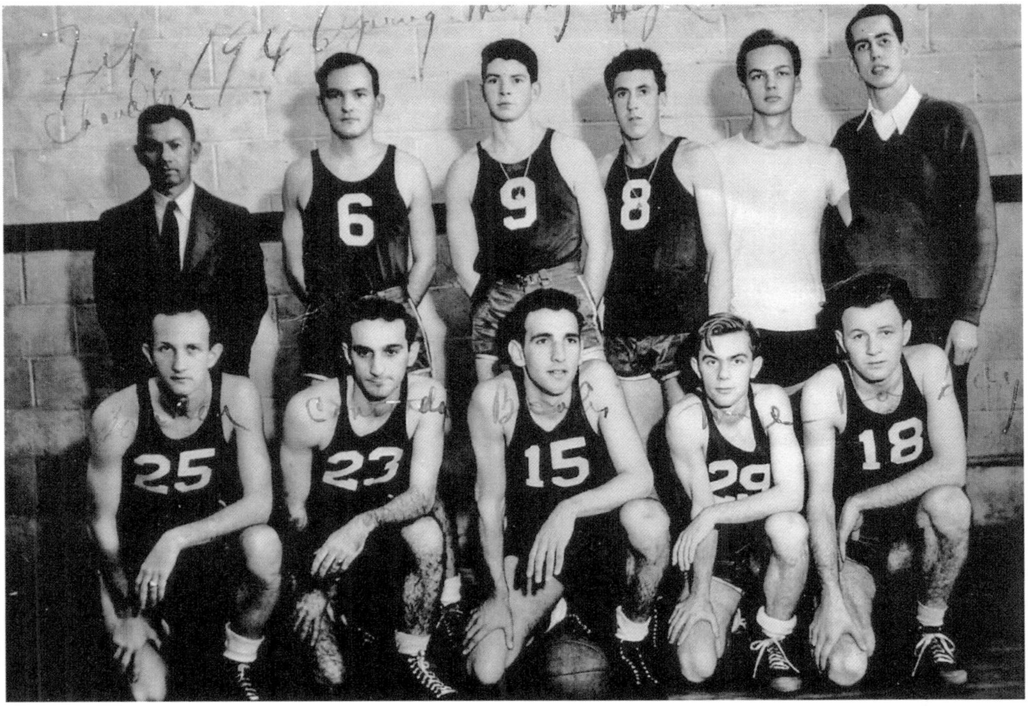

**Norfolk Division Cagers, 1945–1946.** Coach Chandler's cagers went winless during the first month of the 1945–1946 campaign, but the squad's luck changed when two returning war veterans, Skeeter Contrado (23) and Ted Bacalis (15) joined the Braves and turned the season around. Bobby Moye, Hugh Gordon, Frank Bacskay, Jim Young, Bill Murphy, Jack Hogan, Elmer Acey, Bill Hadley, and Ken Askew also contributed to a successful season. (ODU Archives.)

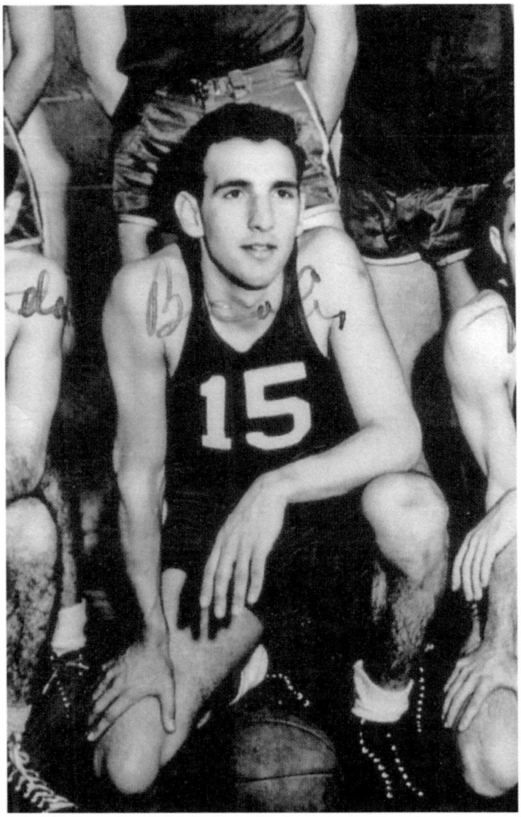

**Cager Legend Ted Bacalis.** After the war, Ted Bacalis enrolled at William and Mary's Norfolk Division and excelled on the local hard court before finishing his collegiate career at Virginia Tech. Bacalis returned to Norfolk to become one of the greatest prep basketball coaches in area history as he compiled 295 victories at Maury High. In 2000, Ted Bacalis became a member of the ODU Sports Hall of Fame. (ODU Archives.)

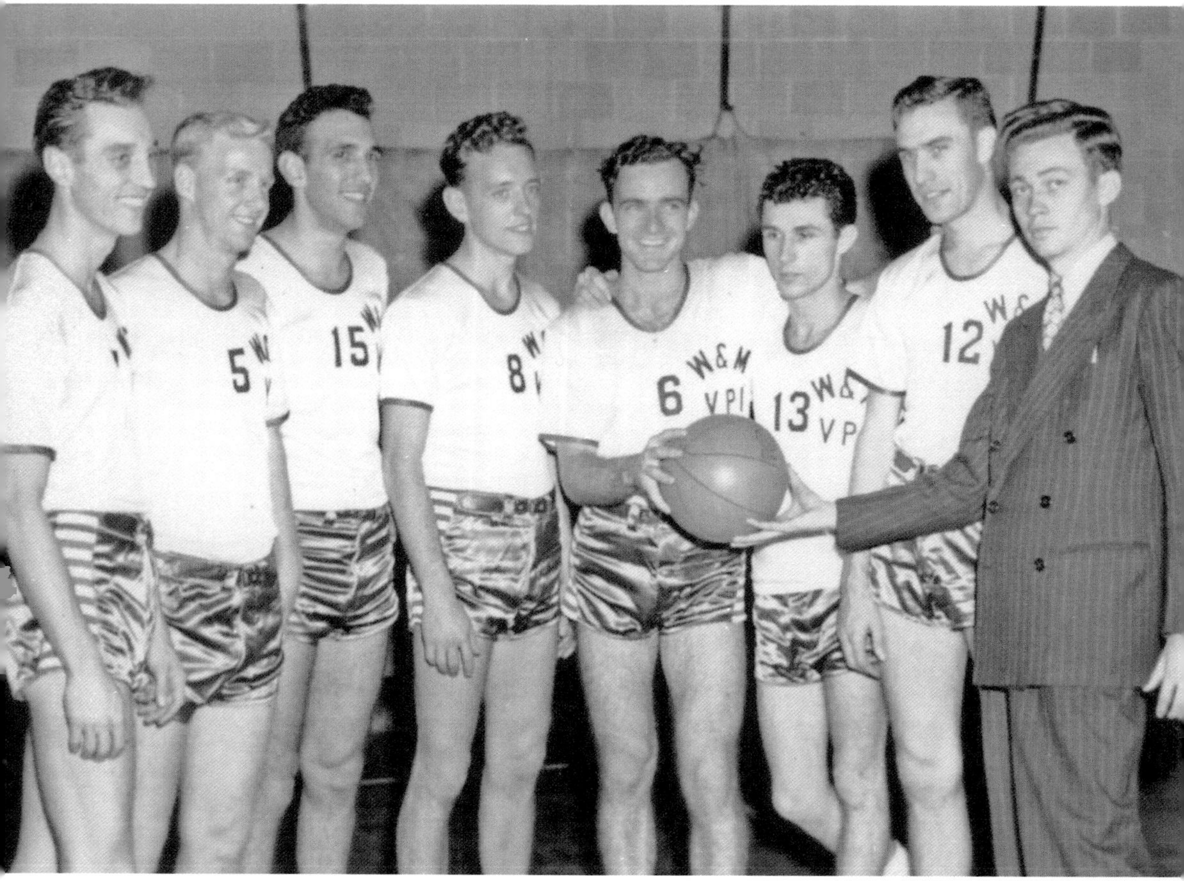


**COACH CALLAHAN'S CAGERS, 1948.** A dapper looking Jack Callahan is shown handing the ball to backcourt ace Charley Kiley (6) as Hershel Beard (13) and John Curfman (12) look on and Bill Roughton (5) and Ted Bacalis (15) are surrounded by brothers Jim and Hodges (8) Viccellio. The Braves had every reason to smile as they were on their way to an impressive 21-8 record for the year. (ODU Archives.)

3

# Coach and Mentor

## The Bud Metheny Years

## 1948–1965

Following the stability and success of the basketball program at the Norfolk Division during the Tommy Scott era, the subsequent decade at the school mirrored the uncertainty and turmoil that gripped the entire nation during the war years. From Stirnweiss to Chandler and Rubin to Callahan, the cager coaches were able to put together only four winning seasons. With the promise of better things to come following the remarkable year the Braves experienced under Coach Jack Callahan and his impressive 21-8 record, it would take the better part of the 1950s before the cagers could muster a string of successful seasons on the hard court. The slow turnaround was not for lack of a knowledgeable and talented coach, for when Callahan's successor took the reigns in the fall of 1948, the Norfolk Division found one of its most charismatic, caring, and motivational leaders in Arthur Beauregard Metheny.

Born on June 1, 1915, "Bud" Metheny developed into an all-around athlete during high school and despite his talented play on the gridiron and hard court, he signed a professional contract with the New York Yankees. By the time he reached his 23rd birthday, he was a member of the Norfolk Tars, a minor league franchise in the Yankees farm system. As he continued his climb to the major leagues, the St. Louis native chose to settle in Norfolk and began to take classes at the Norfolk Division and its parent school in Williamsburg during his time away from the diamond. The fleet-footed outfielder got his call to the majors in 1943 and proved to be a valued member of the Yankees during the war years. During the off-season, he coached at Maury High and South Norfolk High, joined the Norfolk Division's athletic staff in 1948, and was named the school's head baseball and basketball coach.

For the next 32 years, Metheny guided the school baseball team to 423 victories and was crowned National Coach of the Year in 1964. On the hard court, he led the Norfolk cagers to 198 wins and 16 winning seasons from 1948 to 1965. Coach Metheny would be the first to say that the victories came as a result of the sportsmanship personified by the remarkable student athletes under his tutelage, including such legends as Leo Anthony, Randy Leddy, Freddie Edmonds Jr., Joe Agee, Harry Knickerbocker, Marion Carroll, Wayne Parks, and Bobby Hoffman.

In 1948, Metheny made the transition from prep to collegiate coach seem effortless as he led the Norfolk cagers to an impressive 11-5 record during his inaugural campaign. Veteran Bill

Roughton led the team, but it was newcomer Joe Agee that proved to be the catalyst for the Braves. Metheny later described Agee as the quickest player he ever coached. The following season, Agee was named team captain and was one of five-returning letterman to the squad that included starting center "Poochie" Bryant, Nesbitt Riviere, and Billy Beard.

During the 1951–1952 campaign, the team was led by the talented trio of Ralph Muzzey, Mac McCurry, and Montgomery "Monk" Knight with Harry Knickerbocker and Ralph Halstead joining the squad the following season. Over the next four seasons, in spite of the talented play of Knickerbocker and John Casey, the Norfolk cagers put together mediocre seasons at best. In 1953–1954, they won 12 of 22 but then suffered through consecutive losing seasons with records of 7-15 and 8-12. In 1956–1957, the Braves finished out the "Knickerbocker Era" with an 11-10 record.

For most of his early years at the Norfolk Division of William and Mary, Bud Metheny always seemed to be one player short in putting together his dream team. In the fall of 1957, a young freshman donned the No. 5 jersey for the Braves, and Metheny's prayers for a player to fill the role as team sharpshooter and leader were answered. Leo Anthony had arrived.

An all-sport star at Granby High, Anthony soon earned the respect and admiration of Metheny and his collegiate teammates. With veterans Holt Butt and Bob Johnson providing strong support, the Braves began the "Anthony Era" with a record of 12 wins and 9 losses. Over the next three seasons, Anthony and Bobby Hoffman guided the team to records of 15-8, 12-6, and 16-4. In 1959, Anthony was named the school's first All-American and finished his career with 2,181 total points scored while averaging more than 26 points a game. In 1980, Leo Anthony was part of the inaugural group to be named to the Old Dominion University Sports Hall of Fame.

Despite the loss of Anthony, the 1961–1962 Braves were fortunate to have veterans Bobby Hoffman, Marion Carroll, Bill Phelps, Ray Dougan, and Wayne Parks return. This seasoned and talented club surprised everyone but themselves as they dominated opponents and posted an impressive 16-4 record for the campaign. In the fall of 1962, the Norfolk Division was granted independent status from William and Mary and became Old Dominion College. With the change, the athletic teams on campus discarded the moniker "Braves," officially became the "Monarchs," and earned admittance into the Mason-Dixon Conference. The final three seasons of Monarch basketball under Bud Metheny yielded records of 13-13 in 1962–1963, 13-10 in 1963–1964, and 10-13 in his final campaign.

In 1983, Arthur "Bud" Metheny, coach and mentor, was honored for his lasting contributions to the school when he was named to the ODU Sports Hall of Fame.

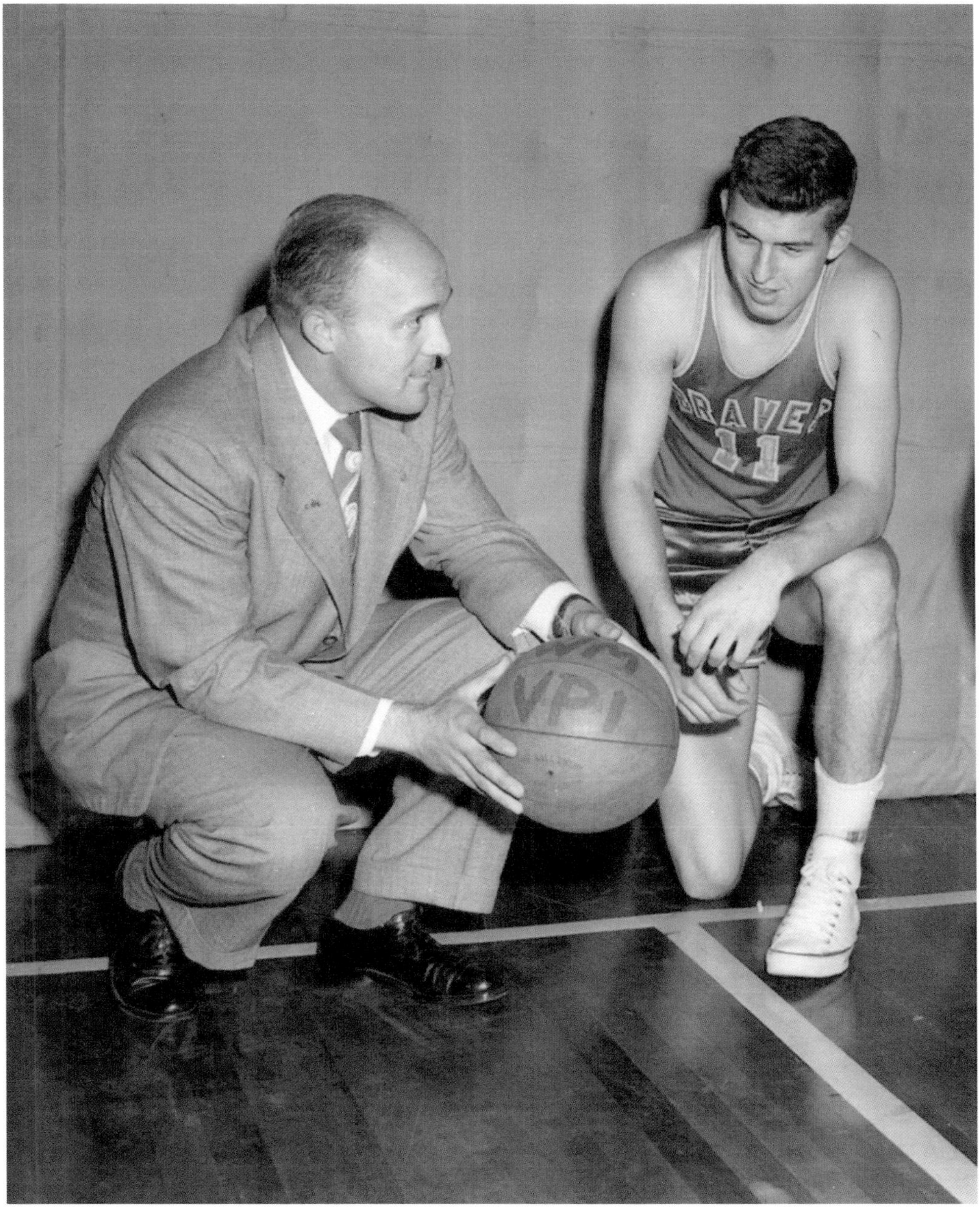


**COACH BUD METHENY AND CAGER BILLY CASEY.** Pictured during a preseason photo session, Coach Metheny and one of his returning lettermen, William "Billy" Casey, pose for the photographer while kneeling on the hard court to discuss the impending 1951–1952 season. Bud Metheny masterfully juggled a number of responsibilities at the school, including head basketball coach (1948–1965), head baseball coach (1948–1980), and athletic director (1963–1970). The multitalented skipper and former New York Yankee outfielder is a member of the Virginia Sports Hall of Fame, the William and Mary Hall of Fame, the Tidewater Baseball Hall of Fame, and the Old Dominion University Sports Hall of Fame. (CSTG.)

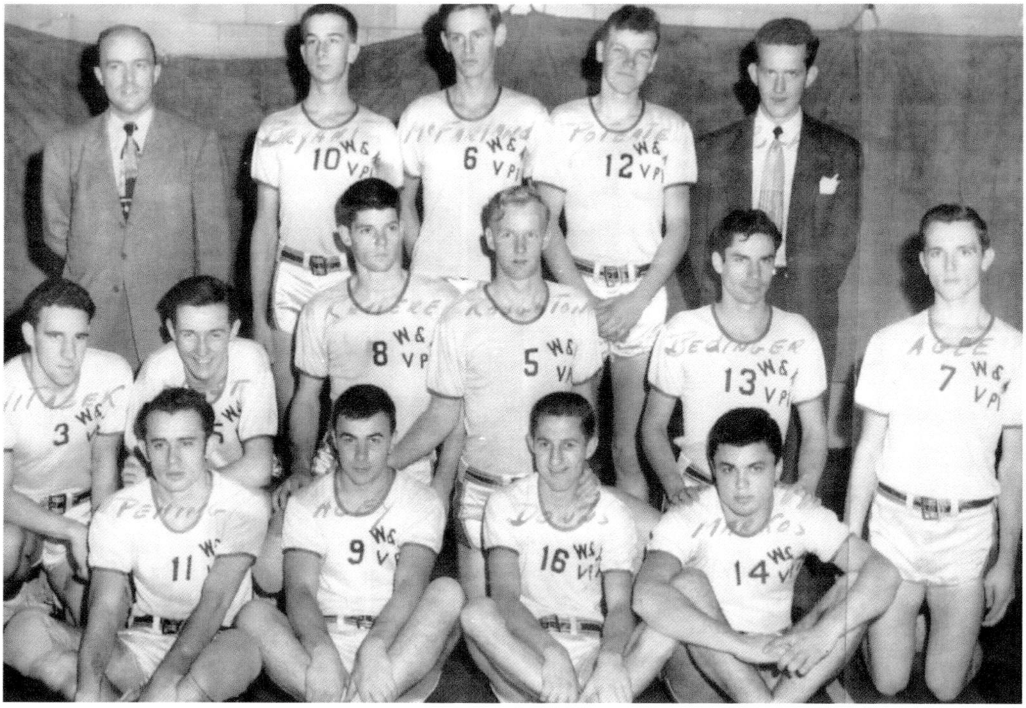

**BUD'S FIRST TEAM, 1948–1949.** When Bud Metheny (back row, far left) took over the head coaching position in 1948, the school was known as the Norfolk Division of the College of William and Mary–Virginia Polytechnic Institute. The team's jerseys show the school's reference to the dual parent institutions. The Braves posted an 11-5 record behind the scoring of Joe Agee (7) and Bill Roughton (5). (ODU Archives.)

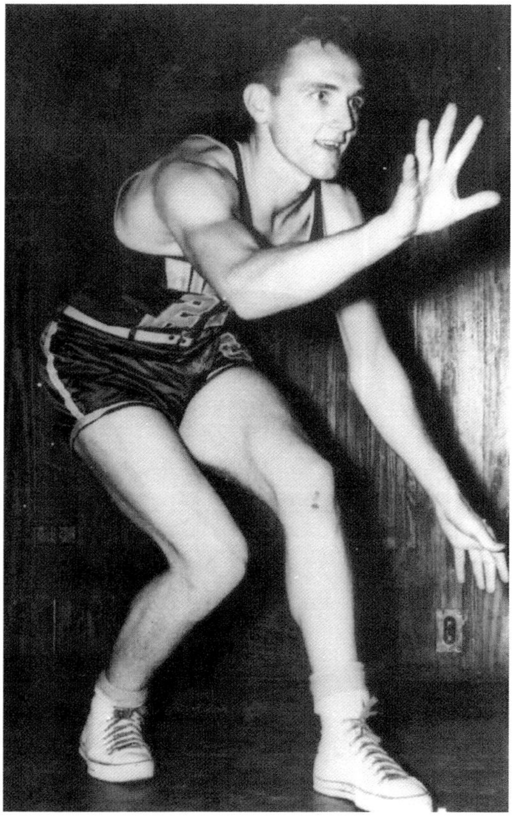

**TWO-SPORT STAR, JOE AGEE.** Following an impressive prep career at Portsmouth's Craddock High, Joe Agee developed into a multitalented sportsman while at the Norfolk Division. In 1949–1950, Agee captained the Braves and was scoring leader for two consecutive seasons; while on the diamond, he was the home run king. Joe Agee is an honored member of the ODU Sports Hall of Fame. (From the collection of Joe Agee.)

**"Monk" and Reggie.** During the 1951–1952 campaign, Montgomery Knight (left) was Bud Metheny's starting forward, while Reggie Watkins (right) provided solid support from the bench. Knight was a multitalented sportsman at the Norfolk Division and excelled on the diamond before continuing his studies and athletic prowess at the College of William and Mary. (From the collection of Montgomery Knight.)

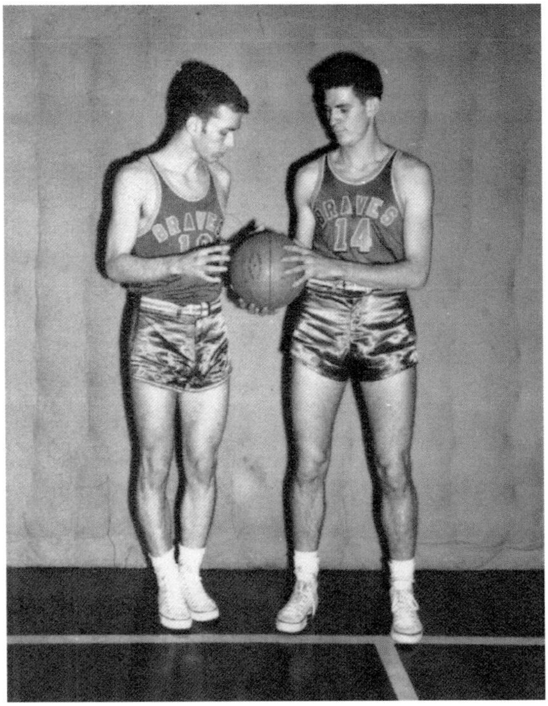


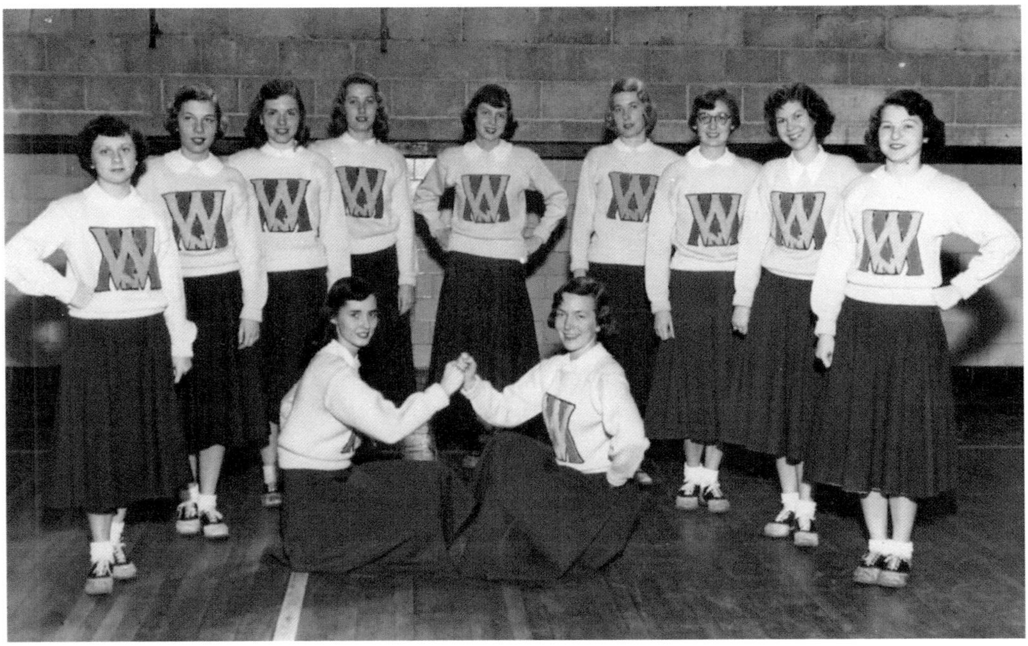

**Bobbie Socks, Saddle Shoes, and the Norfolk Division Spirit.** The 1951–1952 cheerleaders strike a pose as Jerry Seelinger (right front) and Betty Scheek (left front) show a special handclasp used in one of their routines. The rest of the squad (left to right) is Janice Beale, Carlotta Duncan, Verona Willey, Barbara Land, Gay Rice, Betty Land, Ann McDonald, Gloria Smith and Bobbie Lewis. (From the collection of Jerry [Seelinger] Knight.)

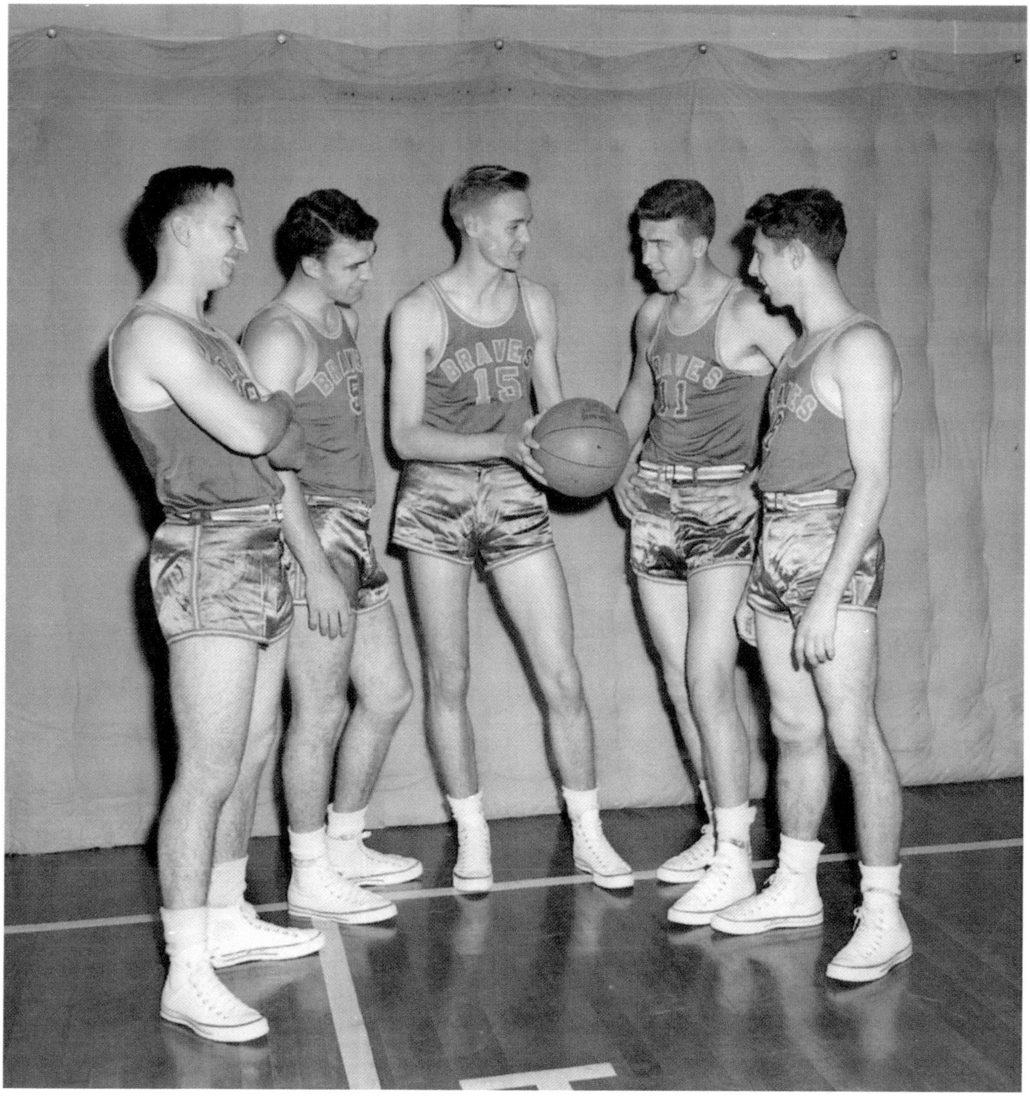

**METHENY'S QUINTS, 1950–1951.** Norfolk Division cager Jerry Burlage (15) holds court with his teammates as they discuss strategies for the 1950–1951 basketball season. Coach Bud Metheny's Braves would post an 11-10 record with a strong starting five that included (from left to right) guard Bobby Williams, forward Otto Franklin, center Jerry Burlage, forward Bill Casey, and guard Sonny Howlett. (CSTG.)

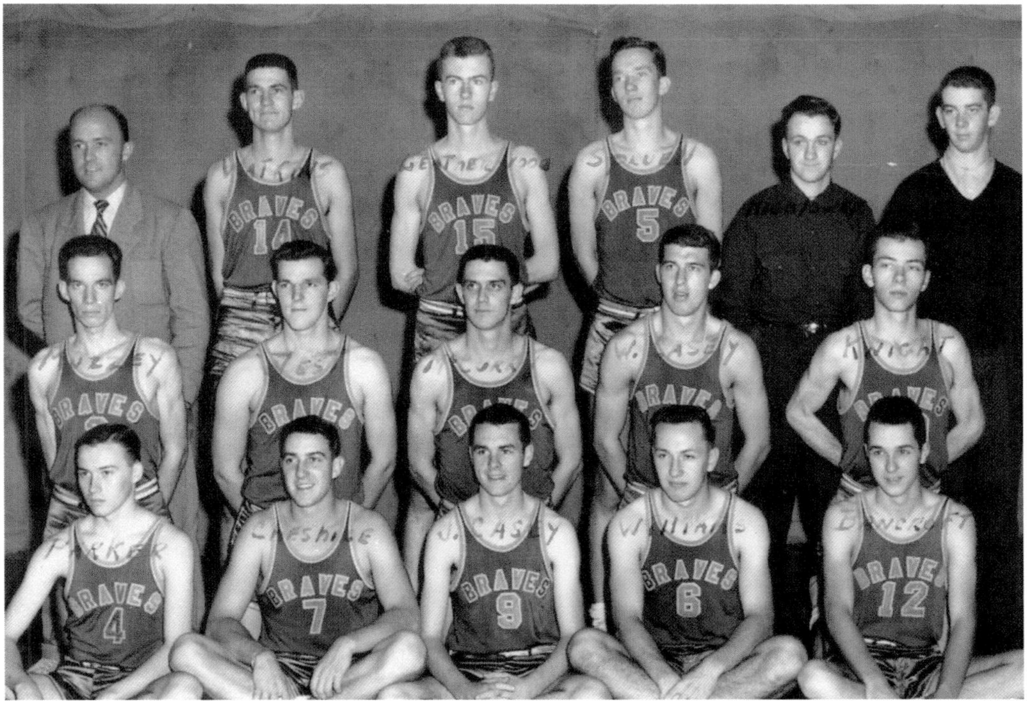


**NORFOLK DIVISION BRAVES, 1951–1952.** Pictured from left to right are (first row) Nick Parker, Ned Cheshire, John Casey, Bobby Williams, and George Bancroft; (second row) Ralph Muzzey, Bubba West, Mac McCurry, Bill Casey, and Montgomery Knight; (third row) coach Metheny, Reggie Watkins, Buddy Leatherwood, Bob Spruell, and managers Hightower and Murphy. (ODU Archives.)

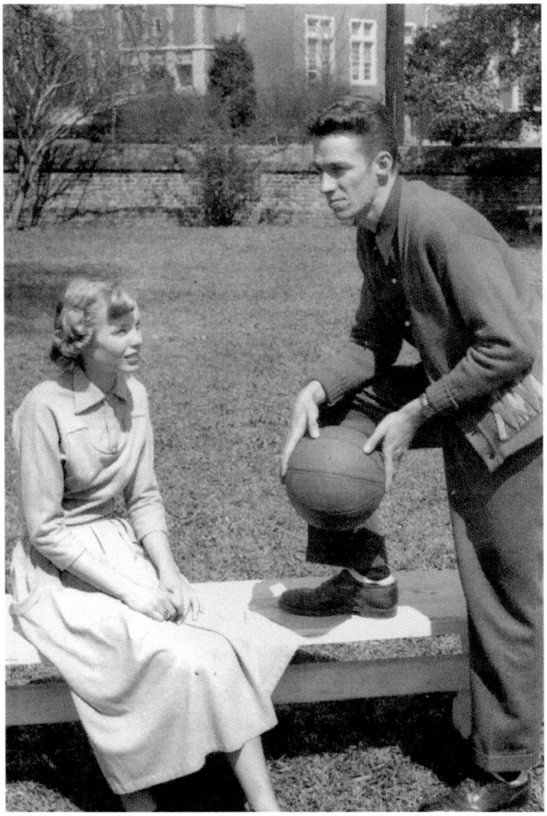

**MOST ATHLETIC ON CAMPUS, 1951–1952.** When the school annual was distributed at the end of the academic year, two triple-threat campus sports stars were selected "Most Athletic" for 1951–1952. Ralph Muzzey, a returning letterman and starting forward for the Norfolk Division cagers, lettered in basketball, track, and baseball, while Kathy Klak excelled in basketball, field hockey, and tennis in women's athletics. (ODU Archives.)

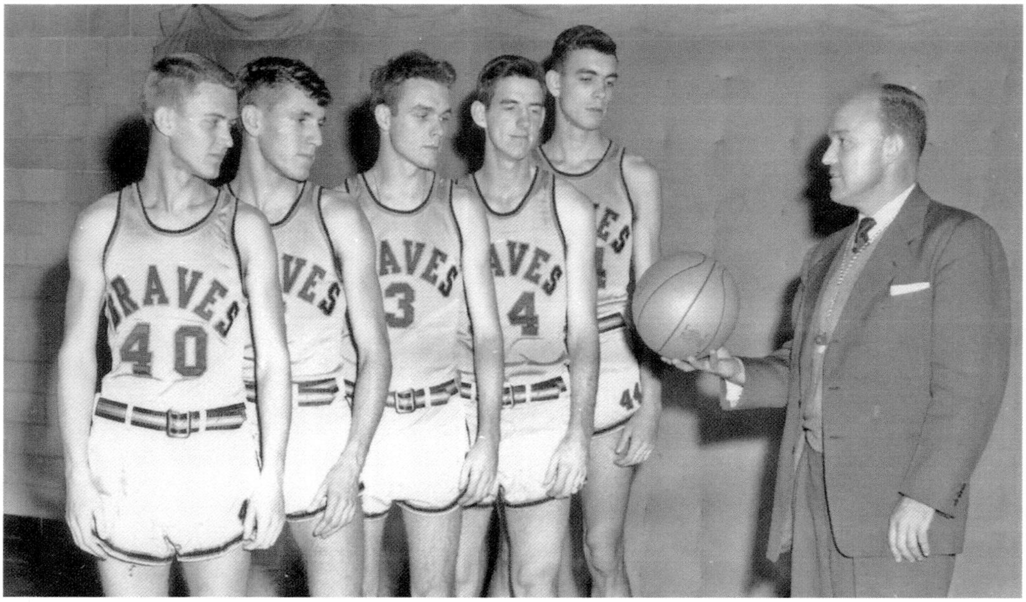


**ALL EYES ON THE BALL.** Coach Metheny's Golden Rule on the hard court was "keep your eyes on the ball." This classic image indeed shows that his 1953–1954 starting five followed Metheny's advice as they stare intently at the basketball. Pictured from left to right are Billy Tyndall, Harry Knickerbocker, John Casey, Ralph Halstead, William McCraw, and coach Bud Metheny. (ODU Archives.)

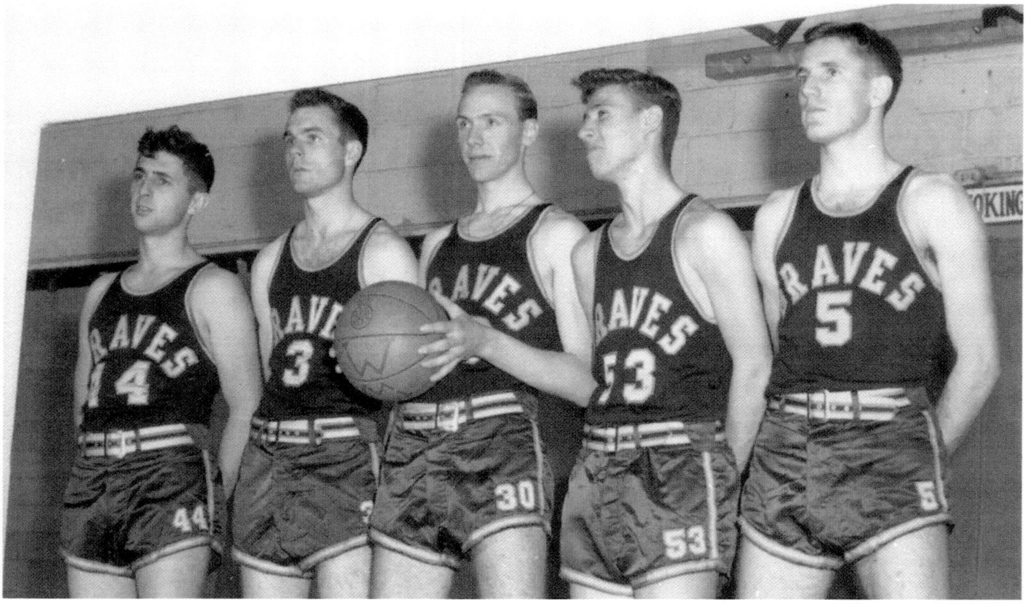


**HARRY AND THE BRAVES FOR 1955.** Wearing No. 5, team cocaptain Harry Knickerbocker poses with his fellow starters for Bud Metheny's Braves for the 1955–1956 season. Pictured from left to right are Malvin Howlett, John Casey, Paul Burlage, Carl Ochsenhaut, and Old Dominion University Sports Hall of Fame honoree Harry Knickerbocker. (ODU Archives.)

**TIP-OFF AGAINST LYNCHBURG.** Norfolk Braves center Bobby Johnson (white jersey) leaps for the opening game tip-off against his Lynchburg College counterpart as the 1956–1957 season begins. Watching to see where the ball goes are Norfolk Division teammates Eric Smith (33) and Ronnie Evans (44). The Braves lost the inaugural game of the season 76-62 in a hard-fought match. (ODU Archives.)

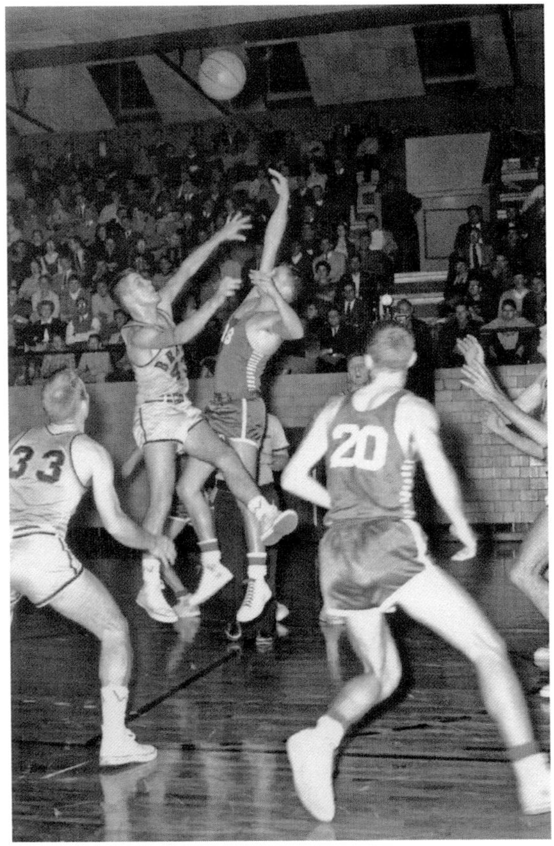

**NORFOLK DIVISION CAGERS, 1957–1958.** Pictured from left to right are (first row) Benn Griffin, Kirkie Harrison, Gene Keel, D. B. Hawkins, Leo Anthony, and Eddie Walsh; (second row) Dick White, Holt Butt, Bobby Johnson, Jim Jordon, and Jim Davis; (third row) coach Metheny, manager Randy Fraiser, Bob Newton, Ronnie Evans, Ray Toleston, Andy Boyce, and manager Jack O'Brien. (ODU Archives.)

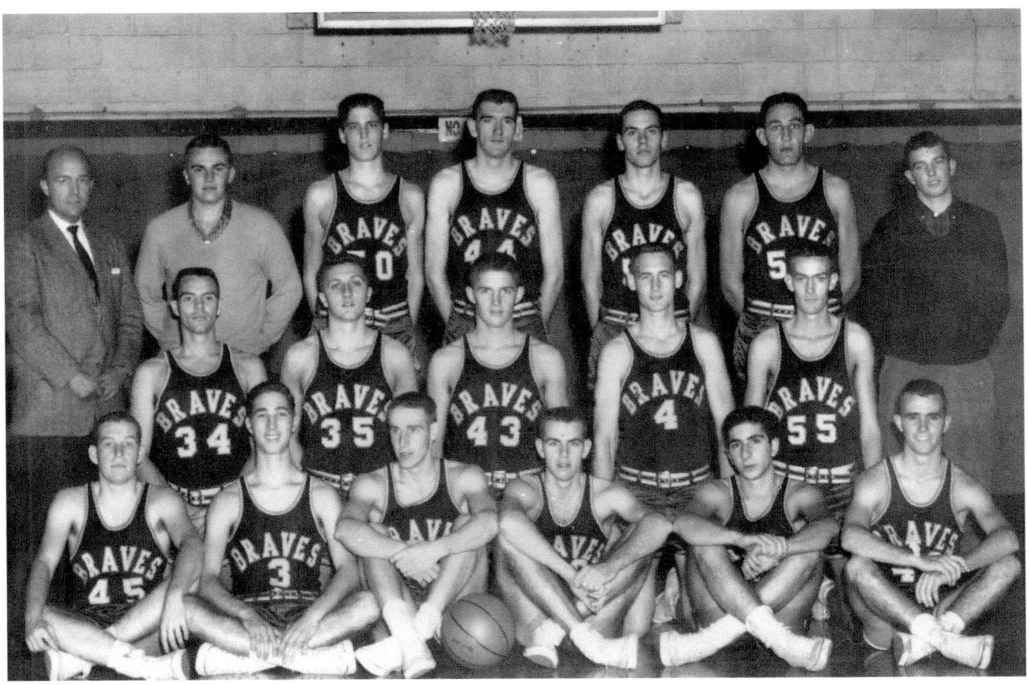

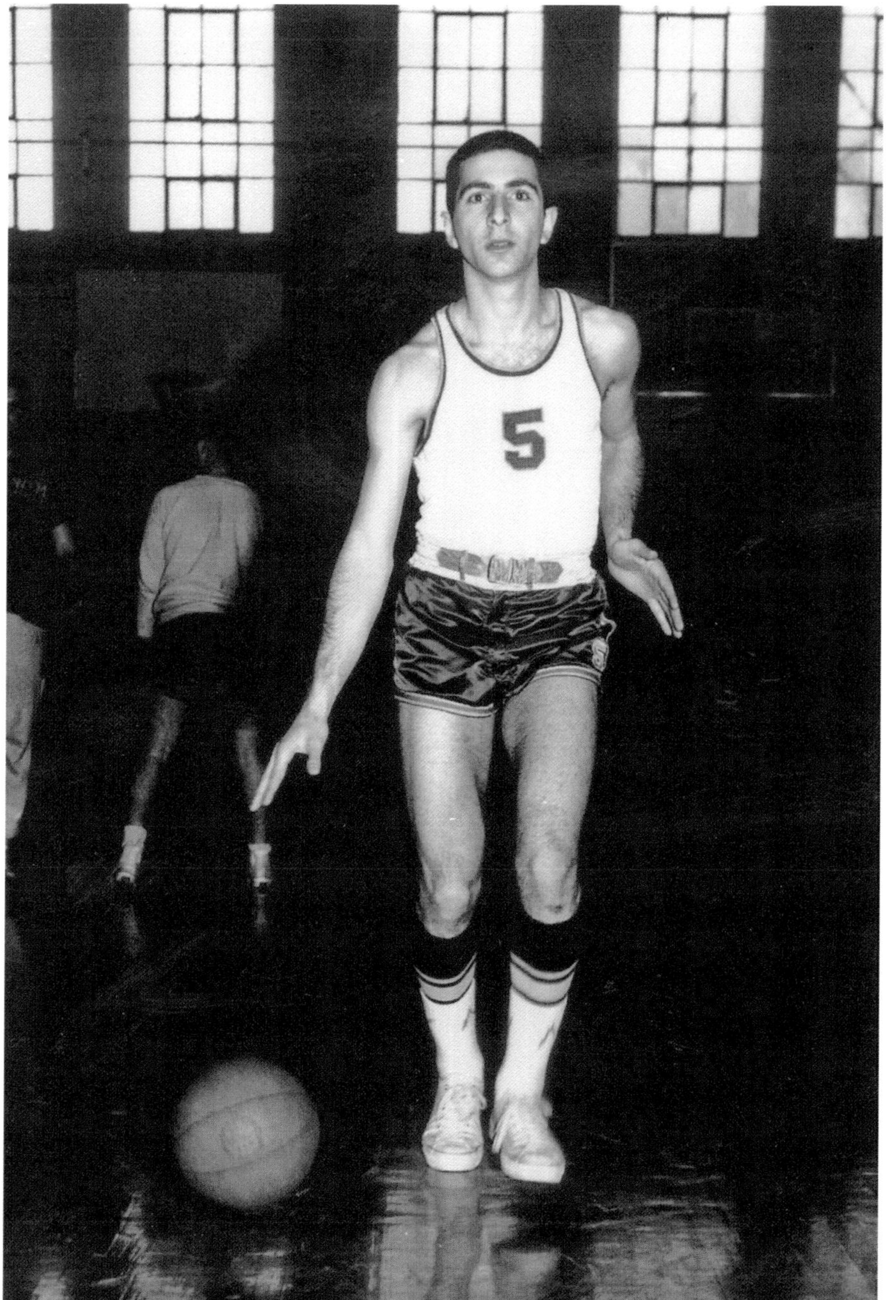

**LEO ANTHONY, ALL-AMERICAN.** One of the most dominating athletes in the history of the school, Leo Anthony was the premier player for Bud Metheny's Norfolk Division Braves from 1957 to 1961. During this era, Anthony was named to the All-Virginia team four times, voted Player of the Year twice for the Commonwealth, and became the school's first All-American. When coach Metheny retired, he was quoted as saying that Leo Anthony was the greatest athlete in the history of the Old Dominion. (ODU Archives.)

**RONNIE EVANS ON THE PROWL.** On a cold night in December 1957, more than 1,000 fans witnessed the Norfolk cagers rough up the University of Baltimore Bees 80-66 in a homecoming celebration. Pictured during some intense game action is Ronnie Evans (44, white jersey), the center for the Braves looking to pounce on a downed opponent. (ODU Archives.)

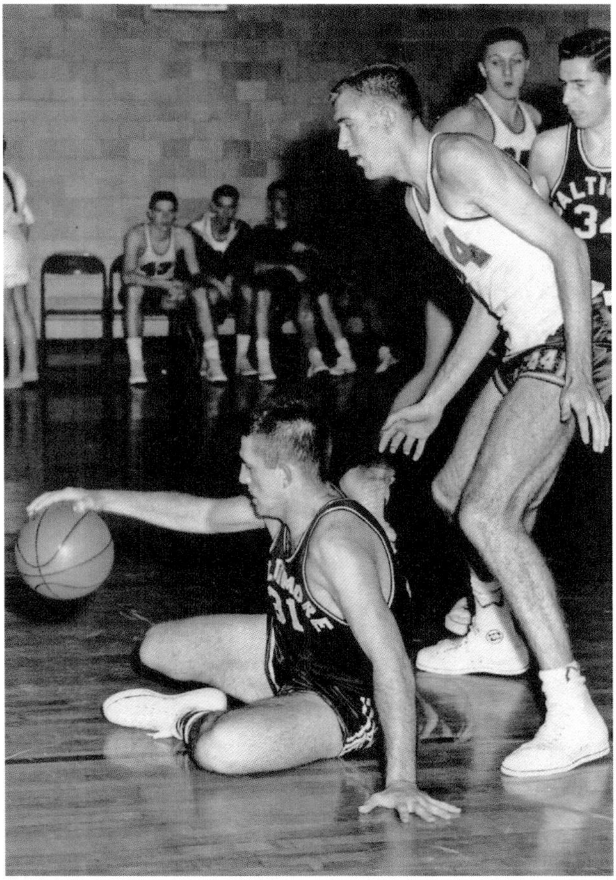

**A VIEW FROM THE HARD COURT.** With the photographer snapping the shutter from this unique vantage point, the reader has a chance to see the stands filled with a good crowd attending a Norfolk Division contest during the 1958–1959 season. (ODU Archives.)

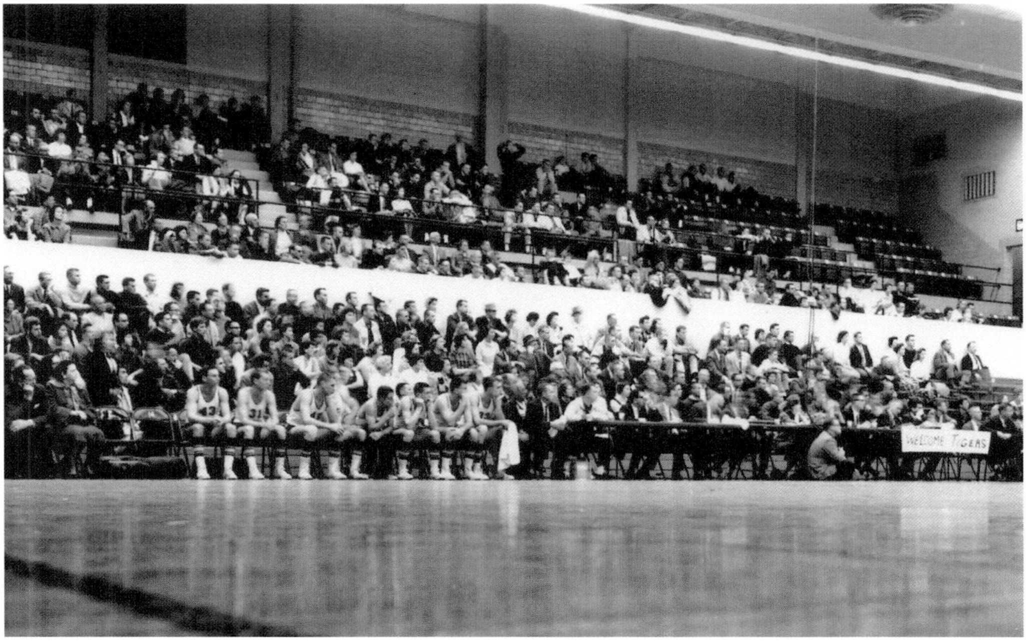

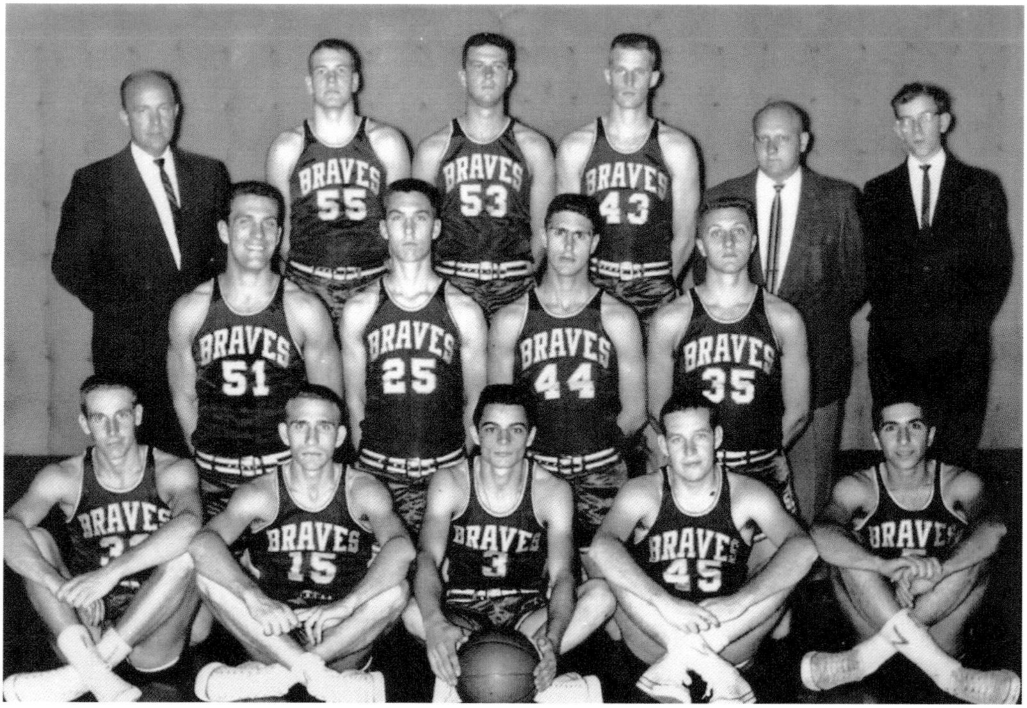



**COACH METHENY'S BRAVES, 1958–1959.** Pictured from left to right are (first row) Gene Keal, Bobby Hoffman, Don Palumbo, Benn Griffin, and Leo Anthony; (second row) Robert Pratt, James Barefoot, Jim West, and Holt Butt; (third row) coach Metheny, Don Ellis, Bob Ainsworth, Horace Williams, and managers Ben Merr and Tom Horton. (ODU Archives.)

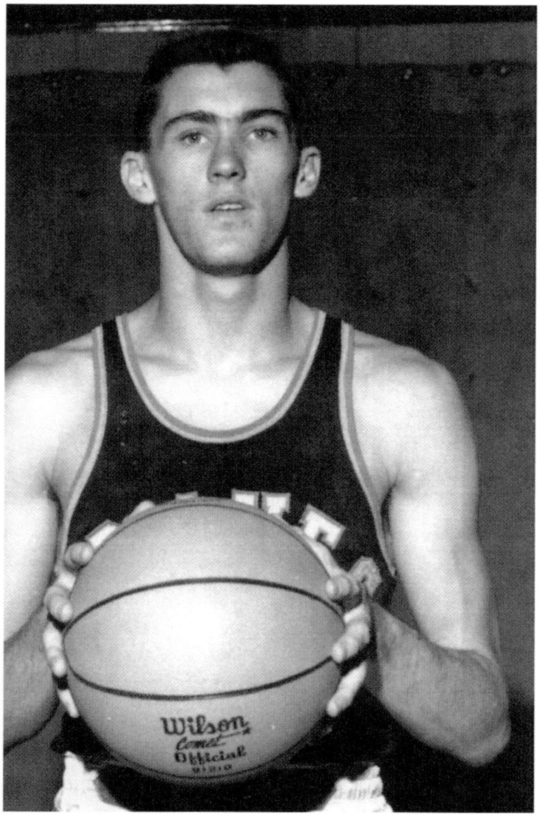



**MARION "MERKY" CARROLL, 1959–1962.** A four-year player who excelled at the guard position, Marion Carroll, nicknamed "Merky" by his teammates, served as an inspirational cocaptain in his junior and senior seasons. The talented cager would return to Old Dominion and serve as an assistant coach under Sonny Allen and later fill the role of assistant athletic director at the school until his retirement. (ODU Archives.)

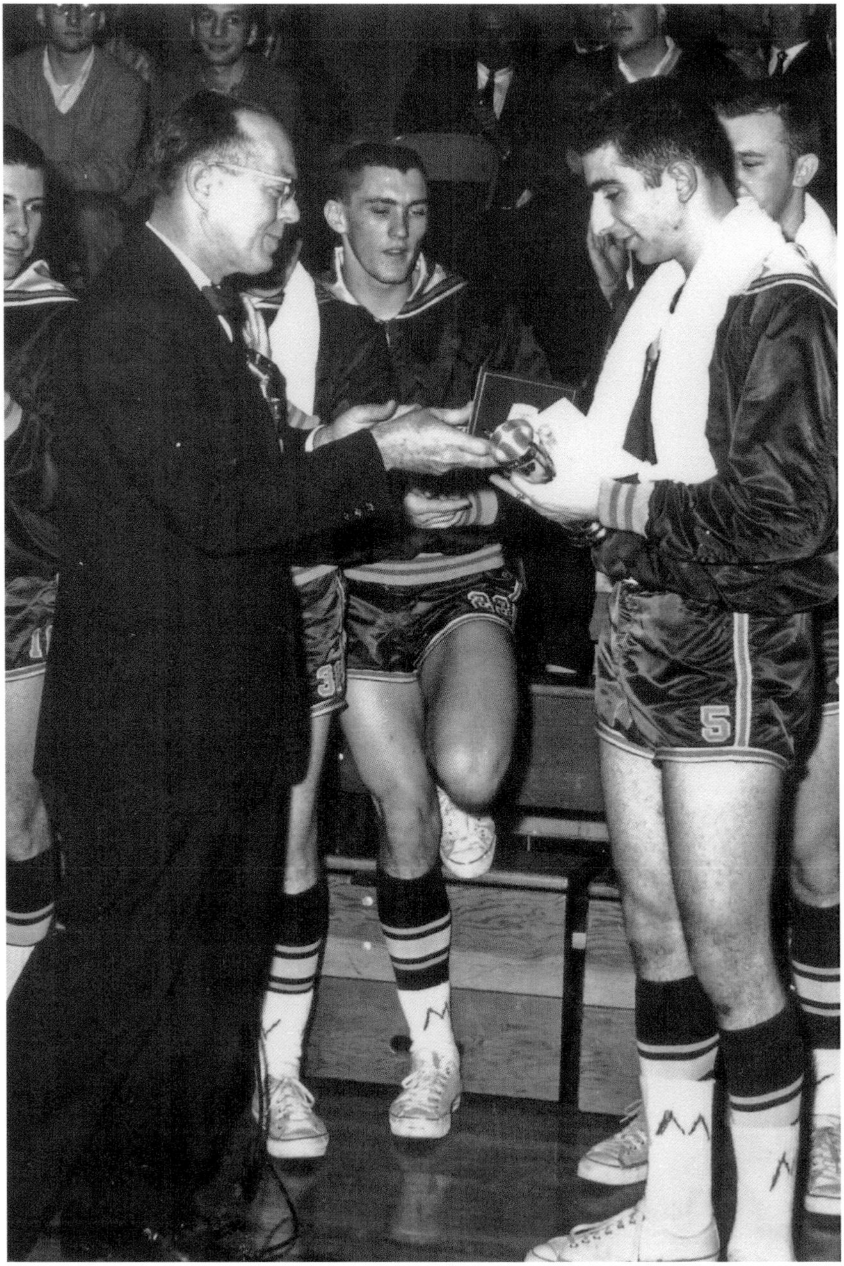

**FEBRUARY 13, 1961, LEO ANTHONY NIGHT.** With teammates and fans providing a backdrop of resounding cheers, Leo Anthony accepts a ceremonial watch and inscribed trophy from Chancellor Louis Webb at half-time of the final game of his career with the Norfolk Division of William and Mary. To top off the festivities, Anthony was awarded the basketball he used to score his 2,000th point for the Braves and the school formally retired his No. 5 jersey. The half-time celebration surely served as inspiration for the school's first All-American as he scored 60 points against Lynchburg College, thus finishing with 2,181 career points. (ODU Archives.)

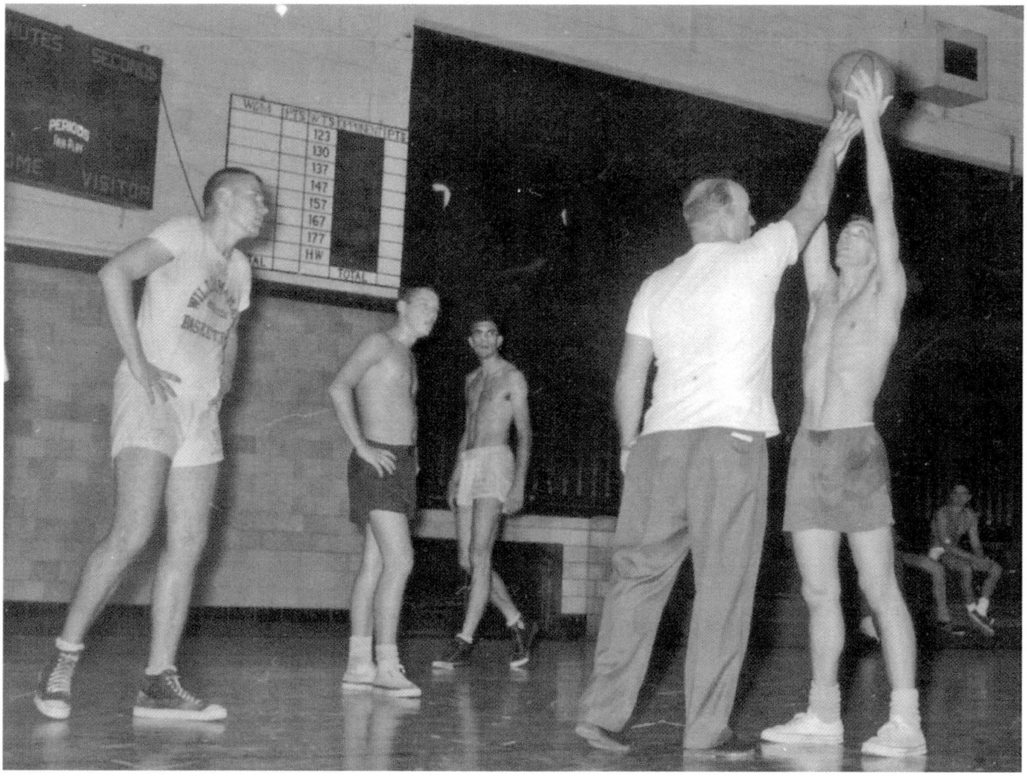

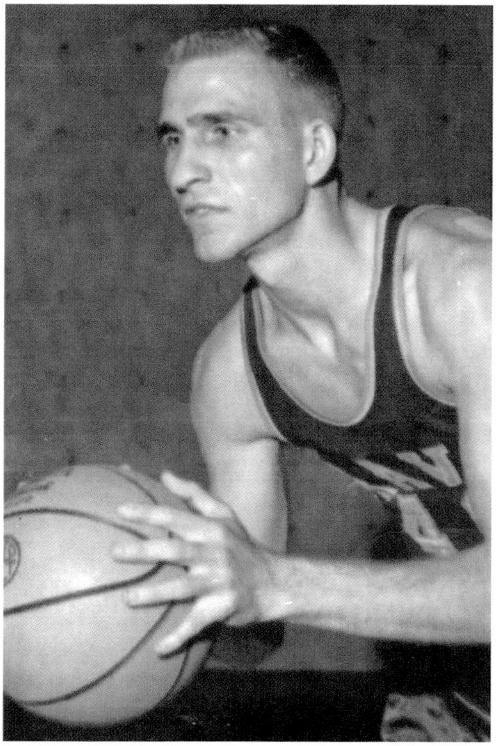

**PRACTICE MAKES PERFECT.** This photograph provides the reader with a behind-the-scenes look at Bud Metheny's coaching technique, especially his hands-on instruction. From the looks of the Norfolk Division of the College of William and Mary cagers, coach Metheny's teaching lesson provided them with a chance to catch a breath. (ODU Archives.)

**HALL OF FAMER BOBBY HOFFMAN.** A native of Portsmouth, Bobby Hoffman served as cocaptain for the Norfolk Division cagers for three seasons from 1960–1962. Over his career, he netted 1,047 points, earned Little Eight All-Conference honors twice, and was First Team All-State in 1962. Bobby is a respected member of the Old Dominion University Sports Hall of Fame. (ODU Archives.)

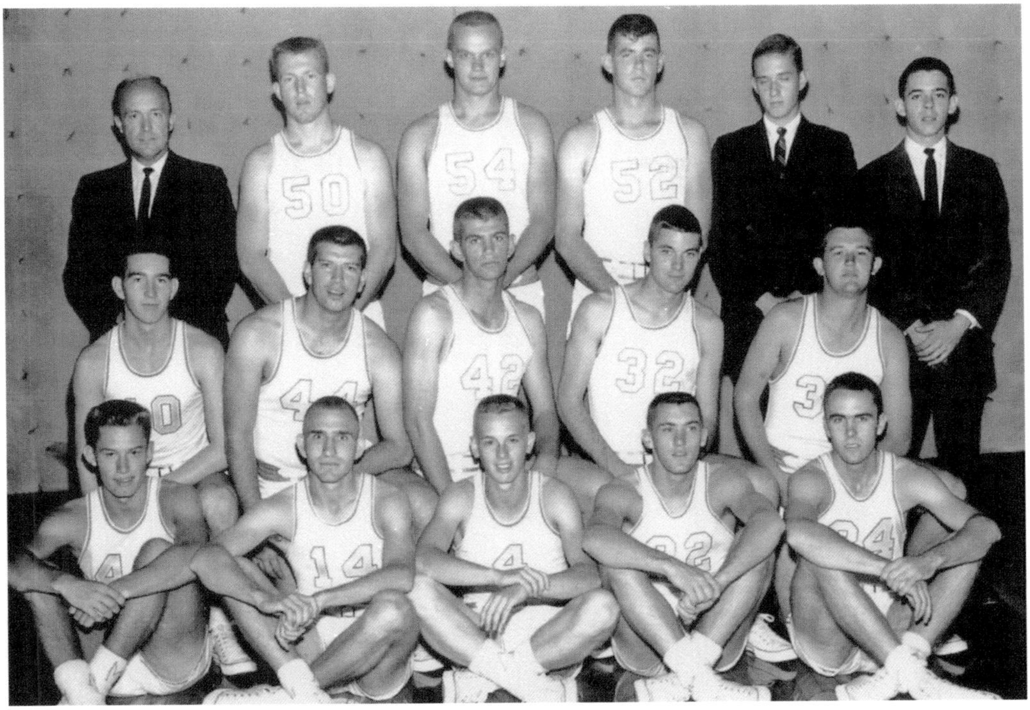

**NORFOLK DIVISION CAGERS, 1961–1962.** Pictured from left to right are (first row) Barry Stokes, Bobby Hoffman, Wayne Parks, Marion Carroll, and Jerry Nichols; (second row) Jerry Hammer, Ron Byrd, Bill Boyce, Fred Edmonds, and Bill Phelps; (third row) coach Metheny, Doug Hollowell, Jim Bettis, Ray Dougan, and managers Vislocky and Pouleris. (ODU Archives.)

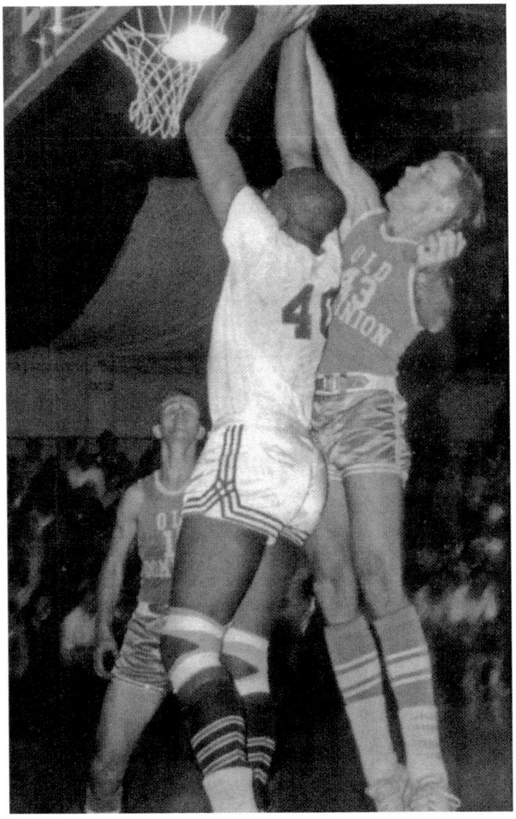

**LEDDY REJECTS AT THE RIM.** Caught in midair, Randy Leddy stops an opponent from scoring during a drive to the basket. Leddy is one of only a few Monarch cagers in the history of the school to grab more than 1,000 rebounds and score in excess of 1,000 points during his career. In 1986, Randy Leddy was named to the Old Dominion University Sports Hall of Fame. (ODU Archives.)

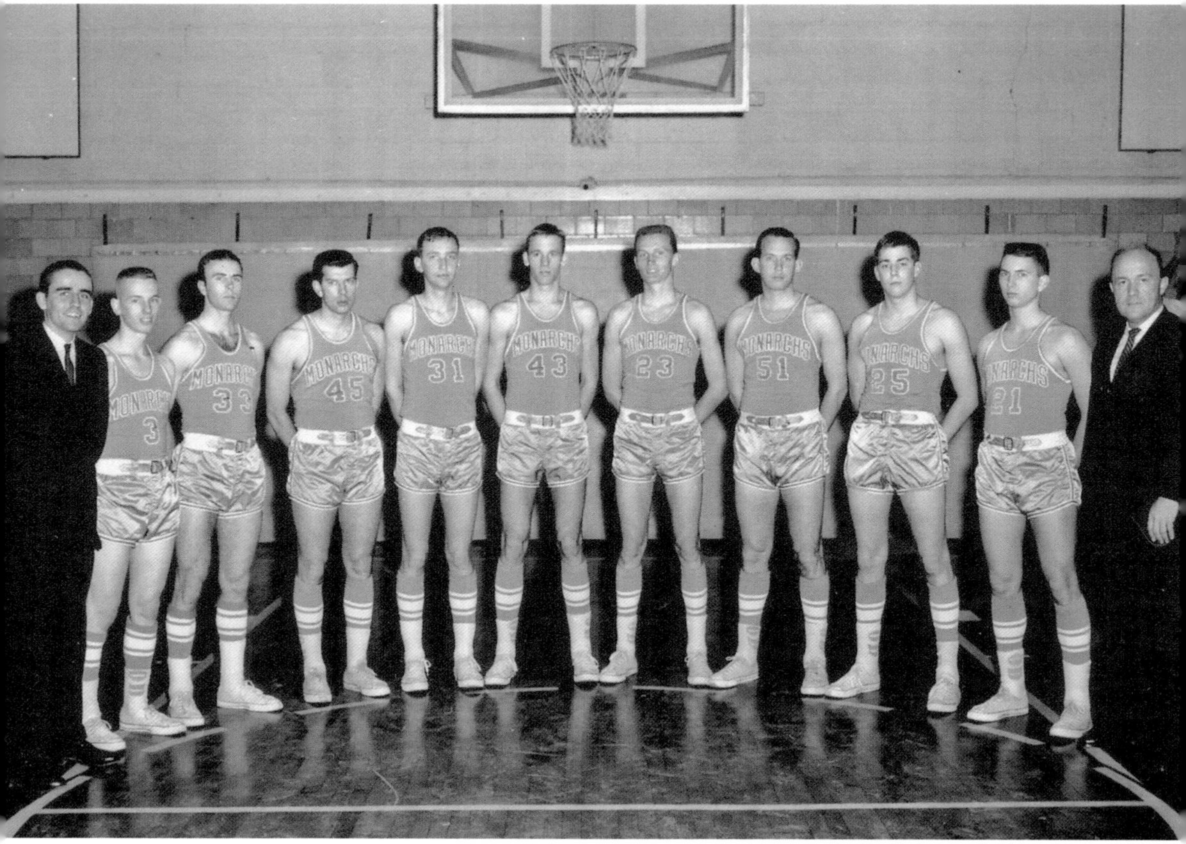

**OLD DOMINION COLLEGE MONARCHS, 1964–1965.** The Norfolk cagers struggled during coach Bud Metheny's final season at the helm and could muster only 10 victories in 23 contests. The Monarchs were led by junior Randy Leddy and team captain Freddie Edmonds Jr. with support coming from Bill Midgette, Jerry Nichols, John Kendall, and Hank Marriott. (ODU Archives.)

# 4

# A Bright Future

## The Sonny Allen Years 1965–1975

More than a dozen men interviewed to replace Bud Metheny as the head coach at Old Dominion College. On March 1, 1965, the school announced the selection of William Russell "Sonny" Allen, a 29-year-old freshman coach and varsity assistant at Marshall University. Allen, not present at the press conference, fielded questions over the telephone from West Virginia. He would begin his new job when the undefeated freshman squad at Marshall completed their season.

A West Virginia native, Allen had played guard for Marshall, which led the nation in total offense during the 1957–1958 season. Asked in the press conference what type of offense the Monarchs would employ, Allen responded, "You know we West Virginians like to run and shoot, and that's the kind of basketball we'll play at Old Dominion." Over the next 10 years, Allen would keep his word, bringing his brand of fast-break basketball to Norfolk.

Allen's first Old Dominion team finished last in the Mason-Dixon Conference's Southern Division with a dismal 7-17 record. That team included nine non-scholarship players, including six holdovers from Bud Metheny's 10-13 squad. Allen's first season left fans wondering if he was the right hire.

The 1966–1967 season would be different, giving Allen his first crop of recruits, specifically chosen for his patented fast break. Sonny recruited Arthur "Buttons" Speakes, a young West Virginian, to run his up-tempo offense. He also acquired National Junior College Player of the Year, Bob Pritchett. Along with Richard Boyce, Ron Drews, Ken Hopkins, and Paul Shepard, Speakes and Pritchett led Sonny to the first of nine consecutive winning campaigns. The Monarchs would go 14-12, including a win against Southern Conference and major college foe, the Citadel. Monarch fans began envisioning an exciting future.

Allen's 1967–1968 team included the return of seven lettermen, including Speakes, Pritchett, and sophomores Harry Lozon and Dick St. Clair. The Monarch's thrived on Allen's philosophy, "run 'em and shoot 'em to death," averaging a school record 98 points per game. Allen's team completed the season 19-7 with four starters averaging double figures.

Sonny's 1968–1969 squad had experience and depth. This team of Speakes, Drews, Lozon, and St. Clair were joined by sophomores Steve Cox and Skip Noble. With a combination of a strong backcourt and inside game, the Monarchs 21-10 record was good enough to capture its first Mason-Dixon Conference title and an invitation to the NCAA Division II South Atlantic Regional.

Before the 1969–1970 season, Allen and the school felt they had outgrown the Mason-Dixon Conference and became an independent. In September, Old Dominion College was granted university status. The future was bright since the Monarchs returned seven letterman, including four starters from a 21-win season. St. Clair went down with an early season knee injury, limiting his playing time and devastating the team and fans. However, sophomore Dave Twardzik, whose play over the next three years would become legendary, proved an able replacement. Beating the likes of Southern Mississippi, St. Francis, Xavier, American University, and Long Island University, Sonny guided this team to a 21-7 record and a second straight NCAA Division II South Atlantic Regional.

During the 1970–1971 season, the Monarchs began playing in the ODU Fieldhouse, a new 5,200-seat, on-campus facility. Allen's team was led by junior guard Twardzik, as well as the inside games of Cox and Noble. The Monarch's success was rewarded when they were asked to host an NCAA Regional. The Monarchs beat Stetson and crosstown rival Norfolk State 102-97, advancing to Evansville and the Division II National Championship final eight. The Monarchs defeated highly favored Puget Sound and Kentucky Wesleyan, earning the chance to meet home-team Evansville in the title game. The Purple Aces dominated ODU and won the championship 97-82. However, that tournament galvanized the Monarch faithful as the team completed a magical season with a record of 21-9.

The return of senior All-American Twardzik, Rick Nau, Joel Copeland, and Jay Rountree for 1971–1972 gave Monarch fans hope for another championship push. The Monarchs were not up to the task and posted a disappointing 14-10 record.

The Monarchs began 1972–1973 without All-American Twardzik, who had graduated. With Copeland back and Oliver Purnell, the guard chosen to replace Twardzik, the Monarchs went 19-9. This was enough to earn another bid to the South Atlantic Regional, where they lost in overtime 88-87 to host Roanoke College, the eventual Division II National Champion.

The following year, 1973–1974, the team returned four starters, including All-American Copeland, and promising freshmen Jeff Fuhrmann and Joey Caruthers. Sonny's Monarchs again won big, finishing 20-7 and making it to the finals of the South Atlantic Regional.

Allen, the team, and the fans were optimistic at the start of the 1974–1975 season. Center Wilson Washington had transferred from Maryland, and veterans Tom Street, Gray Eubank, along with Fuhrmann, Caruthers, Purnell, and Rountree, were back to carry the Monarchs to their big goal, a national championship. The Monarchs' regular-season play again earned them a bid to host the South Atlantic Regional. The Monarchs easily defeated opponents, capturing another trip to Evansville. In its first two games, the Monarchs won big against North Dakota and Tennessee State, and in the finals squeaked out a close 76-74 victory over New Orleans for its coveted NCAA Division II Championship.

On June 10, 1975, the Sonny Allen tenure at Old Dominion University came to an end. Allen announced he was leaving for Southern Methodist University. Losing Allen to SMU was disappointing to Monarch fans, but Allen had accomplished what he set out to do nearly 10 years before, guiding the Monarchs to a national championship, two NCAA Finals, nine winning seasons, 181 wins, and appearances in six postseason tournaments.

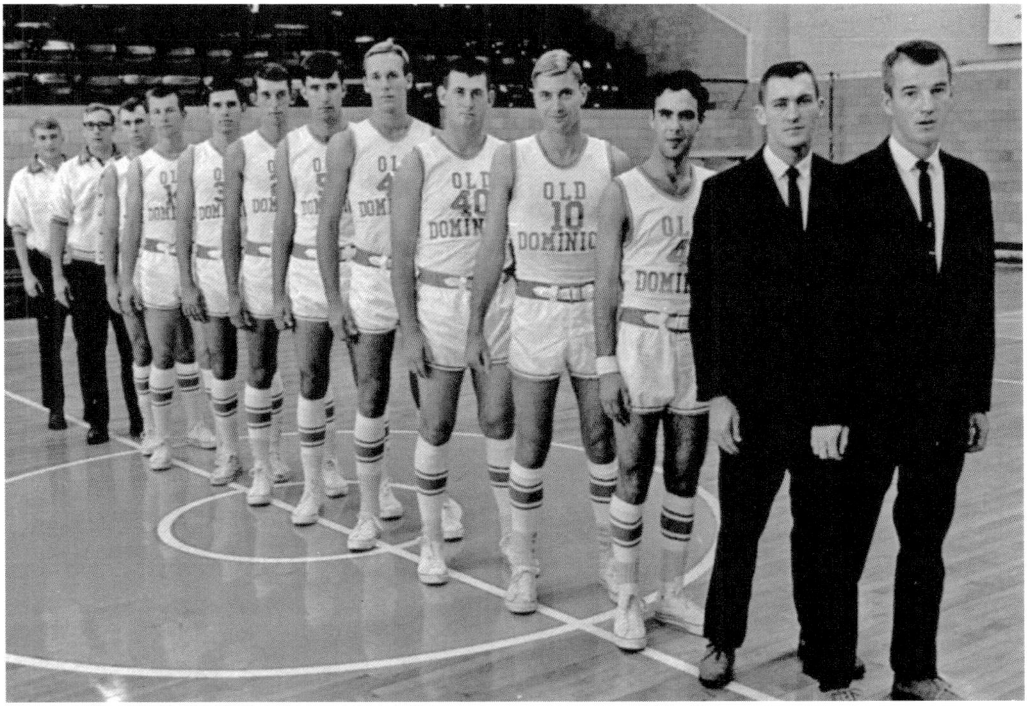

**SONNY'S FIRST TEAM, 1965–1966.** Winning the first four of five games gave the Monarchs optimism, but their lack of size and depth caught up to them as they finished with a dismal 7-17 record. From left to right are two unidentified managers, Richard Boyce, Dennis Riddleburger, Jerry Nichols, Kenny Lanzone, Fred Edmonds, Bill Hill, Randy Leddy, Joe Saunders, Jim Isiminger, and coaches Marion Carroll and Sonny Allen. (ODU Archives.)

**SONNY GETS HIS MAN.** Sonny's wife, Debbie, and freshman coach and varsity assistant Marion Carroll listen with interest as coach Allen talks to a recruit. Soon after arriving at Old Dominion College, Allen began recruiting his freshman class of Button Speakes, Ken Hopkins, Ron Drews, and Paul Sheppard. They would not begin varsity play until the following year. (CSTG.)

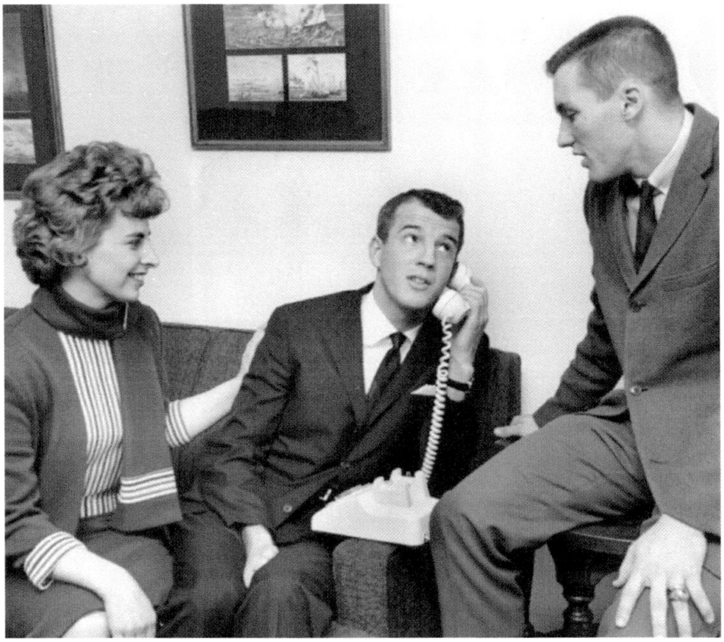

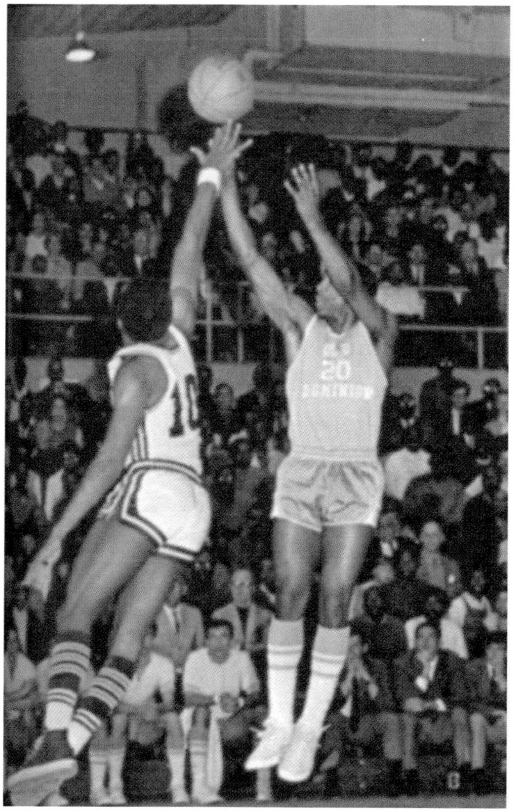

**ARTHUR "BUTTONS" SPEAKES, 1965–1968.** Sonny Allen's first recruit was Buttons Speakes, a 5-foot-11-inch guard from West Virginia. He was the first African American to play for a predominately white college or university in Virginia. Speakes was quick and skilled at running Sonny's fast break, and directed the Monarchs to its first Mason-Dixon title and NCAA berth. In 1983, he was inducted into the ODU Sports Hall of Fame. (ODU Archives.)

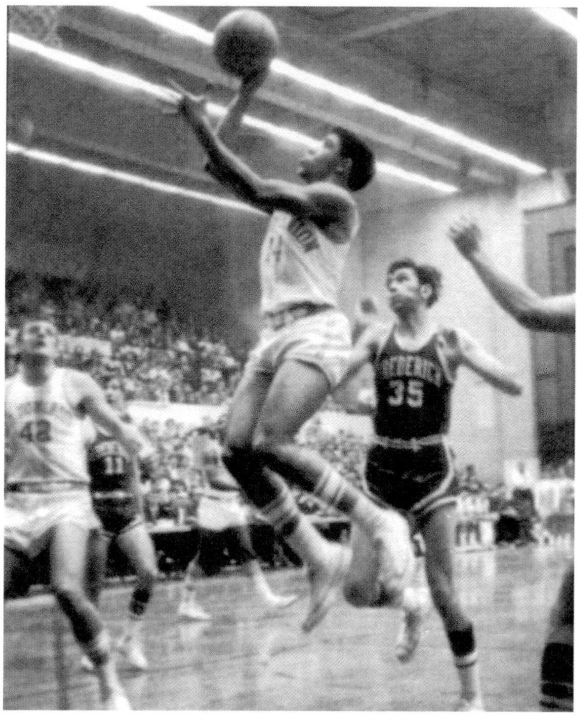

**HOT SHOT HOOSIER.** On February 14, 1968, Bob Pritchett, a 5-foot-10-inch Indiana native, scored a school record 67 points against Richmond Professional Institute (RPI). Pritchett, the 1964–1965 National Junior College Player of the Year at Vincennes Junior College, burned up the nets in his home finale as the Monarchs crushed RPI, 152-110. In his two-year career, Pritchett would average nearly 24 points per game for a total of 1,188. (ODU Archives.)

**RON DREWS, 1965–1969.** A 1991 inductee of Old Dominion University Sports Hall of Fame, this 6-foot-5 center was an exceptional rebounder who ended his career with 796 caroms. In a game against Richmond Professional Institute, Drews hauled down a school record 33 rebounds. Drews, a fierce competitor who lettered in basketball and baseball, was drafted in 1969 by the New York Mets. (ODU Archives.)

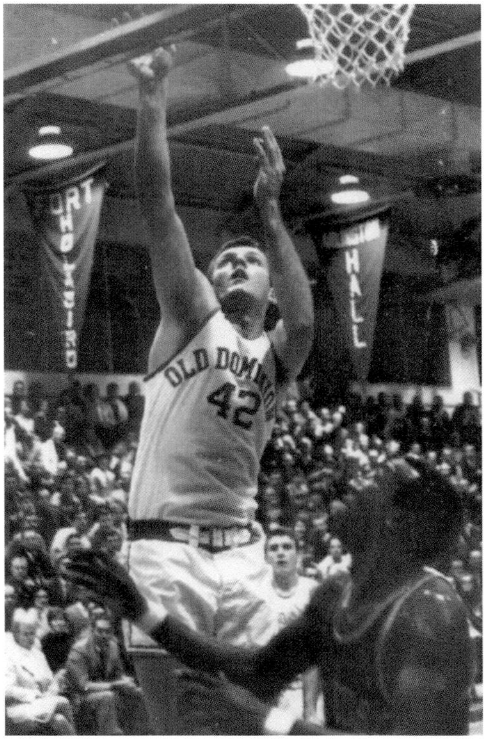


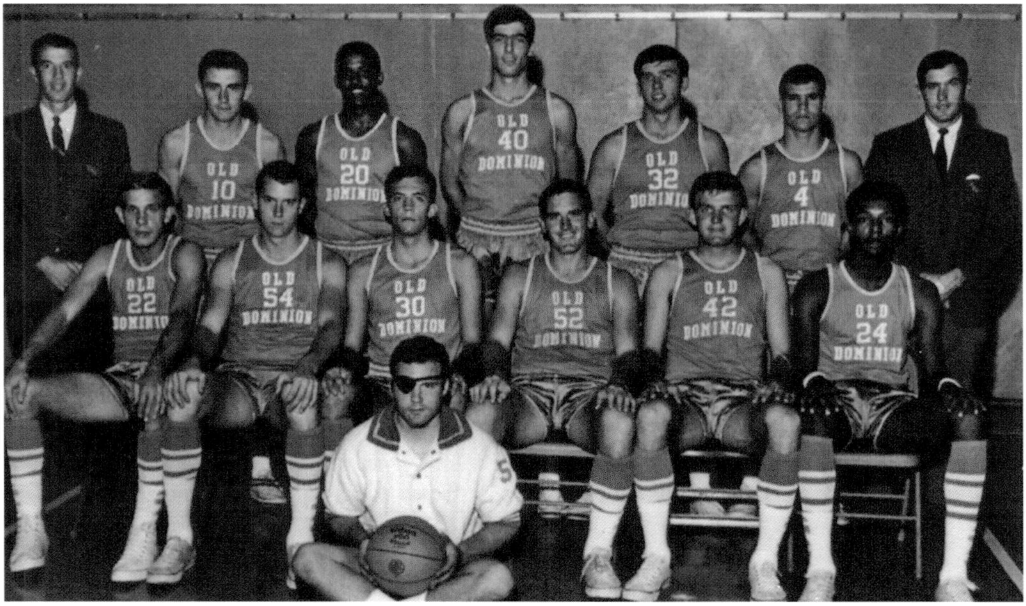


**MASON-DIXON CONFERENCE CHAMPIONS, 1968–1969.** This Monarch team recorded a 21-10 record, winning the school's first conference championship and NCAA bid. Pictured are (seated) Ken Hopkins, Steve Cox, Skip Noble, Harry Lozon, Ron Drews, and Billy Hayes; (standing) Sonny Allen, Dick St. Clair, Buttons Speakes, Barry Roach, Billy Turner, Ken Gathy, and Marion Carroll. Sitting in front is team manager John O'Hara. (ODU Archives.)

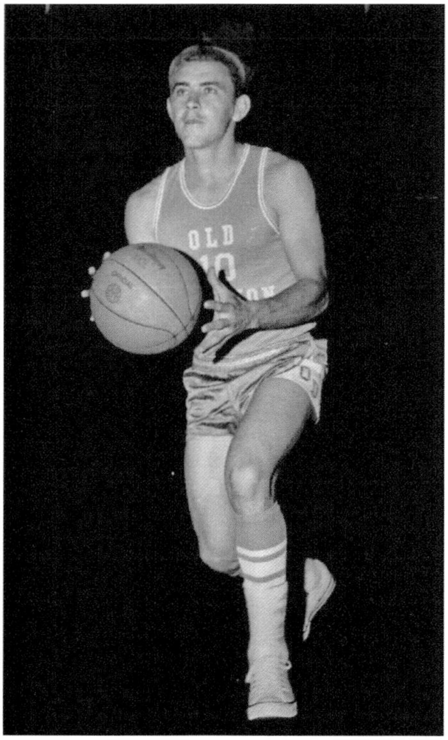

**Dick St. Clair, 1968–1970.** A 5-foot-9-inch guard who could dunk, St. Clair is regarded by many as being one of the school's greatest playmakers. A star for four All-Navy teams before joining Old Dominion, he brought maturity to the court. A Division II All-American, St. Clair scored 1,038 points and dished out 608 assists in his career. In 1983, he was inducted into the ODU Sports Hall of Fame. (VP.)

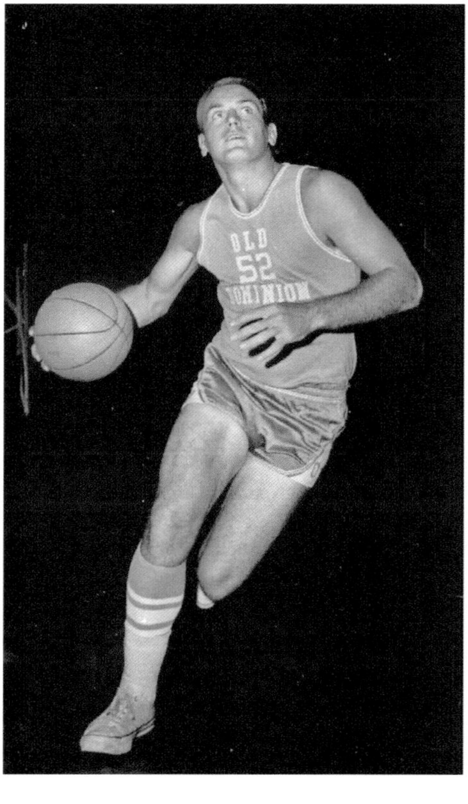

**Harry Lozon, 1966–1969.** Sonny Allen once remarked that this 6-foot-3-inch forward was "probably the most consistent player I ever coached." A powerful and tough player inside and out, Harry Lozon was rewarded with All-American honors in 1970. At the conclusion of his career, Lozon had amassed 1,424 points and 513 rebounds. He was the first Monarch ever drafted, having been selected by the San Diego Rockets. (VP.)

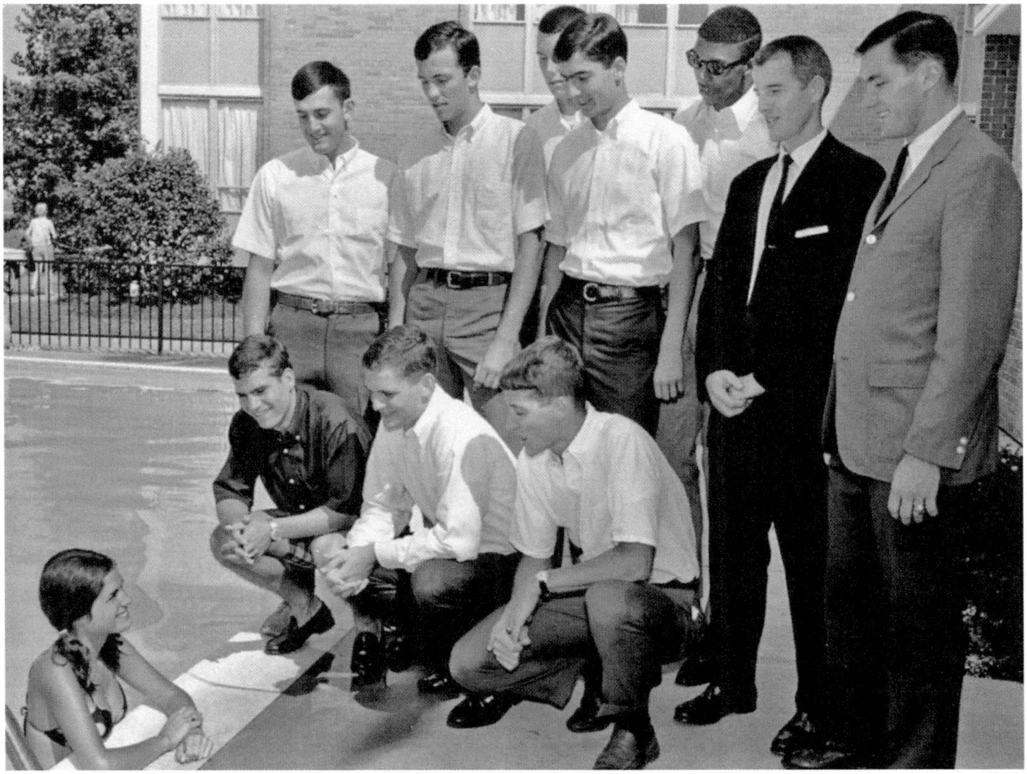

**SONNY'S NEW RECRUITS.** In this photograph, coaches Sonny Allen and Marion Carroll are taking Old Dominion's 1967–1968 recruiting class on a campus tour. They stop at the new pool in front of Rodgers Hall to meet a coed. From the looks on the players' faces it appears they are satisfied with their choice of school. (ODU Archives.)

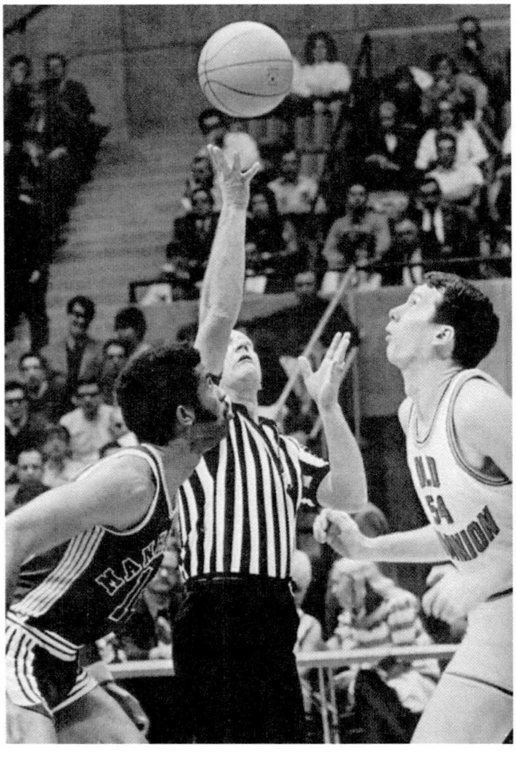

**TIMING IS EVERYTHING.** Monarch center Steve Cox, a native of College Park, Maryland, is intently concentrating on the tip to begin a game against Manhattan. The 6-foot-8-inch Cox was a good rebounder and shooter, a hard worker, and a great team player. Cox played a vital role on Allen's teams from 1967 to 1971. (ODU Archives.)

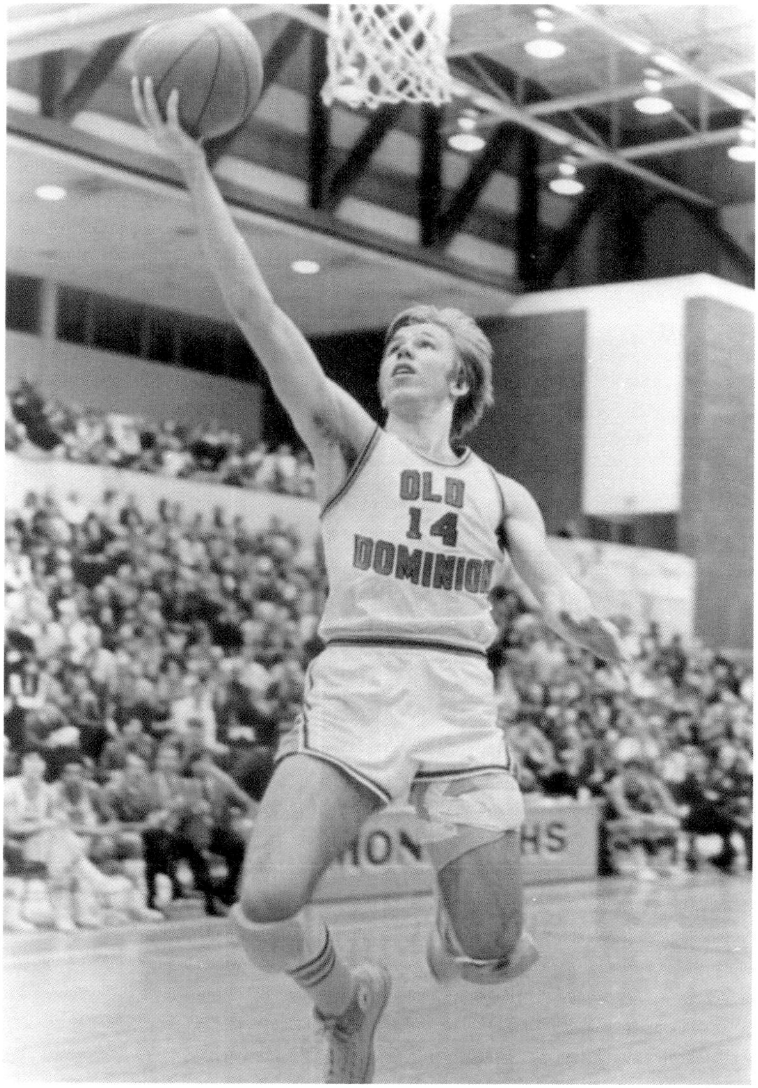


**DAVID TWARDZIK, ALL-AMERICAN.** From 1968 to 1972, this native of Middletown, Pennsylvania, directed Sonny Allen's fast break with a special flair. The first Old Dominion player selected as First Team All-American, Twardzik lead the Monarchs to a runner-up finish in the 1971 NCAA Division II National Championship. Arguably the Monarch's most complete player, Dave was a great passer, clutch shooter, and confident floor leader, guiding the Monarchs to 56 victories during his three-year career. After graduation in 1972, he was picked by the Portland Trailblazers in the NBA draft, but instead, he decided to sign with the ABA Virginia Squires. A four-year player for the Squires, he was named an ABA All-Star in 1975. Following the ABA-NBA merger in 1976, Dave signed with Portland, where he was the point guard for the 1976–1977 NBA champion Trail Blazers. After an injury forced his retirement as a player, he has continued to work in a variety of NBA administrative jobs. His No. 14 jersey hangs from the rafters of the Constant Center as a reminder to the Monarch faithful of his greatness. (ODU Archives.)

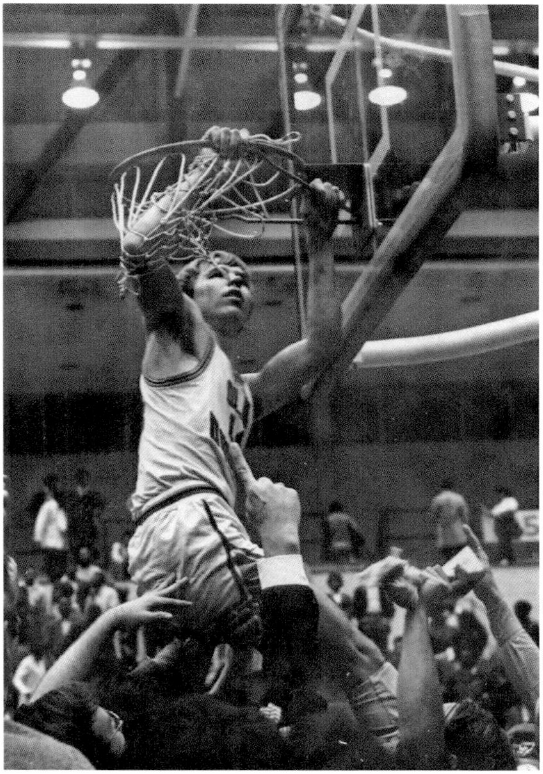

**Twardzik Cuts Down the Net.** After defeating crosstown rival Norfolk State 102-97 in the South Atlantic Regional Finals, Dave Twardzik does the honors of cutting down a net in the ODU Fieldhouse. With the win, Old Dominion was rewarded with a trip to Evansville, Indiana, to play in the 1970–1971 NCAA Division II National Championship. (ODU Archives.)

**Calling it as He Sees it.** Longtime Old Dominion fans can remember sitting around the radio and listening to Dick Fraim, "The Voice of Old Dominion Basketball," call a Monarch victory. Fraim, an Old Dominion graduate, had been a member of Bud Metheny's Norfolk Division teams in 1961–1962. A television-radio executive, he recently retired in Las Vegas, Nevada. (ODU Archives.)

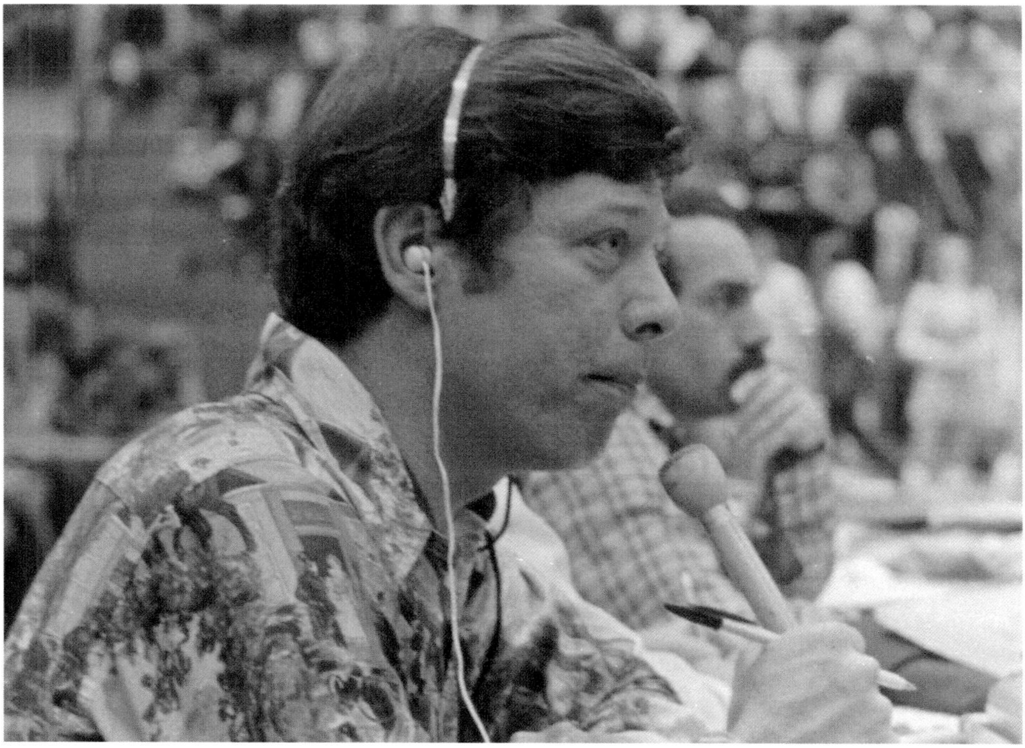

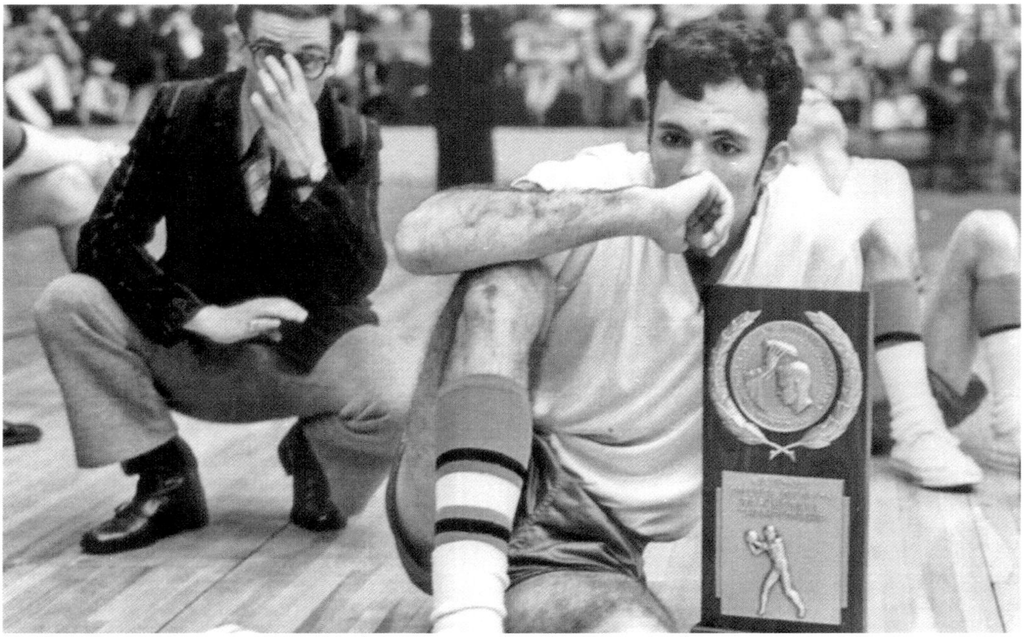

**Contemplating What Might Have Been.** Skip Noble sits next to the NCAA second place trophy after a heartbreaking loss to Evansville in the 1971 NCAA Division II Finals. Noble a 6-foot-5-inch forward, another of Allen's West Virginia recruits, had a quick release on shots and excellent speed. These attributes made him ideal for running the wing in Allen's fast break. (ODU Archives.)

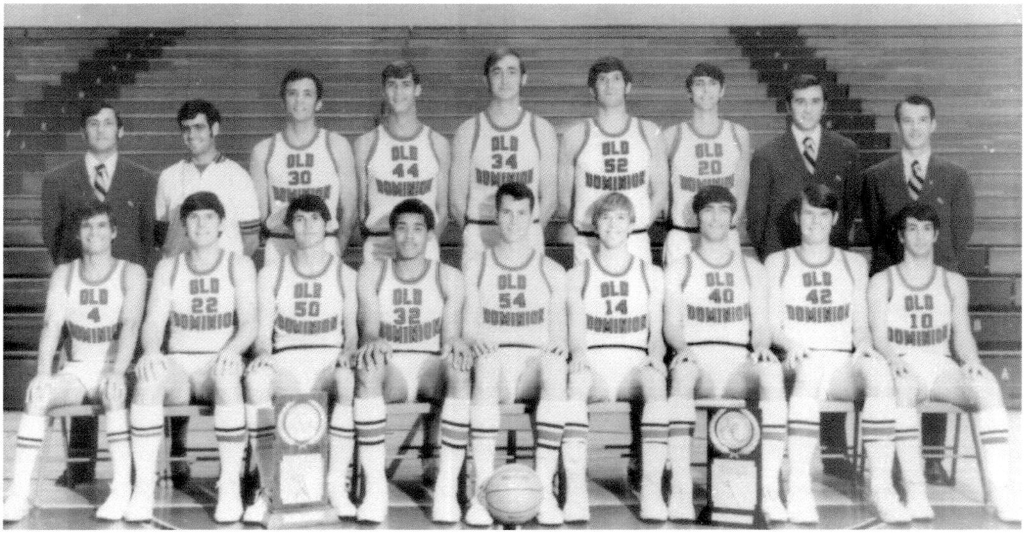

**NCAA Division II National Finalist, 1970–1971.** Members of this 21-9 squad are, from left to right, (first row) Ken Gathy, Parke Congleton, Jack Baker, Joel Copeland, Steve Cox, Dave Twardzik, Barry Roach, Ricky Michaelsen, and Rick Nau; (second row) coach Marion Carroll, manager Larry Crowder, Skip Noble, Terry Foster, Jay Rountree, Randy Coulling, Charles Harrington, coach Steve Cottrell, coach Sonny Allen. (ODU Archives.)

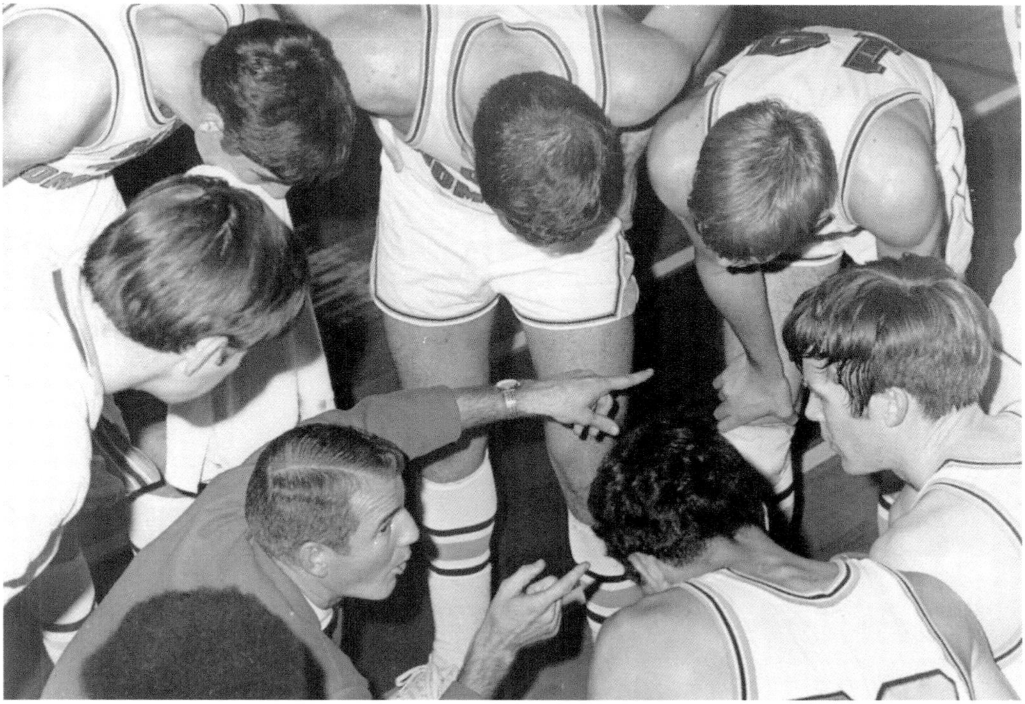

**COACH IN A HUDDLE.** Sonny Allen gives directions to his Monarchs during a timeout. Known nationally for his fast-break offense, Allen was known in practice for placing numbers in certain spots on the floor and assigning individual players to run to each spot in his fast break. (ODU Archives.)

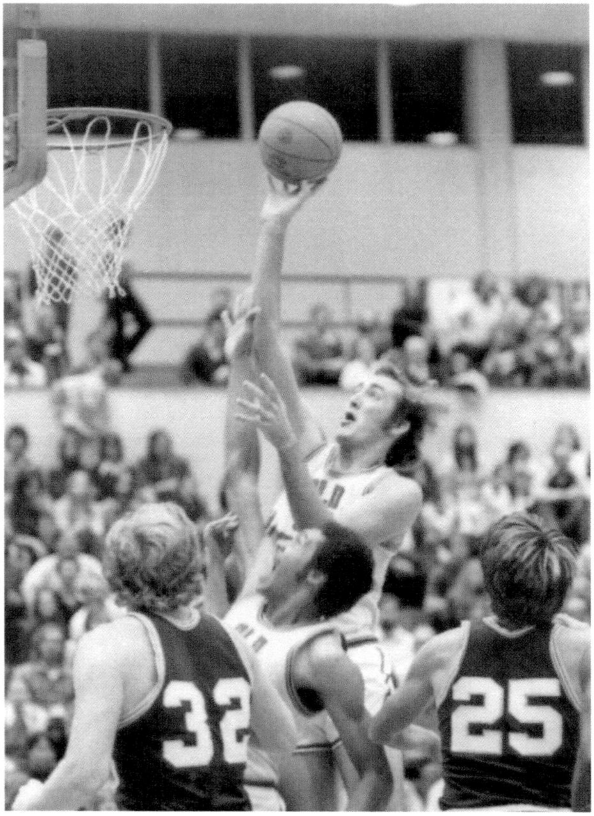


**GOING HIGH FOR A TIP.** Monarch center Jay Rountree goes high for a tip as two Randolph-Macon players watch. At the time the 6-foot-10-inch Rountree, a native of Camp Hill, Pennsylvania, was Old Dominion's tallest player ever recruited. Jay had a nice shooting touch and could run the court well for a big man. For three varsity seasons, Rountree played a crucial role in the school's success. (ODU Archives.)

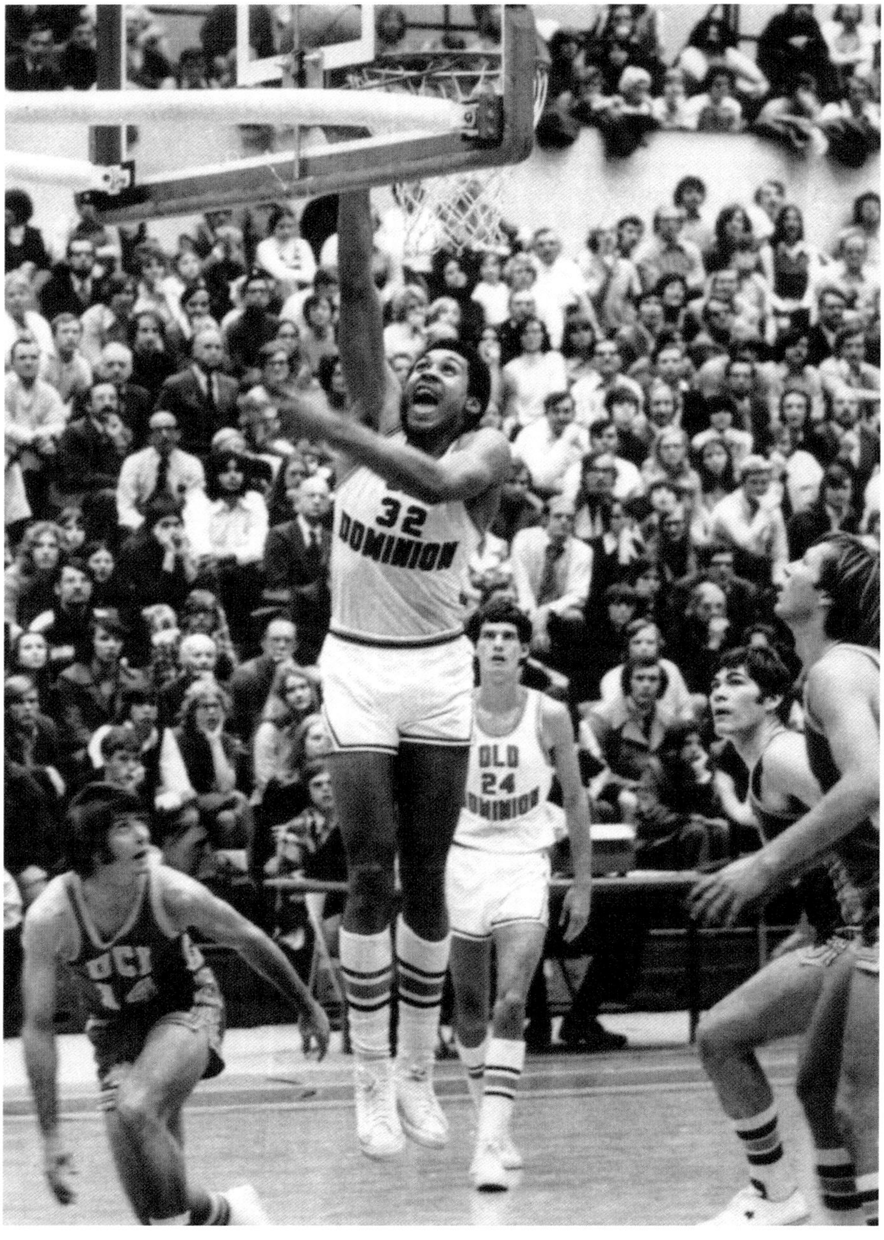

**JOEL COPELAND, ALL-AMERICAN.** In this photograph, Monarch forward, Joel Copeland goes for 2 of his 20 points against the University of California-Irvine. Copeland, a native of Holland, Virginia, was a consensus High School All-American. Joel was a great leaper with an excellent shooting touch both inside and out. A fierce rebounder and defender, he finished his Old Dominion career with 1,657 points and 939 rebounds in just over three seasons. In 1973–1974, Copeland was selected as a First Team Division II All-American. After graduation, he was drafted by the New Orleans Jazz. An inductee of the 1982 class of the Old Dominion Sports Hall of Fame, Copeland's No. 32 jersey was retired and hangs up high in the Constant Center. (ODU Archives.)

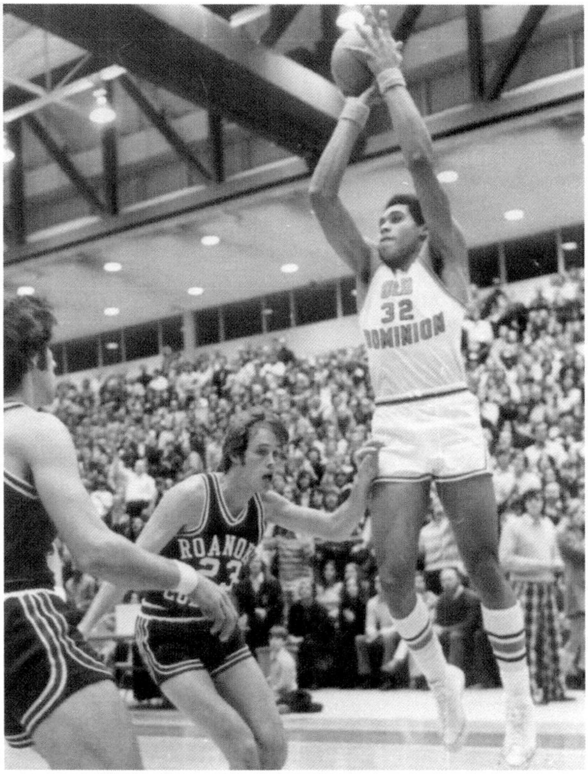


**JOEL HITS TWO, FEBRUARY 22, 1974.** One of the most intense rivalries during Copeland's career was with Division II power Roanoke College. In this image, Copeland squares up and shoots a jumper against Roanoke defenders Denton Willard (23) and Jay Picolla. Copeland scored 21 points and grabbed a game-high 13 rebounds as the Monarchs won 82-76 in a sold-out ODU Fieldhouse. (ODU Archives.)

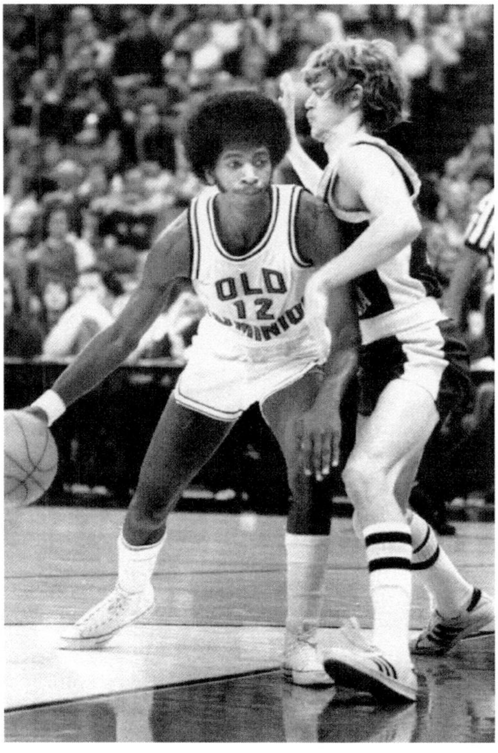


**OLIVER PURNELL, 1972–1975.** This 6-foot-1-inch guard captained the Monarchs to their 1975 Division II Championship and finished his three-year varsity career with 1,090 points and 476 assists. A ferocious defender, he still holds the school record of eight steals in a game. An All-American his senior season, he was a sixth-round draft choice of the Milwaukee Bucks. (VP.)

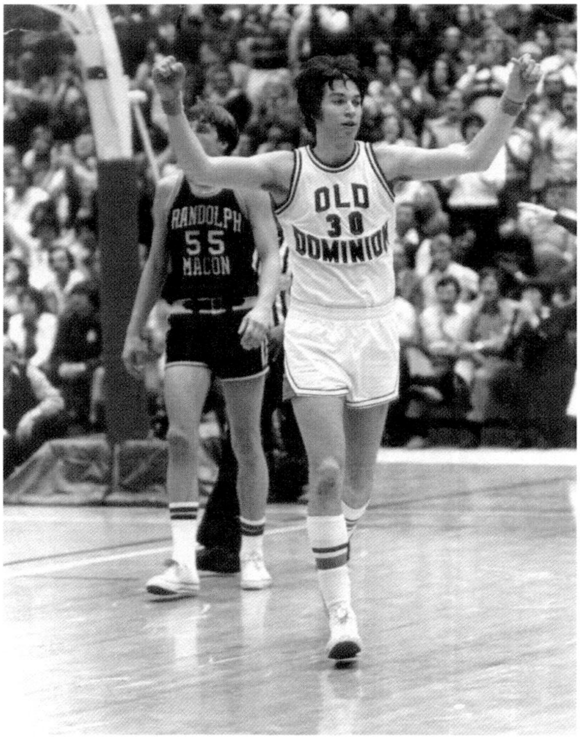


**JEFF FUHRMANN, 1973–1977.** Forward Jeff Fuhrmann clinches his fists in victory after Old Dominion's thrashing of Randolph Macon in the 1974–1975 regional finals, securing a berth in Evansville. Fuhrmann, a member of the ODU Sports Hall of Fame, was a deadly outside shooter who helped lead ODU to postseason play in all of his four seasons. He would complete his career with 1,429 points and 627 rebounds. (ODU Archives.)

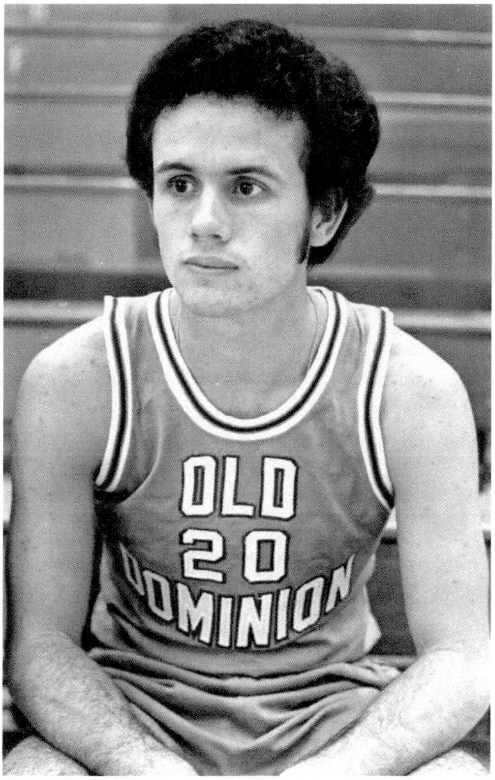


**JOEY CARUTHERS, 1973–1977.** Playing for Sonny Allen and Paul Webb, Caruthers was a member of the 1975 Division II National Championship squad. A quick and accurate guard, he currently ranks among Monarch players as fourth all-time with 188 career steals and 619 assists. Currently a college basketball official, he was honored in 1993 with induction into the ODU Sports Hall of Fame. (VP.)

**VICTORY RIDE FOR SONNY.** After defeating the University of New Orleans to win the 1974–1975 NCAA Division II National Championship, Wilson Washington and team manager Tony Flores, carry coach Sonny Allen in celebration. The win, Allen's 181st victory, would be his last at Old Dominion. Several months later Allen would leave to become the head coach at Southern Methodist University. (ODU Archives.)

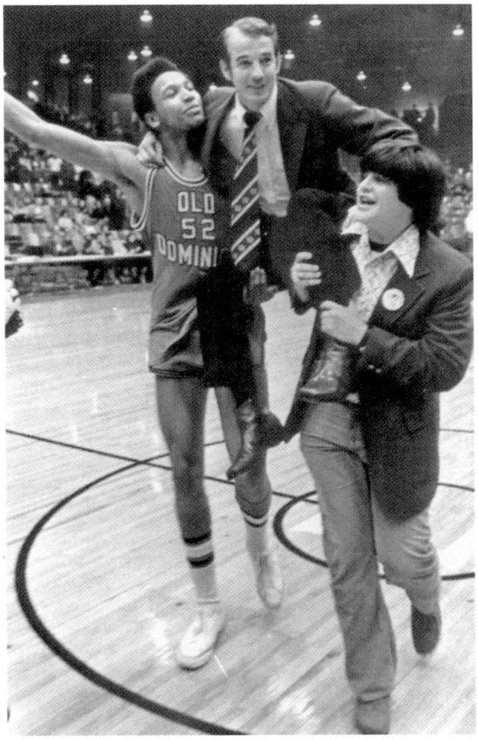


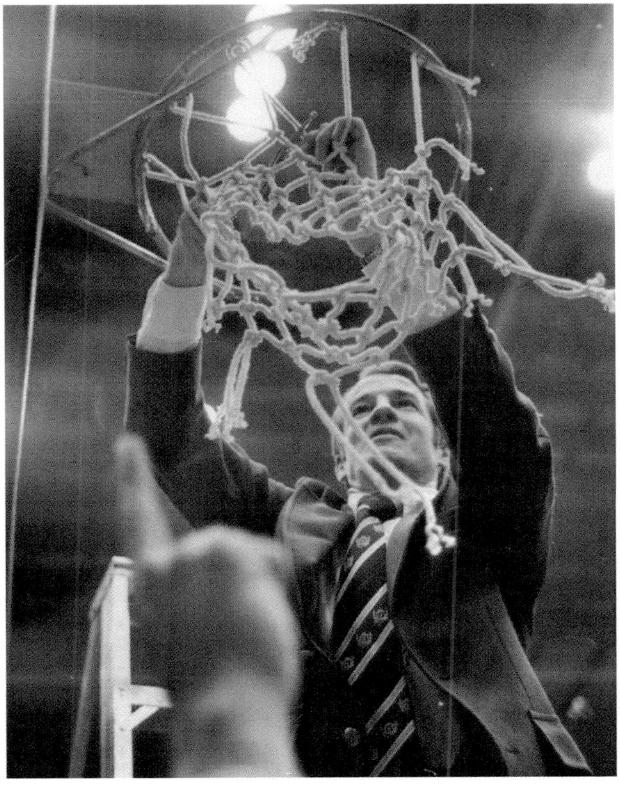

**SONNY CUTS DOWN A NET.** Coach Allen follows the tradition of cutting down the nets after a championship victory in Evansville. With a Division II National Championship, Allen had accomplished what he set out to do nearly 10 years earlier. In the end, he had taken the Monarchs to two NCAA Finals, nine winning seasons, and six postseason tournaments. (ODU Archives.)

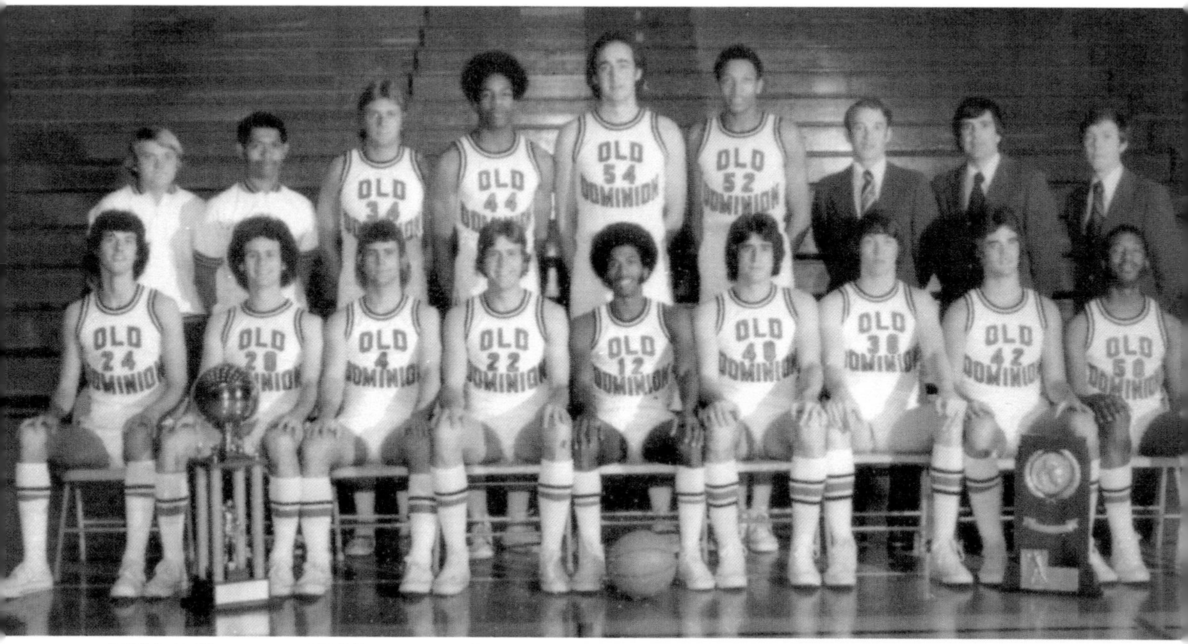

**NCAA Division II National Champions, 1974–1975.** After easily beating North Dakota and Tennessee State in their first two games, the Monarchs met New Orleans in the finals, where they squeaked out a 76-74 win. Members of this 25-6 squad are, from left to right, (first row) Gray Eubank, Joey Caruthers, Windell Morrison, Dave Moyer, Oliver Purnell, Leon Hylton, Jeff Furhmann, Joey O'Brien, and Curtis Cole; (second row) manager Mike Wrigley, manager Carol Hudson Jr., Rich Tackaberry, Tommy Street, Jay Rountree, Wilson Washington, Sonny Allen, Charlie Wollum, and Ed Hall. (ODU Archives.)

5

# A Decade of Excellence

## The Paul Webb Years 1975–1985

After the unexpected resignation of Sonny Allen, Old Dominion moved quickly to name a replacement. Athletic Director Dr. James Jarrett and his selection committee screened a long list of outstanding candidates and quickly found their man. On the afternoon of July 7, 1975, Old Dominion's president, Dr. James Bugg, and Dr. Jarrett introduced Paul Webb as their choice. The 46-year-old Webb was leaving rival Randolph-Macon College, where, after 19 seasons, he had produced a record of 315-158. When asked what type of offense he would employ, Webb responded, "I like to fast break, and we'll run when we get a chance. In comparing my technique with Sonny's, I'd say I stress a little more man-to-man defense." Webb would have approximately five months before his new team would begin defense of their Division II National Championship.

Hopes were high because Webb's first squad included returning starters Wilson Washington, Jeff Fuhrmann, and Joey Caruthers. The team was bolstered by transfers Reese Neyland, Terry Douglas, and freshman recruit Tommy Conrad. Playing a schedule made up of 17 Division I teams, the Monarchs still managed to return to Evansville with hopes of repeating as Division II National Champions. The team was derailed as they lost to eventual champion Puget Sound 83-78 and Eastern Illinois 78-74 in the consolation game.

In 1976–1977, Old Dominion entered the ranks of Division I, joining the Eastern Collegiate Athletic Conference (ECAC). The season was memorable as Washington, Fuhrmann, Caruthers, and Douglas returned for their final campaign and were joined by newcomer Ronnie Valentine. The Monarchs went an impressive 25-4, setting a Virginia state record of 22 consecutive wins. The winning streak included victories against Mississippi State, Virginia, and an 80-58 shellacking of Georgetown in the finals of the ECAC Southern Division Championship on the Hoyas' home court. The Monarchs hosted the ECAC Championship, losing to Syracuse 67-64 and failing to obtain a bid to the 32-team NCAA Tournament. However, ODU hosted Villanova in an NIT contest, losing to the Wildcats 71-68.

Webb's 1977–1978 Monarchs featured the return of forwards Valentine and Neyland, guards Conrad and Richie Wright, and junior center Larry Orton. Poor chemistry contributed to a dismal record of 11-15, Webb's only losing season at ODU.

In 1978–1979, the Monarchs were led offensively by forwards Valentine and newcomer Ronnie McAdoo. Senior point guard Tommy Conrad and sophomore guard Bobby Vaughn as well as 6-foot-8-inch center Mike Ray rounded out the starting five. Freshman Tommy Branch and Billy Mann gave the Monarchs depth. The 23-7 season included wins against SMU, Virginia, Florida State, and an NIT double-overtime win against Clemson.

Webb's 1979–1980 Monarchs returned Valentine, McAdoo, Branch, Mann, and Vaughn. With the addition of four freshman, including guard Grant Robinson and 6-foot-10 Mark West, the year looked promising. In November, they defeated a powerful Soviet National team in overtime, 76-74. The final season record was 25-5, including a nationally televised victory against previously undefeated and third-ranked Syracuse, won on a last-second shot by Vaughn. In the ECAC Championship, ODU defeated Navy, securing the school's first NCAA Division I bid. The Monarchs lost to eventual NCAA runner-up UCLA 87-74 in the West Regional.

Despite the loss of Valentine, prospects for the 1980–1981 campaign were optimistic. Returning starters McAdoo, West, Vaughn, and Robinson were joined by Mann. ODU earned its most significant victory on January 10, 1981, when they defeated top-ranked DePaul on a steal and shot by Mann with only seven seconds remaining, snapping DePaul's 48-game winning streak at home. Despite an undermanned squad with only nine players, the Monarchs managed to earn another postseason bid, losing to Georgia 74-60 in the NIT.

In 1981–1982, McAdoo and Mann returned for their final season along with returning starters West and Robinson. Freshman newcomers included Charlie Smith, Fred Facka, and Horace Lambert. The Monarchs finished the season 18-12, winning the ECAC South Regional and earning an NCAA bid, losing to Wake Forest in the NCAA East Regional.

Optimism was high for the 1982–1983 campaign. West and Robinson were back for their senior season surrounded by sophomore Smith and a freshman class that included Kenny Gattison, Ronnie Wade, and Keith Thomas. The Monarchs were crowned cochampions in their inaugural season in the Sun Belt Conference. They met South Carolina in the NIT, losing 100-90.

The 1983–1984 squad returned juniors Smith and Mark Davis and sophomores Hanley, Gattison, Thomas, and Wade. Webb's squad again earned another winning season, going 19-12 and losing to Notre Dame in the NIT.

With all of his starters returning and the addition of freshman guard Frank Smith and Wake Forest–transfer Sylvester Charles, Webb's 1984–1985 season was one of great expectations. That season Webb coached his 500th career victory, an 86-60 win over the University of North Carolina, Charlotte. Their second consecutive 19-12 record was enough for the Monarchs to receive an NCAA East Regional bid, where they lost to SMU 75-68.

On July 6, 1985, Paul Webb's tenure ended when he resigned as Old Dominion's coach to take an administrative post in the athletic department. Under his direction, he brought ODU into a new era, guiding the school to a successful transition into Division I. Webb's 10 years as head coach included nine winning seasons and seven post-season appearances, including three NCAA Tournaments and four NIT appearances.

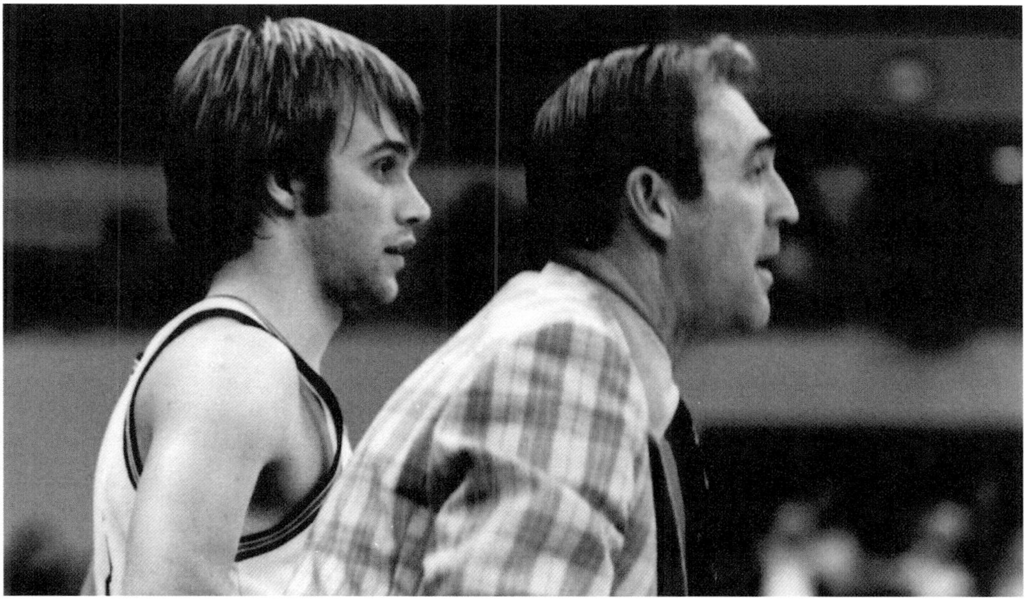

**Coach and Student.** Paul Webb coaches from the sideline as guard Tommy Conrad watches intently before going into the game. Conrad started for Webb's first Monarch squad as a freshman. A defensive specialist at drawing charging fouls, from 1975–1979, this scrappy, hardnosed, and aggressive guard frequently ignited the Monarchs with his on-court enthusiasm. (VP.)

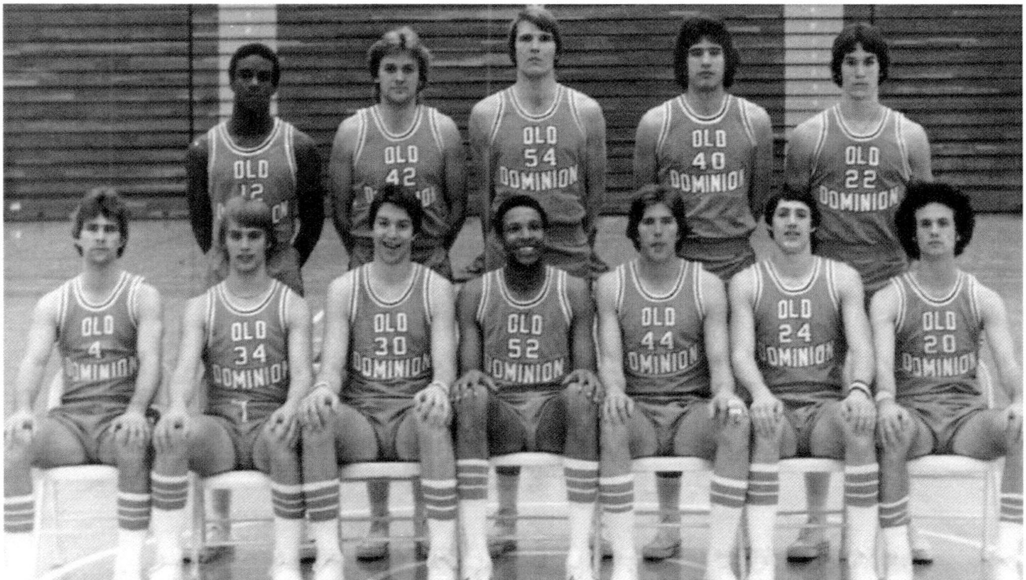

**NCAA Division II Final Four Team, 1975–1976.** Webb's first team at Old Dominion finished 19-12 and journeyed to Evansville for the Division II final four. Members of this squad are, from left to right, (first row) Wendell Morrison, Tommy Conrad, Jeff Fuhrmann, Wilson Washington, Dave Moyer, Reese Neyland, and Joey Caruthers; (second row) Terry Douglas, Rich Tackaberry, Ray Peszko, Leon Hylton, and Bill Herscher. (ODU Archives.)

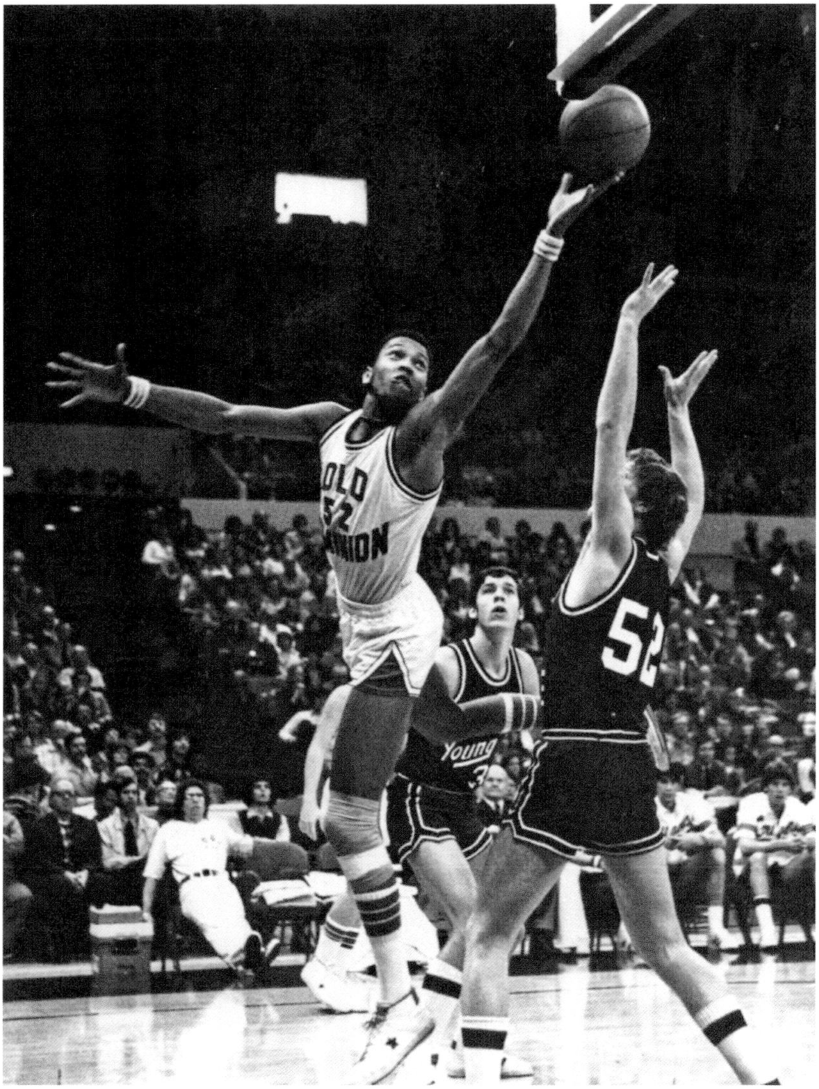


**WILSON WASHINGTON, ALL-AMERICAN.** Old Dominion's 6-foot-9-inch center, Wilson Washington, scores two against a Brigham Young defender at the 1975 Kiwanis ODU Classic. Named the tournament's MVP, Washington scored 43 points and collected 46 rebounds in the two-night event. A transfer from Maryland, the Norfolk native became a fan favorite with his on-court aggressiveness, great leaping ability, and flamboyant style. Probably his greatest game was in 1976 against William and Mary, when he had a 22-point, 20-rebound, 12–blocked shot performance. In his three-year career, Washington scored 1,366 points, collected 1,011 rebounds, and blocked 364 shots. In 1977, he became Old Dominion's first Division I All-American, after previously earning Division II First Team honors in 1976 and third team in 1975. After graduation, Washington was selected in the second round of the 1977 NBA draft pick by the Philadelphia 76ers, where he played for two seasons. In 1978, Wilson Washington's jersey, No. 52, was retired, and today his number proudly hangs from the rafters at the Ted Constant Center. (VP.)

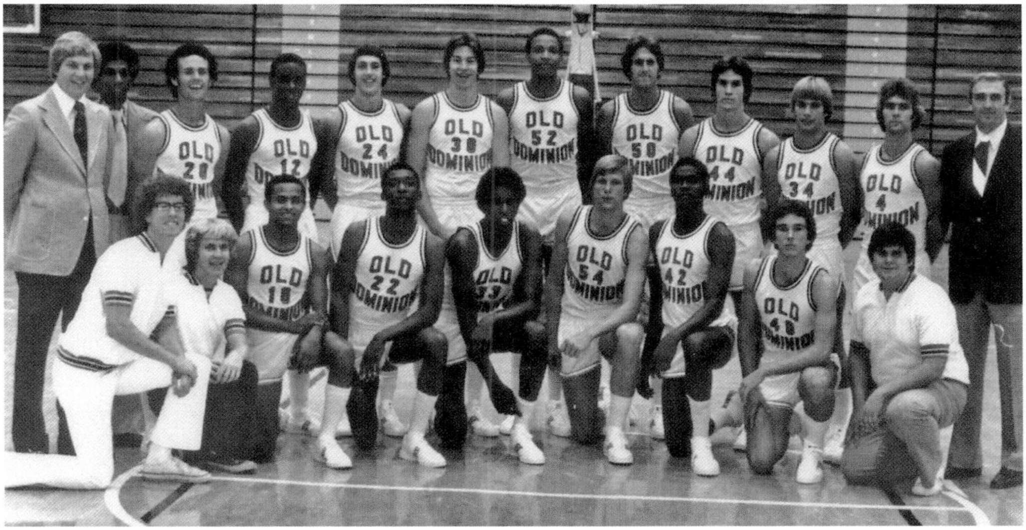

**First NCAA Division I Team, 1976–1977.** This 25-4 squad captured the ECAC South Division Championship. Pictured from left to right are (first row, kneeling) manager Frank Cox, manager Benn Potts, Richie Wright, George Darby, Chris Pickett, Mike Ray, Ronnie Valentine, Bobby Haithcock, and manager Tony Flores; (second row, standing) Mike Polio, Oliver Purnell, Joey Caruthers, Terry Douglas, Reese Neyland, Jeff Fuhrmann, Wilson Washington, Wayne Piscopo, Bill Herscher, Tommy Conrad, Wendell Morrison, and Paul Webb. (ODU Archives.)

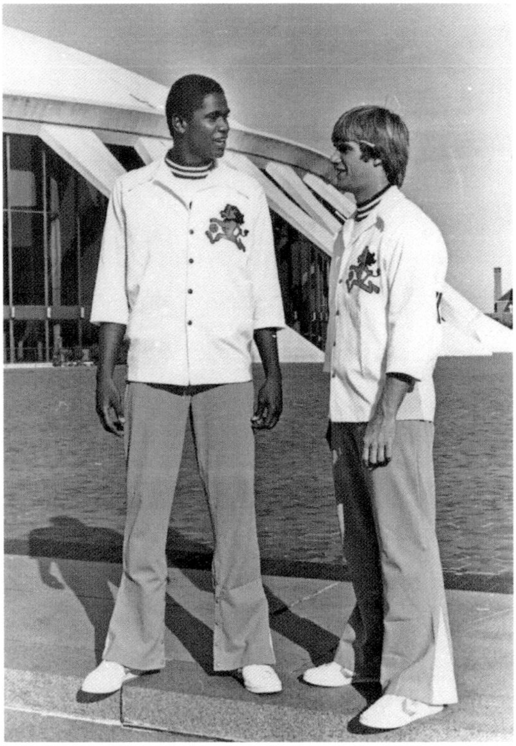

**Monarch Cocaptains, 1978–1979.** Old Dominion University senior guard Tommy Conrad and junior forward Ronnie Valentine stand in front of Scope, the Monarchs' home court, in anticipation of the upcoming season. This young team with only two returning starters was coming off an 11-15 season rocked by dissention. At season's end, the Monarchs would return to their winning ways by playing for the ECAC South Division Championship and finishing the season at 23-7. (VP.)

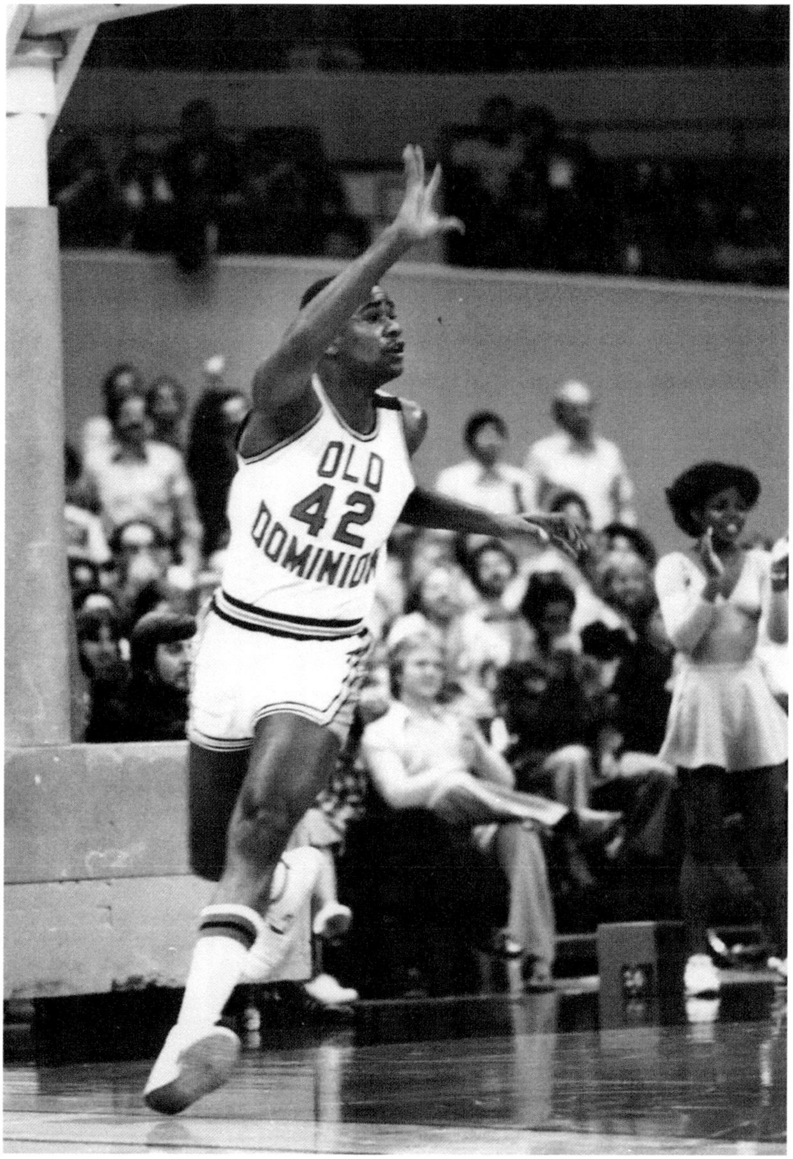


**RONNIE VALENTINE, ALL-AMERICAN.** From 1976 to 1980, Ronnie Valentine was Old Dominion's heart. A Norfolk native, Valentine was talked into becoming a Monarch by another Norfolk native, Wilson Washington. Together they provided a one-two punch for Old Dominion's initial year in Division I. For four years, this 6-foot-7-inch forward was an offensive juggernaut for the Monarchs. A power forward who could score inside and out, Valentine scored in double figures in 101 consecutive games, an NCAA record at the time. Old Dominion's all-time leading scorer, Ronnie scored 2,204 points and grabbed 949 rebounds over his career. Valentine was selected an Honorable Mention All-American in both 1979 and 1980. After graduation in 1980, he was selected in the third round of the NBA draft by the Denver Nuggets. His play was acknowledged in 1985 with his induction into the ODU Sports Hall of Fame. (ODU Archives.)

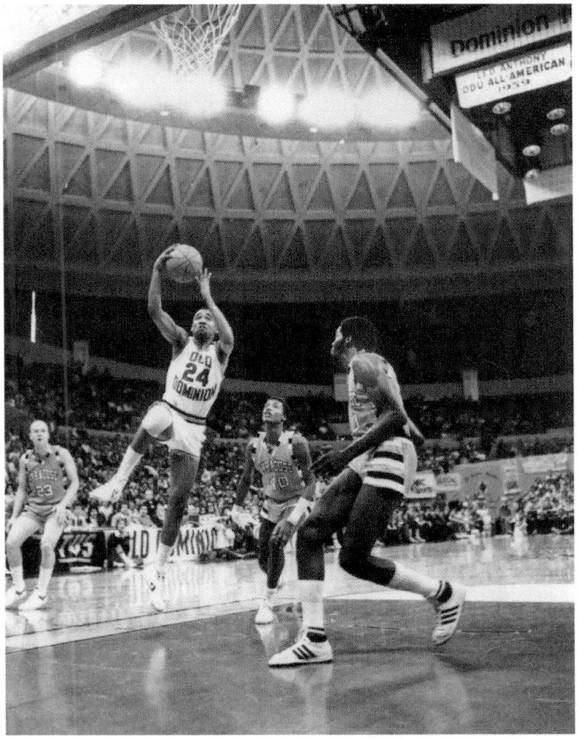


**BRANCH DRIVES FOR TWO.** On January 19, 1980, Old Dominion was on the national stage as they hosted third-ranked Syracuse at Scope. The game was a CBS Television Regional Game-of-the-Week. In this image, Tommy Branch drives for two as three Syracuse defenders can only watch. Branch was a Monarch defensive specialist who had exceptional court awareness. (VP.)

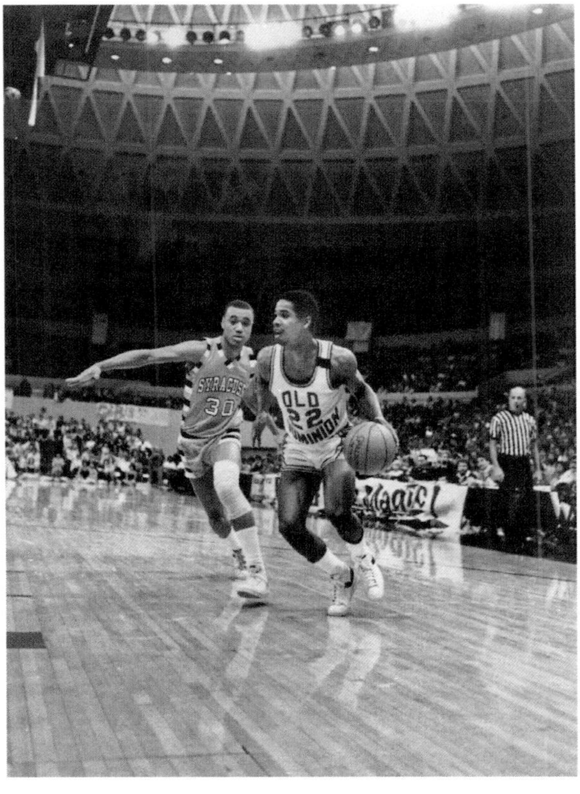


**MAN OF THE MOMENT.** Guard Bobby Vaughn drives against third-ranked Syracuse's Tony Bruin for two points. Down 63-50 with five minutes left in the game, the Monarchs win 68-67 at the buzzer on a Vaughn tip-in. The soft-spoken Vaughn was a hard worker both on and off the court. Recognized for his great floor leadership, he was selected as the Monarchs' captain in 1980–1981. (VP.)

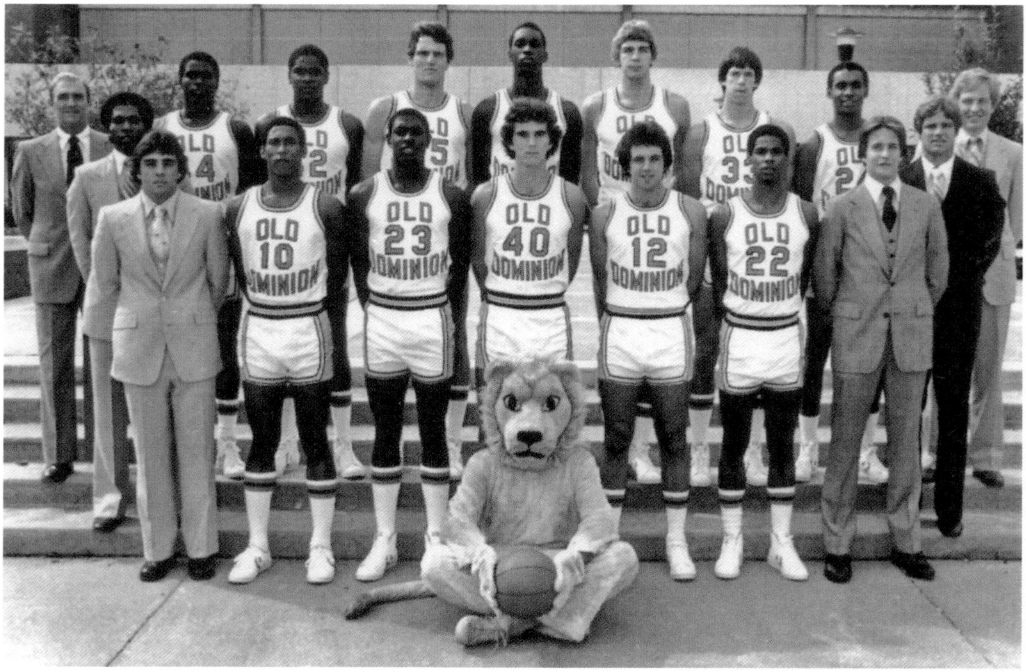

**ECAC South Champions, 1979–1980.** This Paul Webb contingent went an impressive 25-5. Pictured from left to right are (first row) Mike Mouris, Grant Robinson, Billy Mann, Bobby Haithcock, Ricky Adams, Bobby Vaughn, and C. J. Koenig; (second row) Paul Webb, Oliver Purnell, Ronnie McAdoo, Ronnie Valentine, Bert Kragtwijk, Mark West, Eric Griekspoor, Tim Southerland, Tommy Branch, Eddie Webb, and Mike Pollio. (ODU Archives.)

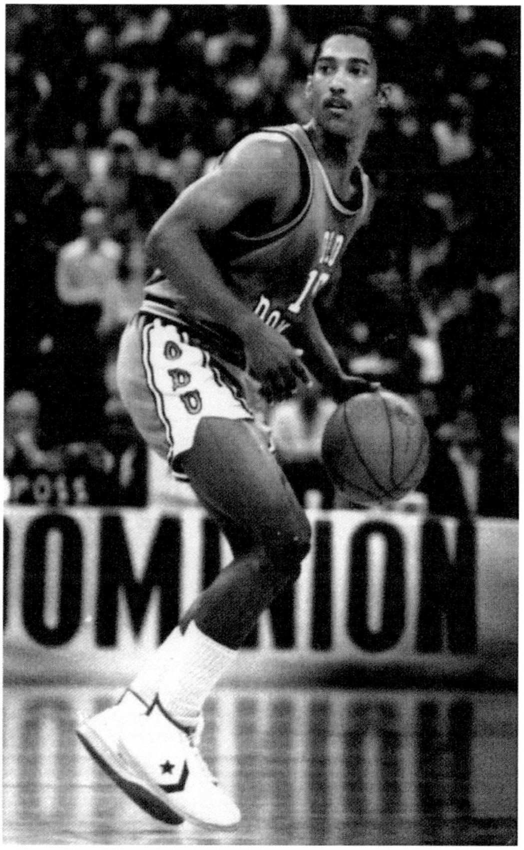

**"General" Grant Leads His Troops.** From 1979 to 1983, Grant Robinson played point guard for the Monarchs. On the court, this 6-foot-1-inch native of Newport News displayed great quickness, speed, and court awareness. His teammates recognized his leadership and in 1982–1983 selected him and Mark West cocaptains of the Monarchs. Grant ended his ODU career with a total of 596 assists and 184 steals over 117 games. (ODU Archives.)

**BIG MAC ATTACK.** Ronnie McAdoo goes high for a tip-in against Wake Forest in a 1982 NCAA Regional clash. The 6-foot-6-inch McAdoo was a Monarch starter at forward from 1978 to 1982. The physically powerful and quick McAdoo scored 1,776 points and collected 953 rebounds for his four-year career. For his play, he was selected a 1980–1981 Associated Press Division I Honorable All-American.In 1989, he was honored with induction into the ODU Sports Hall of Fame. (ODU Archives.)

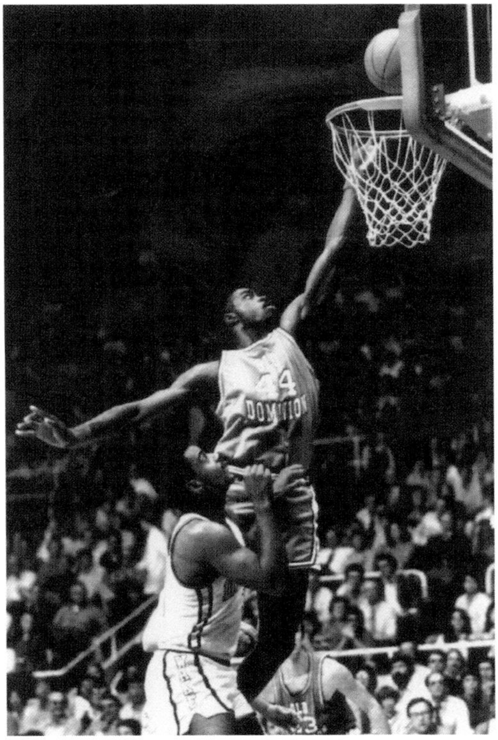

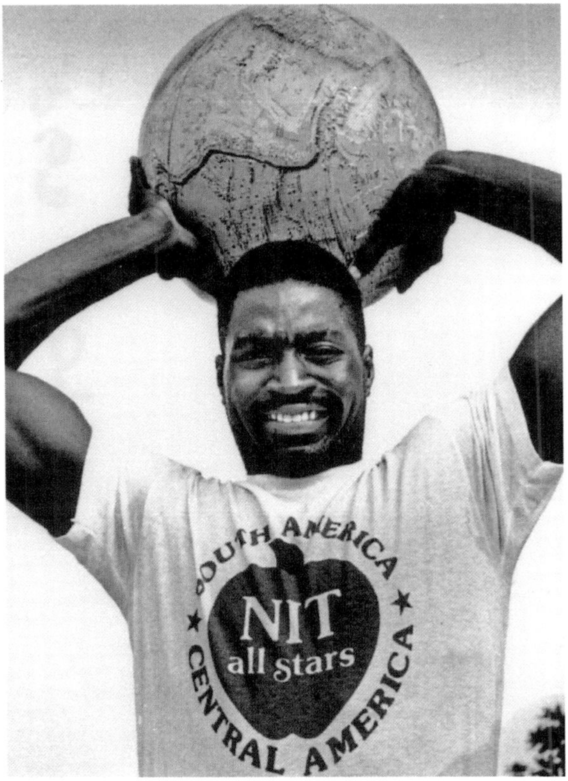


**HE'S GOT THE WHOLE WORLD IN HIS HANDS.** Ronnie McAdoo proudly displays a T-shirt promoting a 1981 South and Central American tour of NIT All-Stars. McAdoo played in the postseason all four of his years at Old Dominion. In 1980 and 1982, he faced UCLA and Wake Forest in NCAA Regionals; in 1979, he faced Purdue in the quarter finals; and in 1981, he faced University of Georgia in the first round of the National Invitation Tournament. (VP.)

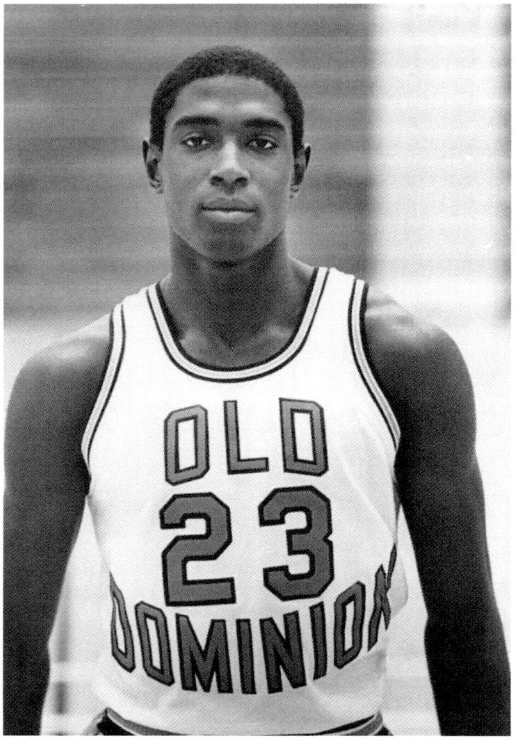


**Billy Mann, 1978–1982.** The 6-foot-4-inch Norfolk native Billy Mann played both the guard and forward position for Old Dominion. He was a skilled and tough rebounder for his size. A good defender, he often was given the task of the toughest defensive assignment. A cocaptain for the 1981–1982 Monarchs, he currently serves as the color analyst for Old Dominion University radio broadcasts. (ODU Archives.)

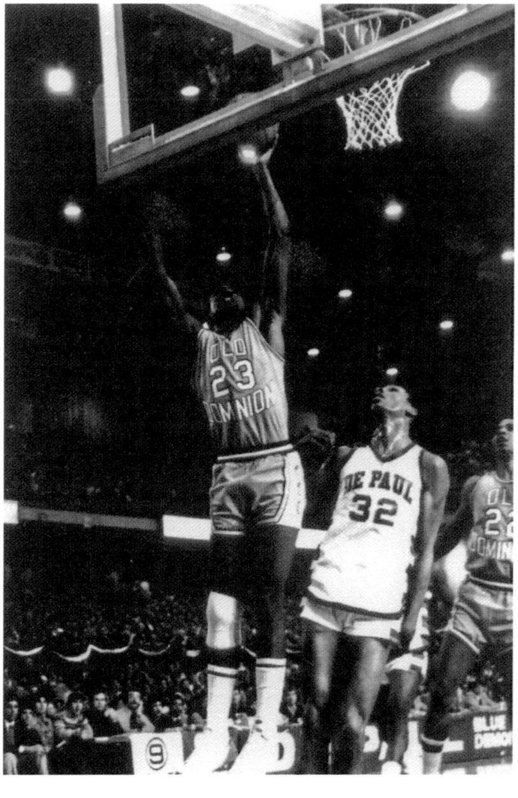


**The Shot Heard round the World.** On January 10, 1981, the Monarchs shocked the basketball world when they defeated top-ranked DePaul on a steal and shot by Billy Mann with only seven seconds remaining. Mann had just hit a short jumper only four seconds earlier to pull ODU within a point. The Monarch victory snapped DePaul's 48-game winning streak at home in the Horizon. (ODU Archives.)

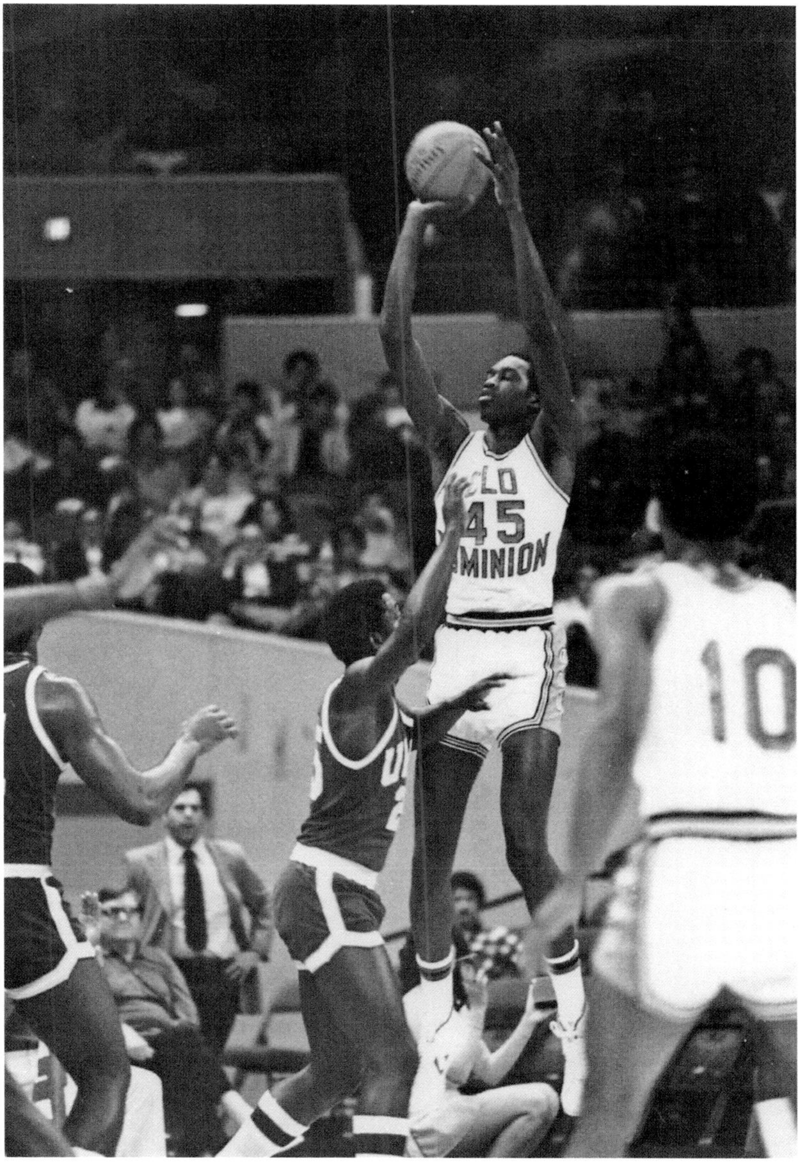


**Mark West, All-American.** This 6-foot-10-inch center was a dominant inside force for the Monarchs from 1979–1983. A two-time Honorable Mention All-American, West led the nation in blocked shots his sophomore and junior seasons. At the conclusion of his career, Mark had become the school's all-time leader in blocked shots with 446. Powerful and authoritative around the basket, West also concluded his ODU career with 1,113 rebounds and 1,308 points. Drafted in the second round by the Dallas Mavericks, he also had stints with Milwaukee, Cleveland, Detroit, Indiana, Atlanta, and Phoenix over 17 seasons. West is currently an assistant general manager for the Phoenix Suns. Besides being a member of the ODU Sports Hall of Fame, in 2006 he was inducted into the Virginia Sports Hall of Fame. In 1984, West's No. 45 jersey was retired and currently hangs beside Old Dominion's other greats at the Ted Constant Center. (ODU Archives.)

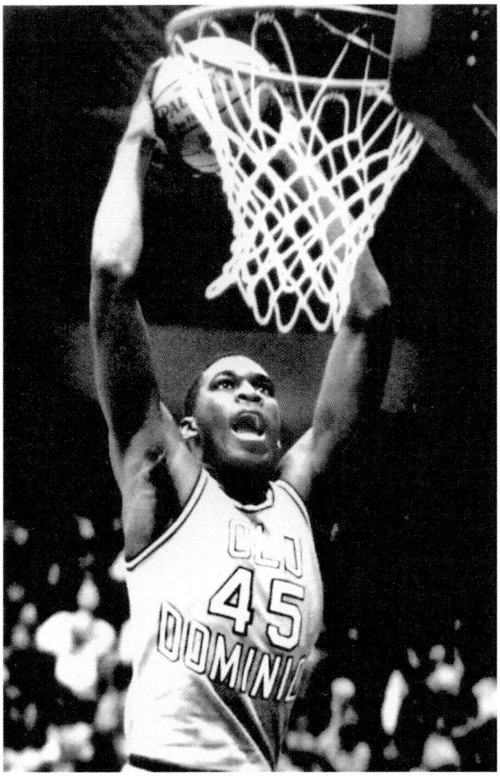


**JAMMIN' WITH AUTHORITY.** From 1979 to 1983, Monarch faithful were treated to numerous authoritative dunks, such as the one shown in this picture. As a Monarch, West had a career field-goal percentage of .559, ranking third all-time. Not to be outdone in the NBA, he had a career field-goal percentage of .580, the second highest in NBA history. (ODU Archives.)

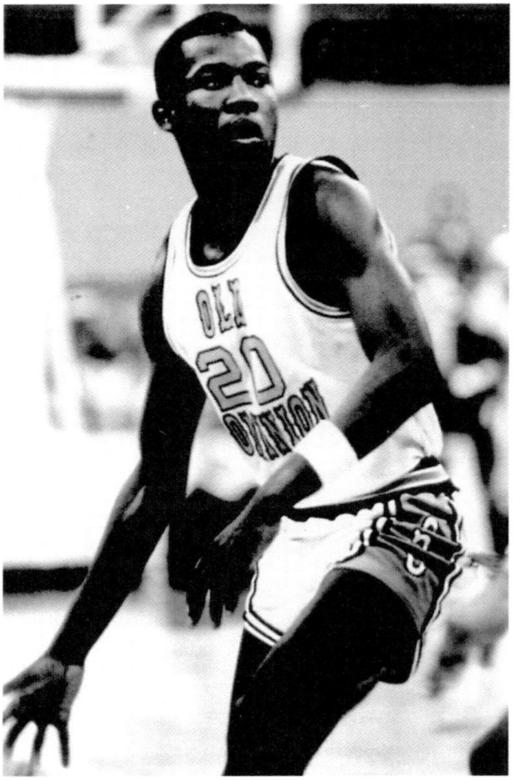


**CHARLIE SMITH, 1981–1985.** This Wilmington, Delaware, native is remembered by longtime Monarch fans as one of the school's greatest clutch performers. On three different occasions, Charlie displayed court heroics by winning games with last-second shots. This ODU captain ended his career with 1,250 points and 385 assists. In May 1998, Charlie passed away from an illness, and in 2004, he was posthumously inducted into the ODU Sports Hall of Fame. (ODU Archives.)

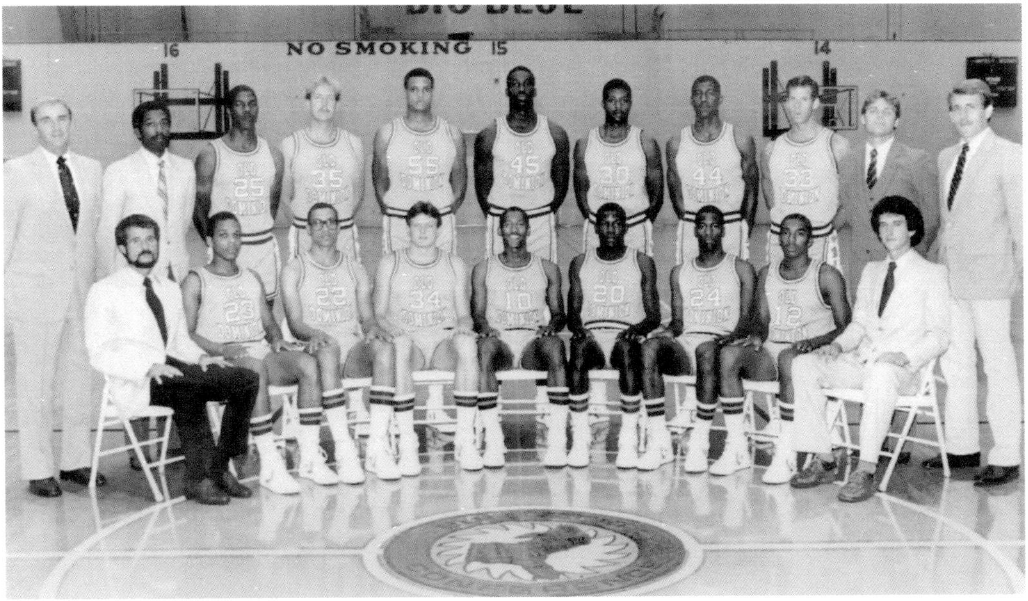


**SUN BELT REGULAR SEASON CHAMPIONS, 1982–1983.** Members of this 19-10 team are (first row, seated) P. Veschi, Mark Dean, Ronnie Wade, Fred Facka, Grant Robinson, Charlie Smith, Keith Thomas, Tom Calloway, and B. Kirkpatrick; (second row, standing) Paul Webb, Oliver Purnell, Mark Davis, Gary Buckland, Clarence Hanley, Mark West, Horace Lambert, Kenny Gattison, Tim Souterland, Eddie Webb, and Tim Franklin. (ODU Archives.)

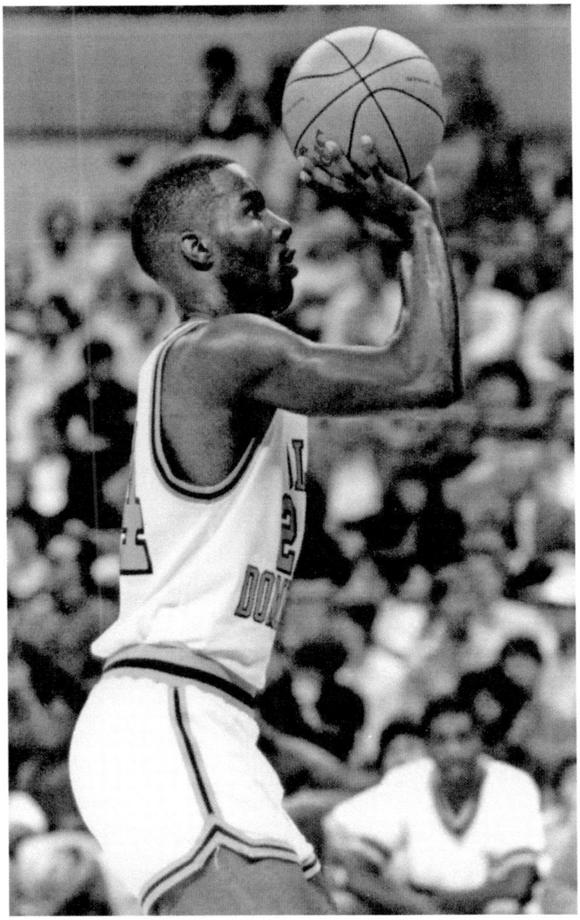

**KEITH THOMAS THE MONARCHS' ZONE BUSTER.** Every team needs a zone buster, and from 1982 to 1986, Keith Thomas was one of the Monarchs' finest. Coming off the bench his freshman season, the 6-foot-3-inch Thomas averaged nearly 10 points a game and caught Webb's attention. Inserted into the starting lineup from 1983 to 1986, this sharp-shooting guard averaged nearly 14 points per game. (ODU Archives.)

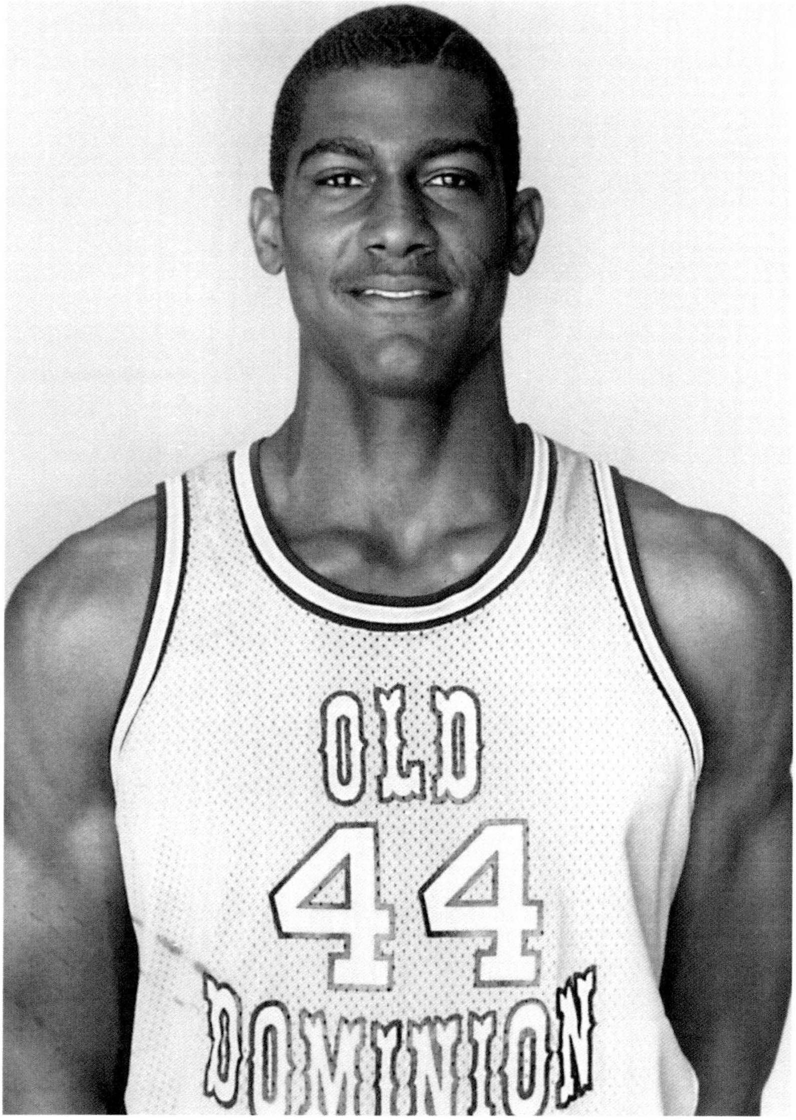


**Kenny Gattison, All-American.** From 1982 to 1986, this 6-foot-8-inch forward was a force down low for the Monarchs. In 1984, in the ECAC Holiday Festival, Kenny scored 48 points and hauled down 22 rebounds against St. Johns and Rutgers. When his four-year career had come to an end, Gattison had scored 1,623 points and captured 963 rebounds for the Monarchs, a Sun Belt Conference record. In 1984–1985 and again in 1985–1986, he was selected to several All-American squads. During his tenure with the Monarchs, Gattison helped take Old Dominion to four postseason appearances. Drafted by the Charlotte Hornets, Gattison played several years until injuries forced his retirement. From 1996 to 1998, he was an assistant coach with the New Jersey Nets. In 2001, Gattison was asked to serve as an assistant coach at his alma mater by Monarch coach Blaine Taylor, and he remained a coach until 2003. He is currently an assistant with the NBA New Orleans Hornets. In 1991, Gattison was inducted into the ODU Sports Hall of Fame and is one of only six Monarchs to have had his jersey number retired. (ODU Archives.)

**CLARENCE "MOOSE" HANLEY, 1982–1986.** Affectionately know as "Moose" by teammates and fans, the 6-foot-10-inch Hanley, a native of Marion, Virginia, was the Monarch starting center from 1983 to 1986. In 1982, his freshman season, he played backup to All-American center Mark West. Hanley shot the ball well from a range of 12–15 feet and averaged a high of 10 points during his junior campaign. (ODU Archives.)

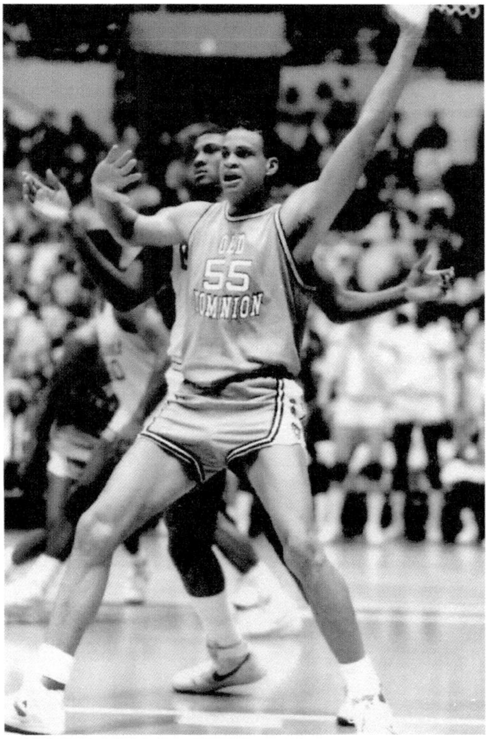


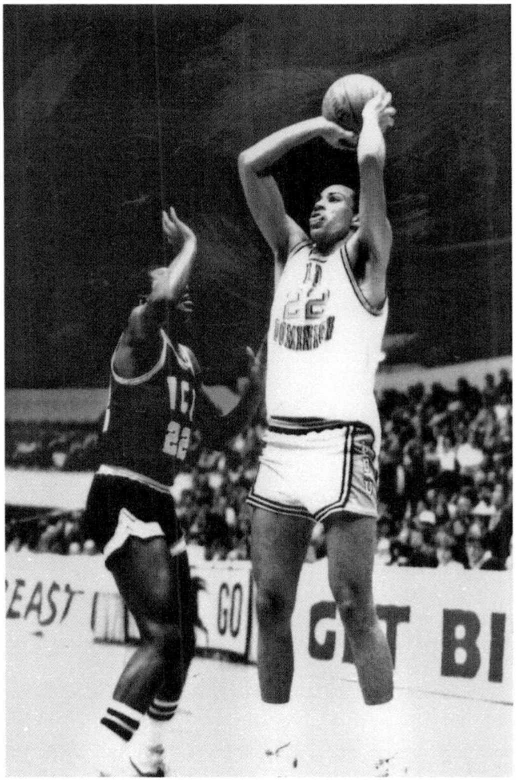


**RONNIE WADE, 1982–1986.** This 6-foot-6-inch forward played a vital role for the Old Dominion teams from 1982 to 1986. A native of Richmond, Wade was a fierce competitor and outstanding rebounder who played excellent defense on his opponent. (ODU Archives.)

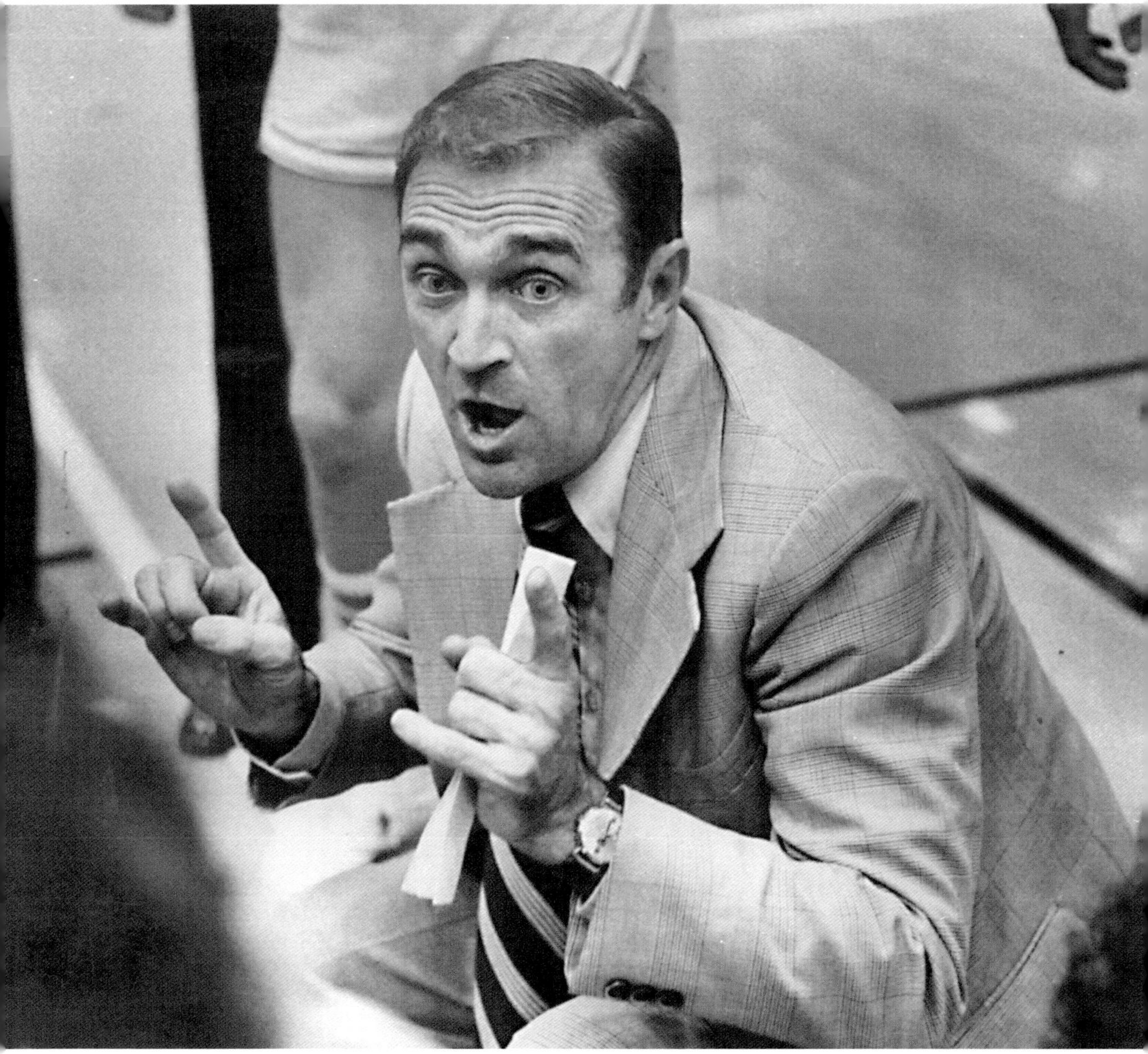

**Coach Webb Gets His Point Across.** Included in Webb's 511 career victories were 196 wins while at Old Dominion. Recognized as a great bench coach, he won 12 overtime games as coach of the Monarchs. In 1978–1979, Webb coached Old Dominion to four overtime victories, including three double-overtime wins against East Carolina, Florida State, and Clemson in the NIT. (VP.)

6

# Closing Out the Sun Belt

## The Tom Young Years 1986–1991

On July 7, 1985, one day after the resignation of Paul Webb, Dr. James Jarrett began compiling a list of possible replacements. Add that list to the more than 100 applications Old Dominion would receive in the next few weeks, and it was apparent that Dr. Jarrett had a massive task ahead. In late July, he began serious negotiations to put together a package to convince University of Maryland coach and Norfolk native Lefty Driesell to take the position. After two weeks of extensive negotiations, Driesell withdrew his name from consideration. Pressure was on the search committee to name a replacement before the beginning of school, which was only weeks away.

On August 22, 1985, forty-seven days after Paul Webb's resignation, Old Dominion announced the selection of 52-year-old Tom Young as the ninth head coach in the school's history. Young had 25 years of coaching experience that included stints at Catholic University, American University, and an illustrious 12-year career at Rutgers University. While at Rutgers, Young had guided his teams to four NCAA Tournament bids (including the 1975–1976 NCAA Final Four) and four NIT appearances.

Young inherited a Monarch team of eight lettermen, including four starters from a squad that had previously gone 19-12 and earned a berth in the NCAA East Regional. Led by forward Kenny Gattison, a senior and All-American; forward Ronnie Wade; center Clarence Hanley; guard Keith Thomas; and sophomore Frank Smith at the point, the Monarchs posted a 22-8 record. Winning the Sun Belt Regular Season Championship, they were awarded a berth in the NCAA East Regional as a No. 8 seed. In the first regional game the Monarch's defeated the West Virginia Mountaineers 72-64. In a second-round matchup with Duke, they were trounced 89-61.

Decimated by graduation, the 1986–1987 campaign was a rebuilding year. Smith was Old Dominion's only returning starter. Joining him at guard was junior Steve Trax, freshman center Howard Morgan, and sophomore forward Bernard Royster. The other freshman recruit, forward Anthony Carver, averaged nearly 16 points a game and immediately made his presence felt. Unfortunately, it was not enough, as the Monarchs finished a dismal 6-22, winning only one Sun Belt game. This was the least number of wins for a Monarch team since the 1940s.

The following season, 1987–1988, Young attempted a three-forward offense, using Carver, Trax, and junior Garrick Davis to anchor the front line. In the backcourt, senior point guard Frank

Smith returned to team with transfer guard Darin McDonald. The Monarchs were winners again, compiling an 18-12 record, including a win over state rival Virginia. Old Dominion was rewarded an NIT bid and traveled to Ohio State, where they were thrashed 86-73 by the Buckeyes.

The season of 1988–1989 gave Monarch fans bona fide optimism. Returning were starters Davis, Carver, and McDonald. New sophomore center Chris Gatling and guard Donald Grant also started. Gatling, a 6-foot-9-inch transfer from the University of Pittsburgh, would make his much-heralded Monarch debut at center. Senior forward Bernard Royster and freshman forward Recardo Leonard added depth to the Monarchs. But nothing seemed to click for the team as they only managed a disappointing 15-13 record.

The hype in several 1989–1990 preseason publications gave Monarch fans another season of high expectations. Seniors Carver and McDonald returned for their final campaign as did junior center Gatling. Joining an already talented squad were three highly touted freshmen: Keith Jackson, Chuck Evans, and Donald Anderson. The season would provide a lofty challenge with arguably the school's toughest schedule. The slate featured games against nationally ranked University of North Carolina, Missouri, Wake Forest, West Virginia, and perennially tough Sun Belt foes. What started in November as optimism quickly turned to March pessimism, as the team, racked with internal dissention, finished with a miserable 13-13 record. The Monarchs failed to earn a postseason bid for the second consecutive season—something that had not happened since 1968.

As the team prepared for the 1990–1991 campaign, an uneasy mood hung over Monarch faithful, who for two previous years had been disappointed by teams that were highly touted. Back for his senior season was All-American candidate Gatling; junior forward Leonard and sophomores Jackson and Anderson also returned. Young added junior college transfers John Robinson and Al Grant to the mix, but team chemistry was missing, and the Monarchs could only compile a disappointing 14-18 record.

Old Dominion's basketball program was on a downward spiral. Attendance at games had dwindled to an alarming low as fans abandoned the program. Young had not been able to win a Sun Belt Tournament Championship and had only taken the Monarchs to two postseason appearances. Old Dominion was planning a move from the Sun Belt to the Colonial Athletic Association the following season, and the only logical step for Dr. Jarrett was to make a coaching change.

After refusing to resign as Old Dominion's head basketball coach, Tom Young was fired on March 7, 1991. In six seasons at the helm Young only managed to compile a 90-87 record. This was definitely not what Monarch fans had come to expect. The Tom Young years, as well as membership in the Sun Belt, were officially over.

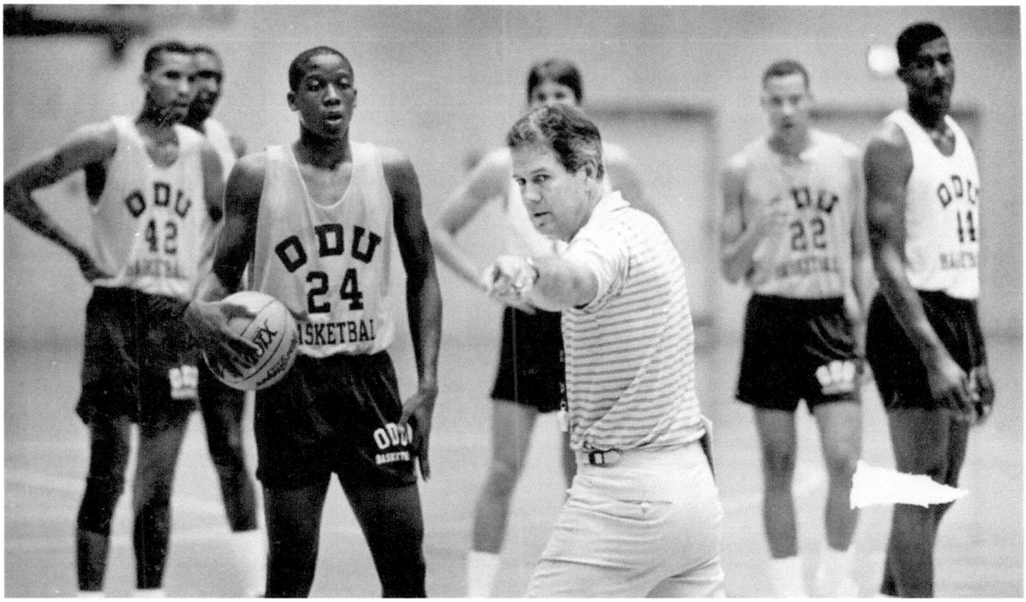


**YOUNG MAKES A POINT.** As players intently listen to his instructions, coach Young points to a position on the court. Under their new coach, the team had two-a-day practices for the first month. When asked the difference between Young and Webb's practices, guard Frank Smith answered, "He keeps the intensity level cranked up the entire practice." (VP.)

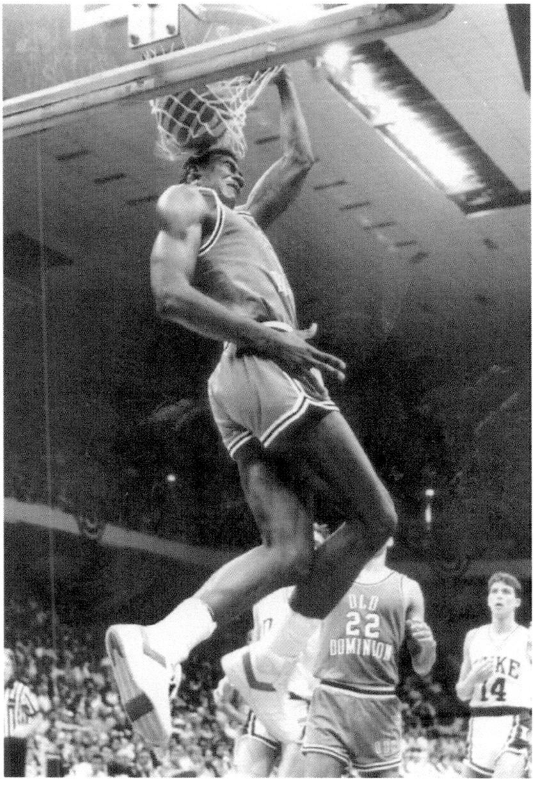


**KENNY'S LAST GAME.** After scoring a game-high 27 points and defeating West Virginia 72-64 in the first game of the 1986 NCAA East Regional, Kenny Gattison and the Monarchs met Duke in the championship. In what would be his last game in a Monarch uniform, Gattison dunks for two of his 17 points against the Blue Devils, who destroyed the Monarchs 89-61. (ODU Archives.)

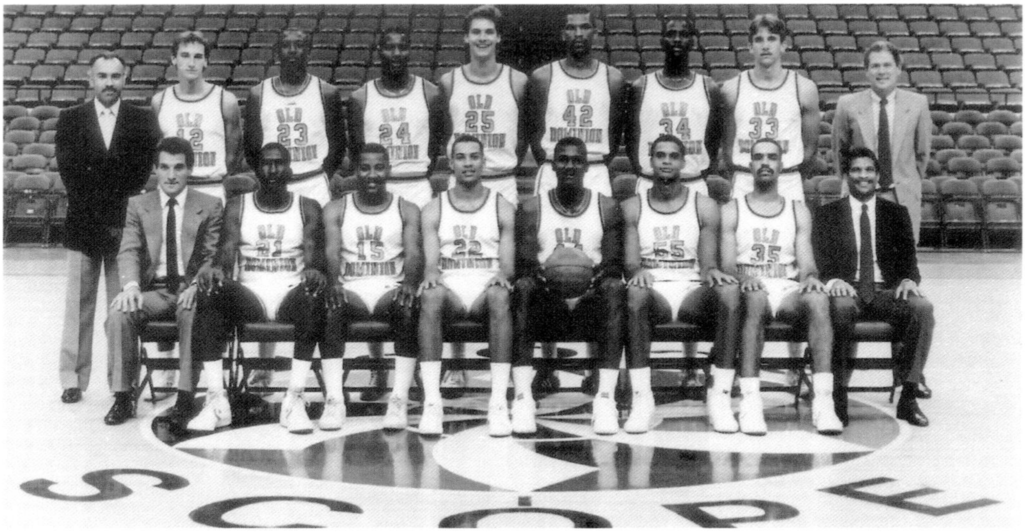

**SUN BELT REGULAR SEASON CHAMPIONS, 1985–1986.** Tom Young's first team at Old Dominion finished 23-8. From left to right are (first row) Ron Ganulin, Sylvester Charles, Frank Smith, Ronnie Wade, Kenny Gattison, Clarence Hanley, Darryl Tolson, and Eddie Jordan; (second row) coach Art Perry, Dee Pritchett, Kennell Jones, Keith Thomas, David Carlyle, Garrick Davis, Bernard Royster, Steve Trax, and Tom Young. (ODU Archives.)

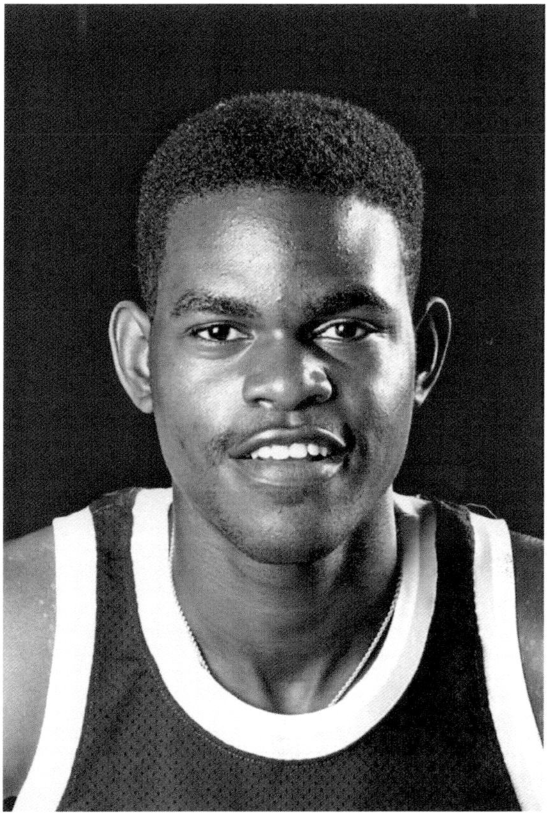

**ANTHONY CARVER, 1986–1990.** This 6-foot-7-inch forward was Young's first signing at ODU. "A. C.," as teammates and fans called him, was an offensive juggernaut. A. C. led the team in scoring during his freshman, sophomore, and senior seasons. A deadly shooter, in 1989–1990, A. C. shot a school record 94 threes. At the conclusion of his career, 657 points of his 1,958 had come from beyond the arc. (VP.)

**TRAX CONCENTRATES AT THE LINE.** Steve Trax, a forward/guard for the Monarchs from 1984 to 1988, concentrates before he shoots. During 1986–1987, this 6-foot-6-inch Maryland native averaged nearly 13 points a game as guard. The following year he was moved to forward, averaging 11 points for an 18-12 team that earned an NIT bid. Trax is vice president of SFX Sports, a financial advisory group to some of the biggest names in sports. (VP.)

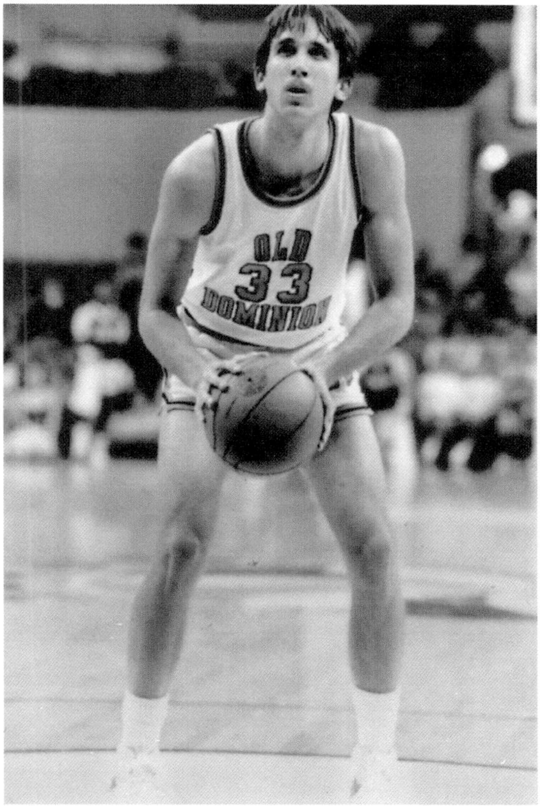


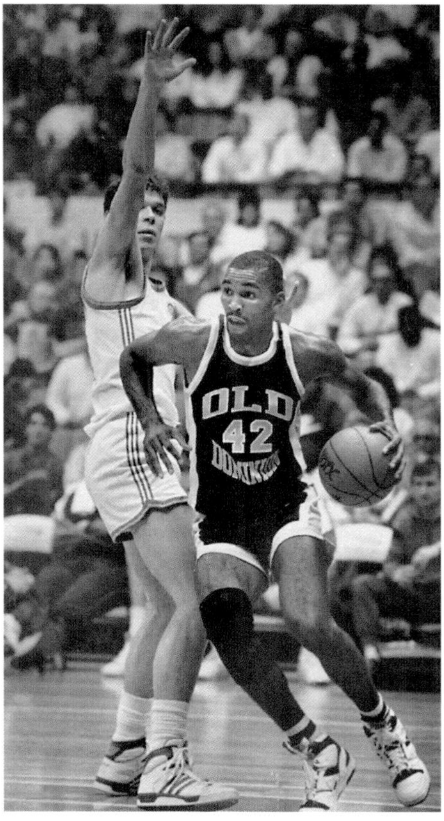


**MONARCH DETENTE.** Chesapeake native Garrick Davis, a 6-foot-7-inch forward, drives against towering Alexander Volkov, 6-foot-10-inch forward of the Soviet Union national team, in a 1988 exhibition game. Several months earlier, the Soviet team had been crowned gold medal champion at the Seoul Olympics. The Soviet depth and size proved too much for Monarchs, as they succumbed by a score of 95-86. (VP.)

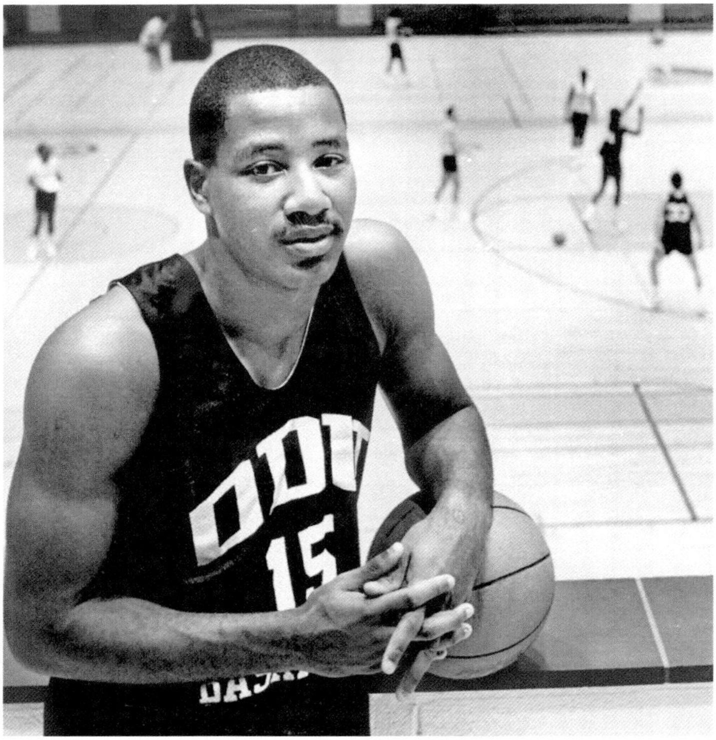


**FRANK SMITH, 1984–1988.** Smith was a Virginia All-State quarterback who had scholarship offers to Notre Dame, Southern California, and Nebraska, among others; it's lucky for the Monarchs that he chose basketball. After playing 120 games in his four years of running the Monarchs offense, this 6-foot, 180-pound guard presently holds ODU career records for assists (883) and steals (295). Smith is currently an assistant at Clemson with Oliver Purnell. (VP.)

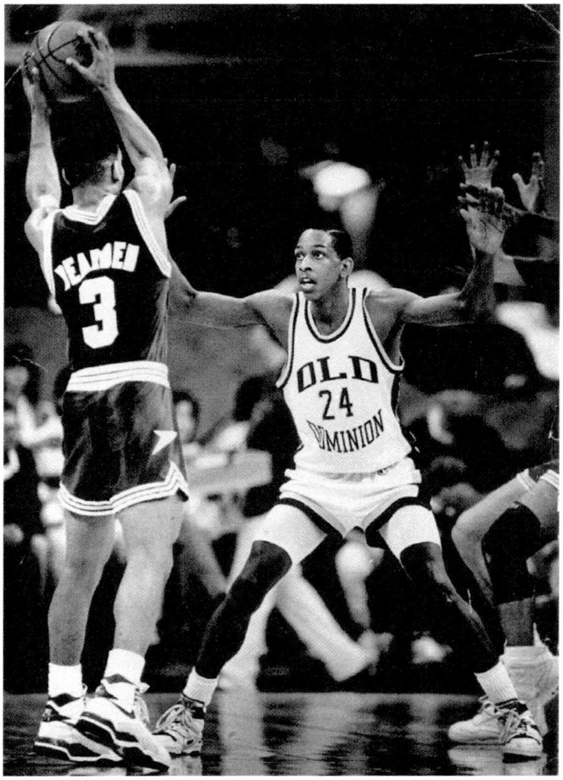


**DARRIN'S DEFENSE.** In a game against University of Alabama, Birmingham, Monarch guard Darrin McDonald keeps his eye on the ball as he guards an opponent. The Monarchs won in overtime 80-74. A native of Milwaukee, Wisconsin, McDonald scored 21 points and grabbed nine rebounds in the contest. Before transferring from VMI, McDonald had been the Southern Conference Rookie of the Year. An excellent offensive and defensive player, McDonald had great court awareness. (VP.)

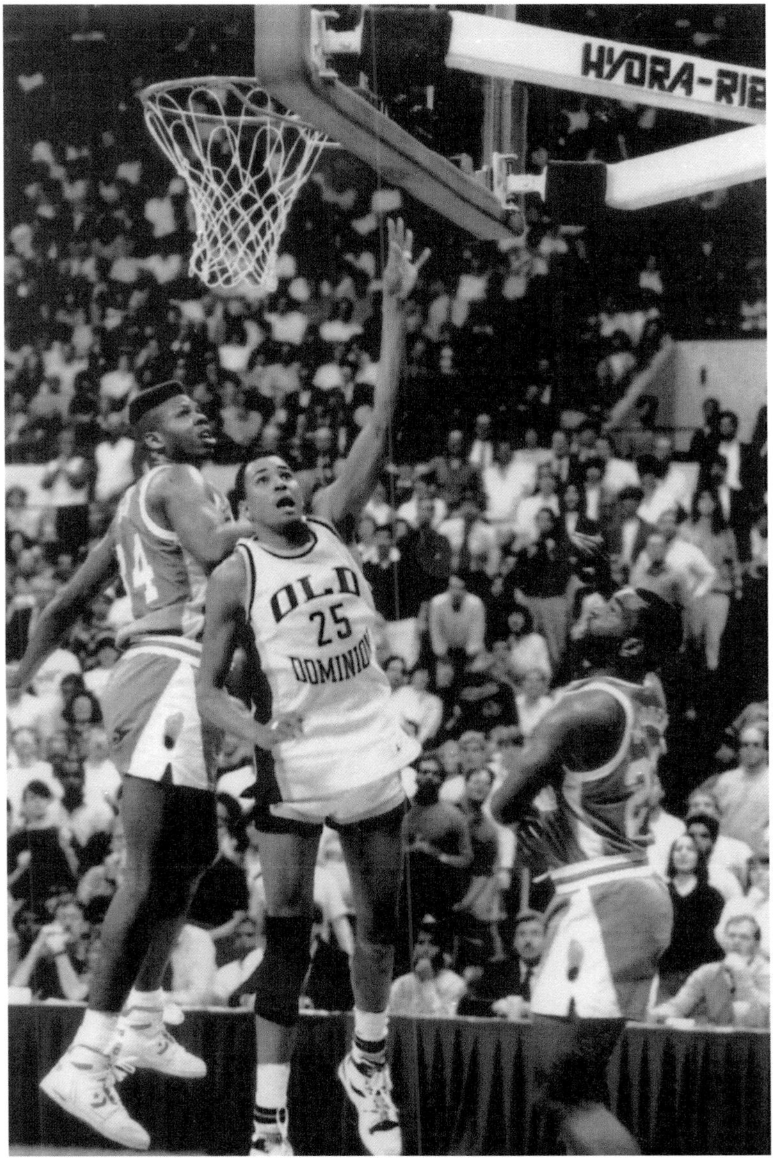


**CHRIS GATLING, ALL-AMERICAN.** Monarch center Chris Gatling boxes out University of North Carolina's J. R. Reed for a rebound in a February 14, 1989, game at Scope. The, 6-foot-10-inch, 225-pound center was a much heralded transfer from the University of Pittsburgh. Gatling earned many accolades during his three-year Monarch career, including the Sun Belt Player of the Year in 1990 and 1991 and the 1991 Sun Belt Tournament MVP. During his junior and senior seasons, he was selected Division I Honorable Mention All-American by the Associated Press, *Basketball Weekly*, and the *Sporting News*. Gatling concluded his Monarch career with 1,811 points, 859 rebounds, and 195 blocked shots. The biggest knocks on Gatling were the fact that during his career, the Monarchs never received a postseason bid and compiled a losing record of 43-45. Selected in the first round with the 16th pick overall by the Golden State Warriors, Gatling went on to an 11-year NBA career with eight different clubs. (ODU Archives.)

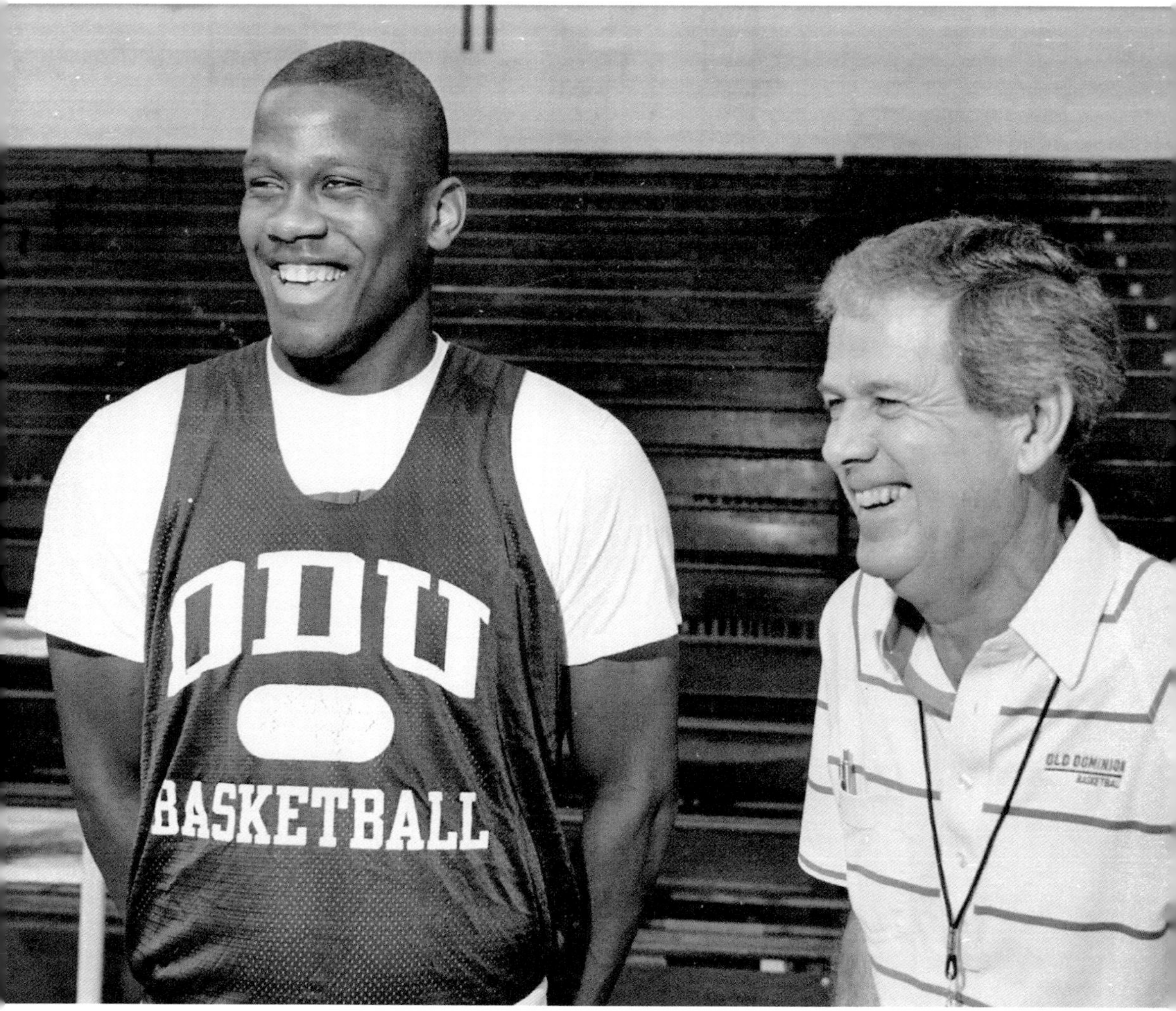


**YOUNG AND THE RESTLESS.** Coach Young and Old Dominion power forward Ricardo Leonard share a laugh together before the 1989–1990 season. Their days together were not always as jovial, as Leonard had been dismissed from the squad his previous season. Allowed to return by Young for his junior season, Leonard averaged 16 points for the Monarchs. Leonard would average 20.4 points his senior season under new coach Oliver Purnell. (VP.)

7

# A Favorite Son Returns

## The Oliver Purnell Years 1991–1994

Only hours after the firing of Tom Young, there was wide speculation on who would be the next coach at Old Dominion University. The names at the forefront were two Monarch greats: All-American Dave Twardzik, arguably Old Dominion's greatest and most popular player; and Oliver Purnell, the point guard on the 1975 Division II National Champion team. Both Twardzik and Purnell were recognized as having brilliant basketball minds, even though they had traveled different roads. Twardzik's career as a professional player, coach, and front-office executive had spanned a total of 18 years. Purnell had been a college assistant at Old Dominion, Maryland, and a head coach at Radford University for the previous 16 years. In the end, it was Purnell's college coaching experience that was the deciding factor. On March 27, 1991, Pres. James Koch and Athletic Director Dr. James Jarrett introduced Purnell as the Monarchs' 10th coach.

Purnell inherited a Monarch team that returned four starters and nine lettermen in what would be the school's first season in the Colonial Athletic Conference. The team had compiled a disappointing 14-18 record the previous year. The 1991–1992 edition of the Monarchs were led by senior forwards Richardo Leonard and Al Grant and guard John Robinson. Juniors included guards Keith Jackson and Donald Anderson. Freshman newcomers included 6-foot-8-inch center David Harvey, 6-foot-5-inch guard Mike Jones, and 6-foot-7-inch forward Petey Sessoms. For the next four years, Sessoms would provide Monarch fans with many great memories.

Purnell promised Monarch fans the same type of play employed while he was a player and assistant for Old Dominion, a fast-break offense and an aggressive style of defense. In addition to games in their new conference, the Monarchs had a challenging out-of-conference schedule that included West Virginia, Penn State, Alabama, South Florida, George Washington, and Virginia Tech. Before the start of the season, ODU was picked by the CAA coaches to finish sixth in the conference. With a new coach and a new style of play, many felt the Monarchs had a difficult season ahead.

In his first season, Purnell challenged the Monarchs to focus on getting better each week with the goal of being ready for the CAA Tournament. The team did just what their new coach had suggested. Entering the tournament with a record of 12-14 and seeded fourth, the Monarchs defeated UNC Wilmington, top-seeded Richmond, and James Madison to win an NCAA Tournament bid, the first for the Monarchs in six years.

ODU faced Kentucky in the first round of the NCAA East Regional in Worcester, Massachusetts, losing 88-69. Finishing with a flurry, in one season Purnell pumped vitality and optimism into a program that had lacked both in recent years.

Key players returning for the 1992–1993 campaign were Anderson, Jackson, and Sessoms. Purnell had the satisfying job of blending a talented recruiting class that included 6-foot-7-inch forward Mario Mullen, 6-foot-9-inch center Odell Hodge, and junior transfer guard 6-foot-2-inch Kevin Swan with returning players from the previous year. With a schedule that included powers like North Carolina, Virginia, Alabama, Auburn, Southern Mississippi, and Virginia Tech, it was difficult to know what to expect. The team, led by a balanced scoring attack that included Sessoms's and Jackson's 17-point averages, as well as Hodge's 14- and Mullen's 11-point averages, exceeded expectations by going 21-8 and earning a postseason NIT bid. In the NIT, the Monarchs defeated rival Virginia Commonwealth 74-68 at Scope. The team then traveled to Ohio, where they lost a close game to Miami of Ohio, 60-58.

The 1993–1994 season offered high hopes to the Monarch faithful as Old Dominion returned their frontline of Hodge, Sessoms, and Mullen. The loss of both starting guards left question marks at the position. Swan and Larkin were tapped to start and immediately added value to the lineup. With wins against state rivals Virginia, Richmond, George Mason, James Madison, and William and Mary, as well as against South Carolina and UC Santa Barbara, the Monarchs were able to carve out a 21-10 record and earn another NIT bid. The Monarchs met Manhattan at Scope where they squeaked out a 76-74 win. Traveling to Peoria, Illinois, Old Dominion lost 78-74 to Bradley University. In three seasons, Purnell had revived Old Dominion basketball by taking the Monarch's to three consecutive postseason tournaments, a feat last accomplished by Paul Webb. The future was looking bright for the program.

On the morning of April 5, 1994, Monarch fans awoke to the news that the University of Dayton asked for and were given permission to interview Purnell. Oliver was torn about leaving his alma mater, but in the end it was apparent that this opportunity was to be a stepping stone to his dream of becoming a coach in a major conference. Thus, on Friday, April 8, 1994, after three very successful seasons, Oliver Purnell, a favorite son, stepped down as the Monarchs' coach to take a more lucrative position at Dayton. The Monarchs once again were faced with the daunting task of looking for a head coach.

**MEET THE MONARCHS' NEW COACH.** Only hours after signing a long-term contract to coach the Monarchs, Oliver Purnell waits for a live interview with WTKR sportscaster Ross McCullum. A cocaptain and MVP of the 1975 Old Dominion team that won the Division II National Championship, Purnell served as an assistant under Paul Webb from 1975 to 1985. From 1985 to 1988, he served as an assistant at Maryland. Prior to coming to ODU, he had been the head coach at Radford from 1988 to 1991. (ODU Archives.)

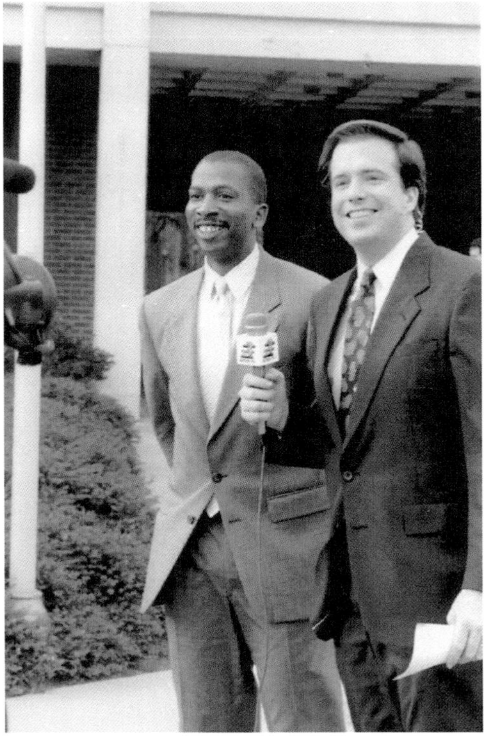

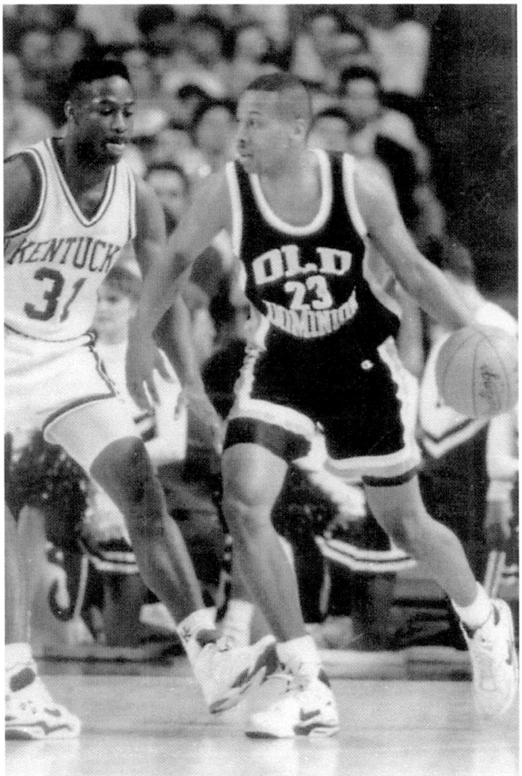

**KEITH JACKSON, 1989–1993.** In this March 20, 1992, photograph, Keith "Action" Jackson attempts to drive around a University of Kentucky defender in the first round NCAA East Regional in Worcester, Massachusetts. Jackson would score 12 points in an 88-69 loss to the Wildcats as 13,514 watched on. Recruited by Tom Young, Jackson played two years under Oliver Purnell, averaging nearly 17 points his senior season. The Monarch guard scored 1,592 points during his 117-game career. (ODU Archives.)

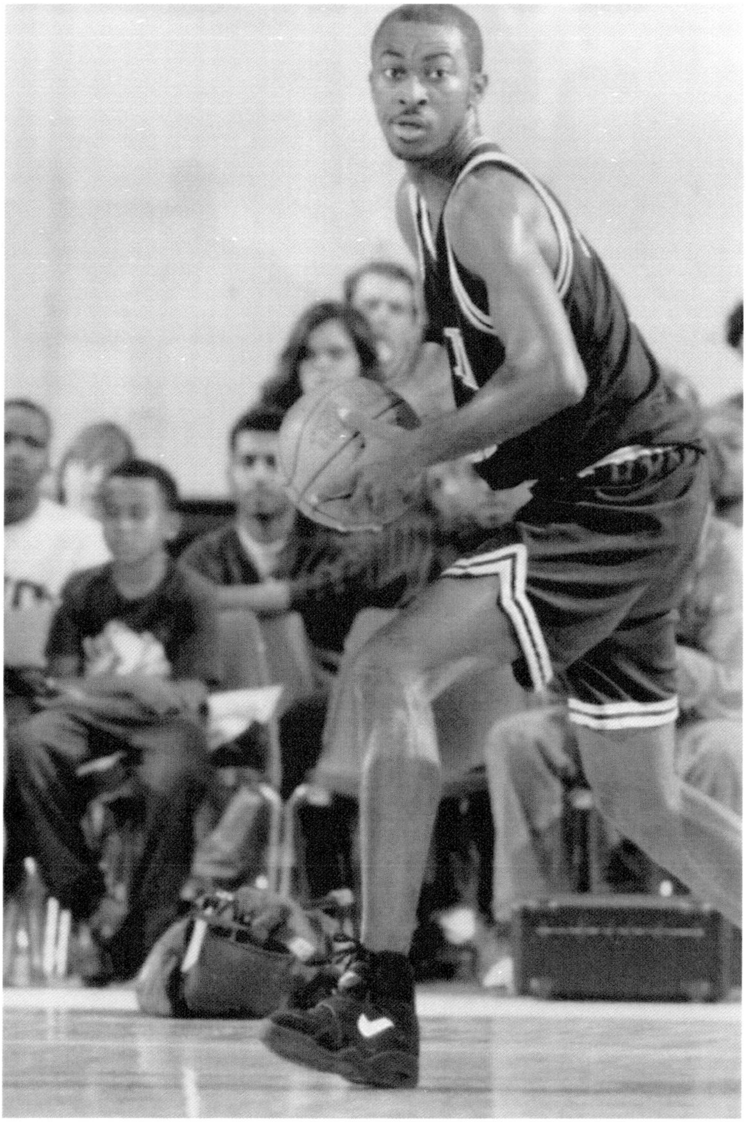

**A BIG-TIME PERFORMER.** Arguably no Monarch performed larger on the big stage than Petey Sessoms. The 6-foot-7-inch forward from Portsmouth averaged 16 points per game over his four years at Old Dominion. A great outside shooter who was deadly on the wing, Petey hit 270 three-point shots as a Monarch. In this March 20, 1992, image, taken at the first round of the NCAA East Regional, Sessoms looks to drive against the University of Kentucky. For his 21-point and 12-rebound performance, he was selected as the CBS Player of the Game. However, he saved his best performance for last. On March 17, 1995, Old Dominion met Villanova in an NCAA East Regional contest. ODU, behind a 35-point performance by Sessoms, upset the third-seeded Wildcats 89-81 in a triple-overtime contest. The win, Sessoms's last as a Monarch, is one of the most memorable in the school's history. In four years, Sessoms scored 1,985 points for fourth-place all-time in Monarch history. In 1994, he was inducted into the ODU Sports Hall of Fame. (ODU Archives.)

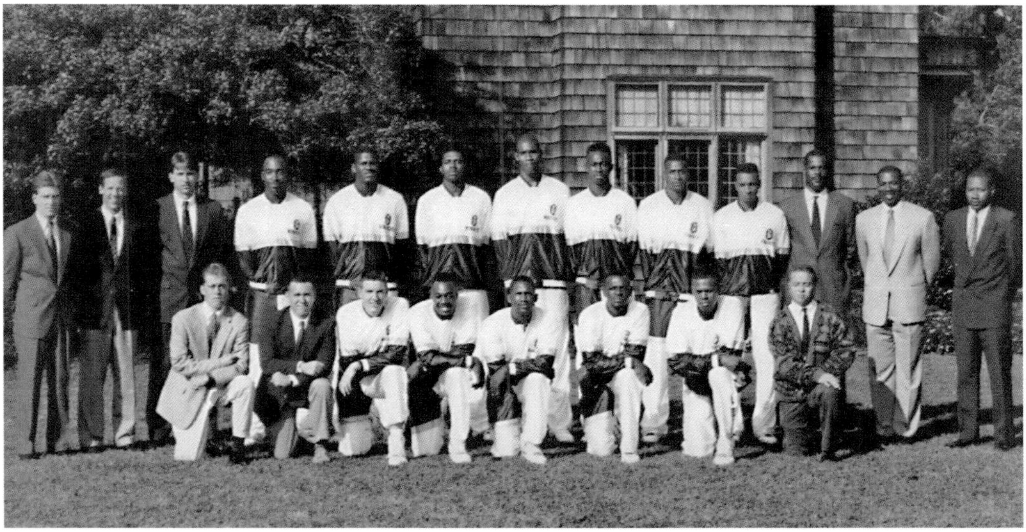

**COLONIAL ATHLETIC ASSOCIATION CHAMPIONS, 1991–1992.** Purnell's first Monarch squad finished 15-15 and earned an NCAA bid. Pictured from left to right are (first row, kneeling) manager Brian Sheffler, manager Jason Barnett, Kevin Larkin, John Robinson, Barrty Smith, Donald Anderson, Mike Jones, and manager Tom Rouse; (second row, standing) trainer Scott Johnson, Pete Strickland, assistant coach Steve Trax, Al Grant, Ricardo Leonard, David Harvey, Allon Wright, Petey Sessoms, Keith Jackson, Joe Leake, asstistant coach Tic Price, coach Oliver Purnell, and assistant coach Frank Smith. (ODU Archives.)

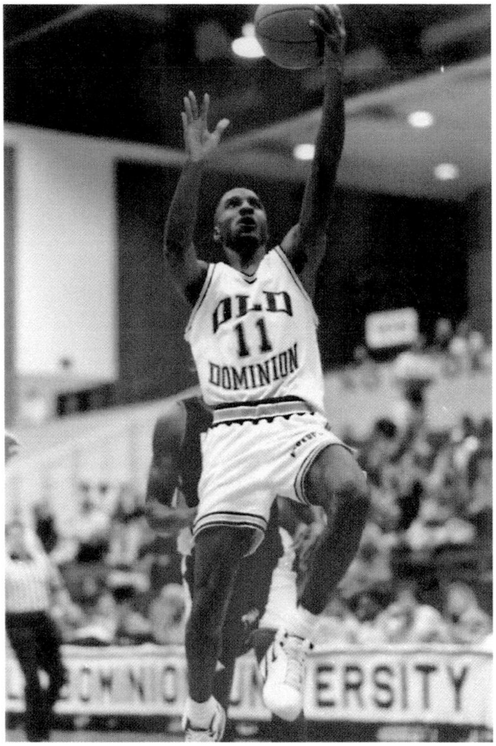


**KEVIN SWANN, 1992–1994.** This 6-foot-2-inch guard from Hampton, Virginia, transferred to ODU from Central Connecticut State, where he had started all 28 games and led his team in assists and steals. During the 1992–1993 season, Swan was mostly used as a backup to point guard Donald Anderson. After Anderson's graduation, Swann was called on to run Purnell's offense for the 1993–1994 campaign. His on-court leadership and nearly 17 points a game helped the Monarchs post a 21-10 record. (ODU Archives.)

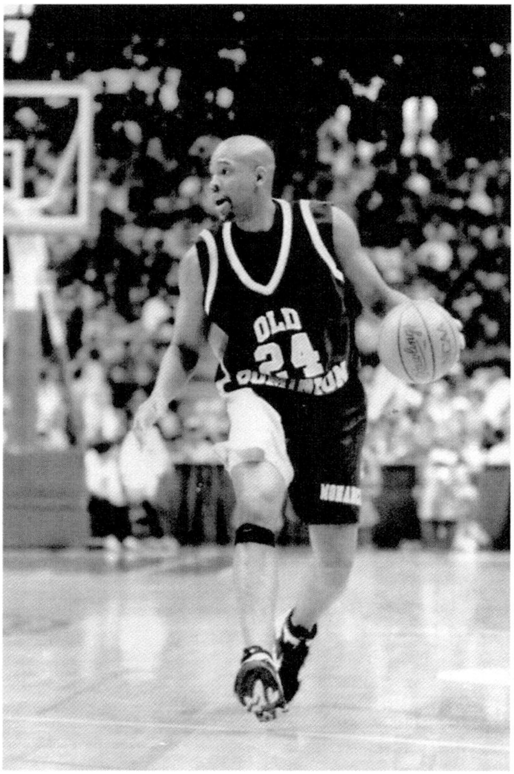

**MARIO MULLEN, 1992–1996.** This 6-foot-6-inch forward was a native of Virginia Beach where he attended Bayside High School and led the school to two consecutive AAA State crowns. Mario started in all 29 games as a freshman and was selected to the CAA All-Freshman squad in 1992–1993. In 1993, Mullen was involved in a car accident, which required surgery to repair a ruptured disc. He would be hampered by this injury for the remainder of his collegiate career. (ODU Archives.)

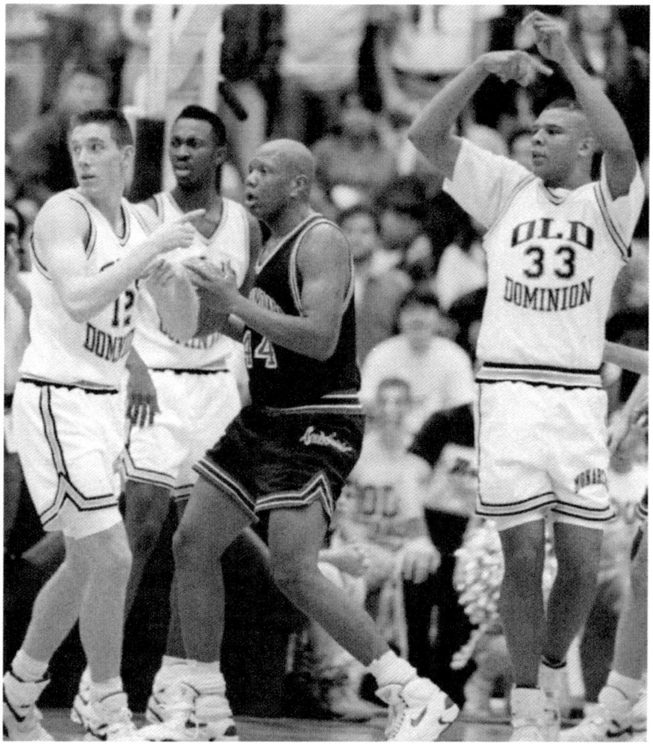

**CONFUSION ABOUNDS.** In a January 16, 1993, game against CAA rival University of Richmond, Old Dominion junior guard Kevin Larkin (12) and freshman center Odell Hodge (33) point to an infraction committed on the court. Richmond forward Kenny Wood (44) displays disbelief as he is called for a foul. In the background, ODU sophomore Petey Sessoms shows his familiar scowl after the play. The Monarchs completed the season with a record of 21-8 and earned an NIT bid. (V.P.)

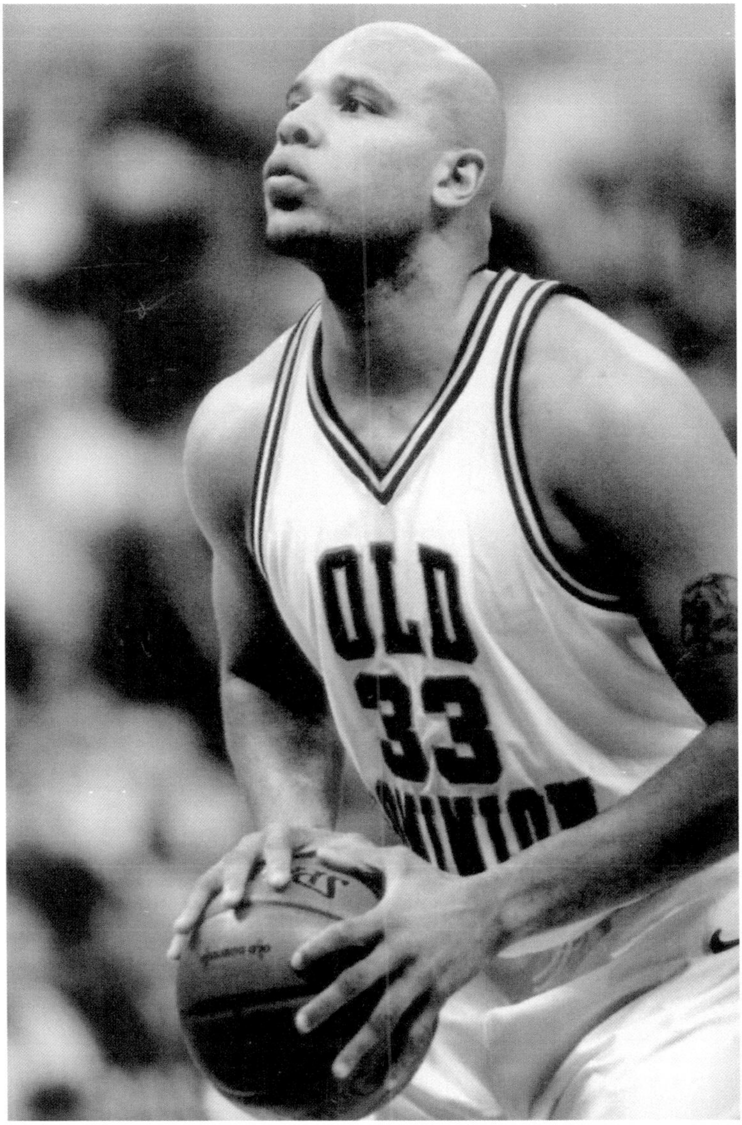

**ODELL HODGE, ALL-AMERICAN.** A two-time Virginia State Player of the Year from Martinsville, Virginia, who for several years held the distinction of being the all-time scorer in Virginia High School history. Hodge amassed 2,530 points and over 1,000 rebounds in his four-year high school career. A powerful center/forward for the Monarchs from 1992 to 1997, Hodge was a force down low. Hodge garnered a number of CAA honors during his Monarch career. In 1992–1993, he was chosen the CAA Rookie of the Year. The next year, 1993–1994, he was selected as the CAA Player of the Year, the first sophomore since David Robinson to do so. Out the following season with a medical red shirt after tearing his anterior cruciate ligament (ACL), Hodge won his second CAA Player of the Year award in 1997. A leader and intimidating figure on the floor, Hodge finished his Old Dominion career with 2,117 points and 1,086 rebounds. These statistics put him third all-time in both Monarch categories. In 2005, Hodge was selected to the ODU Sports Hall of Fame. (ODU Archives.)

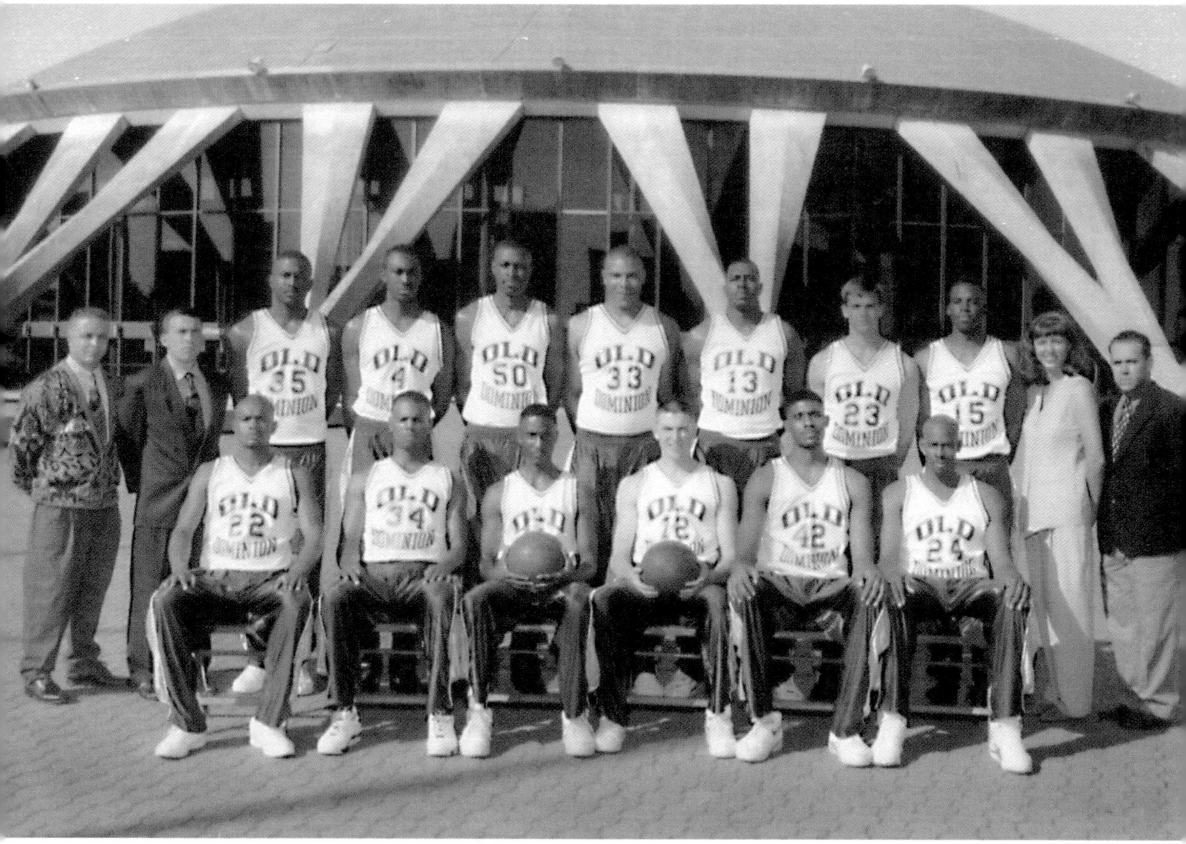

**COLONIAL ATHLETIC ASSOCIATION REGULAR SEASON CHAMPIONS, 1993–1994.** Oliver Purnell's final team at Old Dominion finished a respectable 21-10. Pictured from left to right are (first row) Corey Robinson, Mike Jones, Kevin Swann, Kevin Larkin, Allon Wright, and Mario Mullen; (second row) manager Tom Rouse, manager Rob Dalby, Corey Parker, Petey Sessoms, Derrick Parker, Odell Hodge, David Harvey, Mark Johnson, E. J. Sherod, manager Kristen Peiffer, manager and Jason Barnett. (ODU Archives.)

# 8

# Highs and Lows

## The Jeff Capel years 1994–2001

Dr. Jarrett hoped to hire a new coach within two weeks to continue the success and positive momentum Purnell had brought to the program. Over the next few days, several names surfaced. Most notable were Colorado coach Joe Harrington, Radford coach Ron Bradley, and Bowling Green's Jim Larranaga. In the end it was a late applicant who was introduced on April 26, 1994, as Old Dominion's 11th coach in 64 years. He was 41-year-old Jeff Capel, who had previously coached at North Carolina A&T and Fayetteville State.

For Capel's first season, he inherited a solid team from Purnell, with returning senior stars 6-foot-7-inch forward Petey Sessoms and 6-foot-5-inch guard Mike Jones. Junior forward Mario Mullen also returned healthy after a year filled with injuries. Joining Jones in the backcourt was 5-foot-11-inch freshman Brion Dunlop. But all eyes were on 6-foot-10-inch center Odell Hodge, the returning CAA Player of the Year, who led the league in scoring and rebounds during the previous year. The Monarchs had a difficult schedule that included games with Virginia, South Carolina, North Carolina, St. Joseph's, Arizona State, and the usual CAA foes.

Four games into the season, Hodge went down with a torn anterior cruciate ligament. David Harvey, a 6-foot-8-inch senior, served as a capable fill-in over the season. At the conclusion, the Monarchs had crafted a 21-12 season, including winning the CAA regular season championship. Next up for the Monarchs in the NCAA Tournament was Big East Champion, Villanova. The Monarchs played one of the NCAA's most memorable contests, as they defeated the Wildcats 89-81 in triple overtime. The Monarchs were defeated by Tulsa 64-52 in the second round.

The 1995–1996 season presented Capel with an opportunity to build on the success from the previous year. Hodge was set to return from his knee injury. Joining him in the frontcourt were Joe Bunn (averaging 16.1 points per game), a transfer from North Carolina A&T; and freshman Mark Poag, a 6-foot-6-inch sharpshooter. Poag was part of a highly touted freshmen class that included 6-foot-8-inch forward Skipper Youngblood, 6-foot-9-inch Reggie Bassett, and 6-foot-10-inch center Cal Bowdler. Returning guards Jones, Dunlop, and Samuels handled the backcourt duties. The Monarchs ended the season with an 18-12 record and no postseason bid.

The 1996–1997 season, Capel's third at Old Dominion, was one of much promise. Returning were starters Hodge, Dunlop, Byers, and Poag. The Monarchs displayed depth with returning players Edmond Sherod, Bassette, Bowdler, and Youngblood. The 22-11 Monarchs earned a trip to the NCAA Tournament by winning the CAA Championship with a 62-58 overtime victory against James Madison. Up next was 11th-ranked New Mexico in the East Regional in Pittsburgh, Pennsylvania. ODU kept it close, losing to the Lobos 59-55.

Picked in the preseason to repeat as CAA Champions, the Monarchs were optimistic about the upcoming 1997–1998 campaign. Hodge was gone, but returning were juniors Poag, Bassett, and Bowdler. Dunlop returned at point for his senior season, and Mike Byers returned at the other guard position. With a challenging schedule, ODU found itself in fourth place in the CAA with an overall record of 12-16, its worst record in 11 years.

The 1998–1999 season was one in which the Monarchs had much to prove. Selected again as the CAA preseason favorite, this time the Monarchs were determined to live up to expectations with a senior-laden team of Byers, Poag, Bassett, and Bowdler. ODU had the most experienced team in the CAA with only one non-senior starter, sophomore point guard Mike Williams. The Monarchs finished with a 25-9 record and an NIT bid. Defeating Seton Hall 75-56 in a first round game at ODU, the team then traveled to Indianapolis to play Butler in the second round. The Monarchs lost to the Bulldogs, 75-62.

The 1999–2000 season was a rebuilding year, as an inexperienced team took the court. The only returning starter was Williams, who was joined in the backcourt by 6-foot-2-inch sophomore Pierre Green. Returning for his red shirt senior season was center Youngblood. At forward were 6-foot-7 junior Andre McCullum and 6-foot-8 freshman Ricardo Marsh. The season began with a challenging non-conference schedule that included Kansas, North Carolina State, Washington, and Virginia Tech and ended with another losing record of 11-19.

Capel was optimistic about the prospects for 2000–2001 because of returning forwards McCullum and Marsh and guard Green and the addition of Rasheed Wright in the backcourt. The low-post position was anchored by 6-foot-6-inch senior Clifton Jones. The schedule was challenging with games against Washington, North Carolina State, Stanford, Kansas State, and Dayton. After losing seven of its first eight games, optimism vanished, and fan support reached its lowest point in the Monarch's 25 years in Division I. The season ended at 13-18, the second consecutive losing record, a first for ODU since the mid-1960s.

With three losing seasons in four years and declining fan support, it was evident that ODU needed to go in a different direction. On March 5, 2001, Jeff Capel's seven-year tenure at Old Dominion ended, as he resigned, citing personal and family concerns.

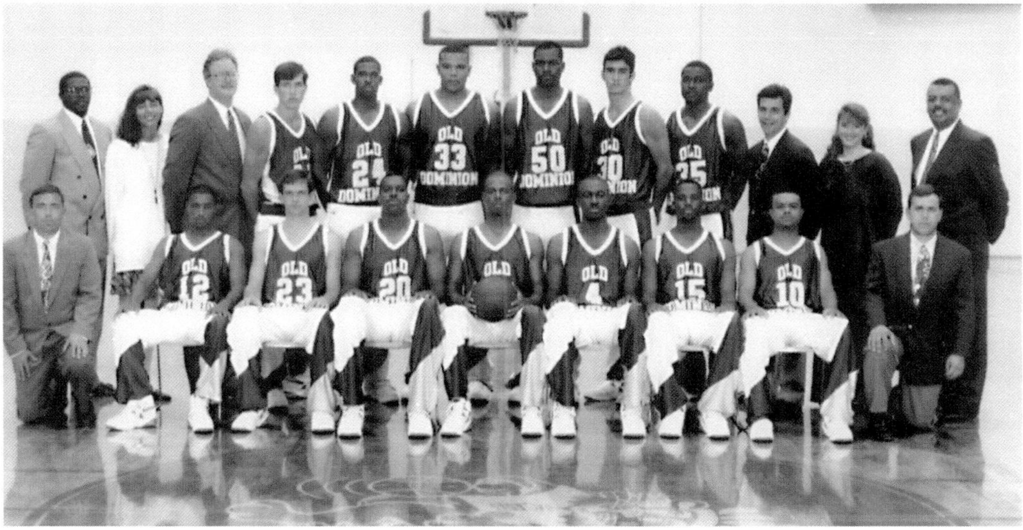

**COLONIAL ATHLETIC ASSOCIATION CHAMPIONS, 1994–1995.** Capel's first Monarch squad finished 21-12 and earned an NCAA bid. Pictured from left to right are (first row) manager Rob Dalby, Duffy Samuels, Mark Johnson, David Harvey, Mike Jones, Petey Sessoms, E. J. Sherod, Brion Dunlop, and manager Jason Barnett; (second row) assistant coach Bobby Collins, manager Kristen Pfeifer, assistant coach Mark Cline, Jason Nickerson, Mario Mullen, Odell Hodge, Derrick Parker, Jeff Mordica, Corey Parker, assistant coach Jim Corrigan, manager Piper Blye, and coach Jeff Capel. (ODU Archives.)

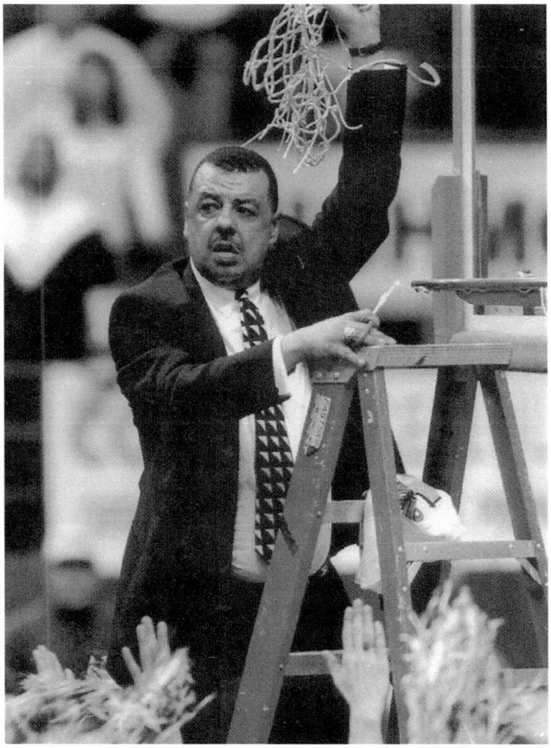

**A WAVE OF VICTORY.** Jeff Capel waves a net high after defeating James Madison 80-75 in the finals of the 1994–1995 CAA Tournament and earning an automatic NCAA bid. Next up for the Monarchs was a trip to the East Regional in Albany, New York, and a game against the 11th-ranked and Big East Champ Villanova. The Monarchs played one of the NCAA's most unforgettable contests, defeating the Wildcats 89-81 in triple overtime. (ODU Archives.)

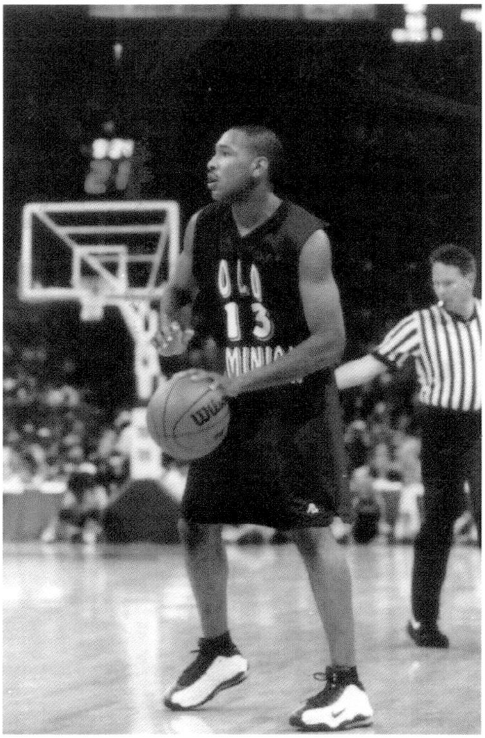

**MIKE BYERS, 1995–1999.** This 6-foot-2-inch guard started all four years for Old Dominion. A solid competitor, Byers scored 1,175 points, garnered 363 assists, and had 189 steals as a Monarch. In 1995, he earned a position on the CAA All-Rookie team. In 1997, he was selected on the CAA All-Tournament squad, and he helped lead the Monarchs to an incredible 62-58 overtime win against James Madison in the CAA Finals in Richmond, Virginia. (ODU Archives.)

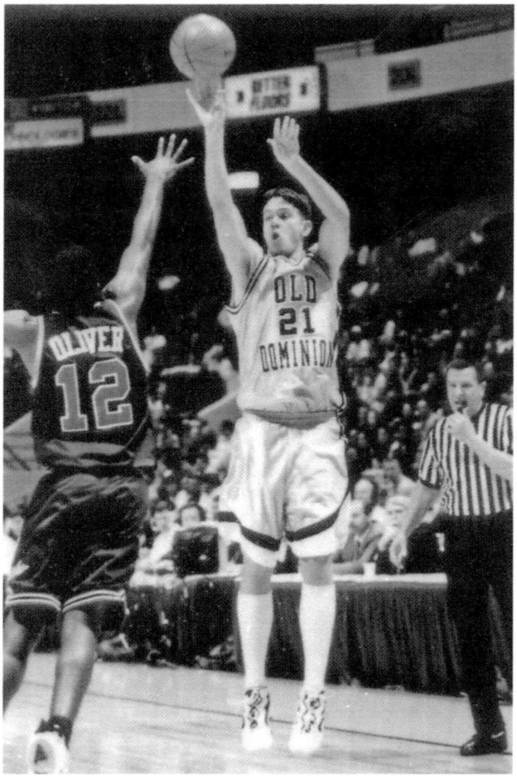

**MARK POAG, MONARCH SHARPSHOOTER.** This 6-foot-6-inch forward from Knoxville, Tennessee, is remembered as a deadly outside shooter who rained down threes for the Monarchs. Poag would complete his ODU career with 1,475 points. Leading the Monarchs with three-pointers from 1995 to 1999, he finished his career hitting 328 three pointers. In 1997–1998, he set an NCAA single-game three-point shooting mark by going 9 for 9 in a game against VMI. (ODU Archives.)

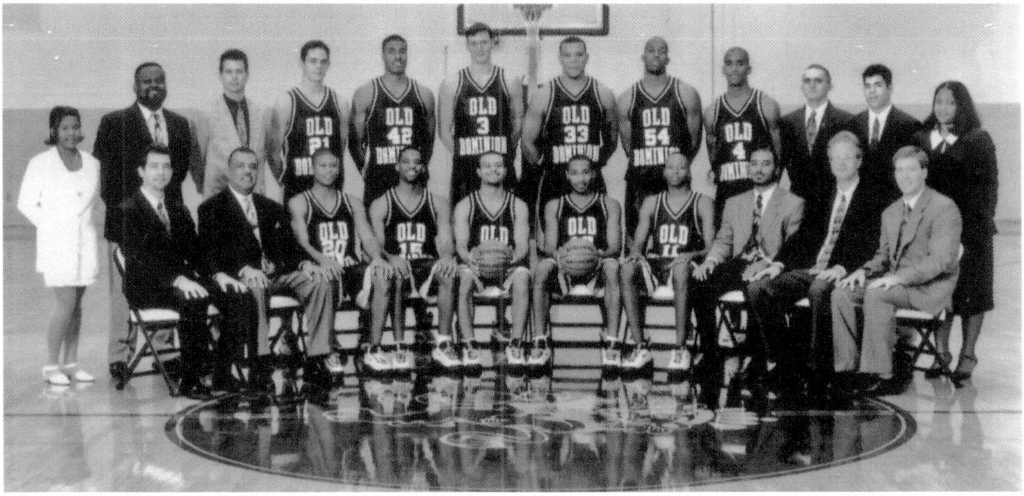

**Colonial Athletic Association Champions, 1996–1997.** Capel's third Monarch squad finished 21-12 and earned an NCAA bid. Pictured from left to right are (first row, seated) assistant coach Jim Corrigan, coach Jeff Capel, Brett Harper, E. J. Sherod, Brion Dunlop, Mike Byers, Freddie Bryant, assistant coach Milan Brown, assistant coach Mark Cline, and trainer Scott Johnson; (second row, standing) manager Andria Bane, manager Tracy Binson, manager Mike Tyree, Mark Poag, Reggie Bassette, Cal Bowdler, Odel Hodge, Skipper Youngblood, Brandon Jones, manager Michael Roundtree, manager Jose Irizarry, and manager Jackie Jones. (ODU Archives.)

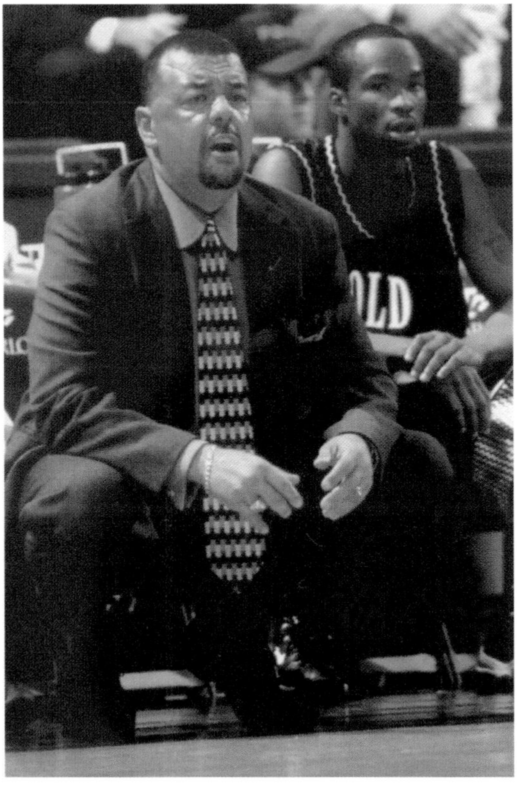

**Coach's Game Face.** Jeff Capel watches intently as ODU battles an opponent. His style was to play an up-tempo offense and swarming defense. During his seven years as coach of the Monarchs, he built a record of 122-98. During his tenure, he took ODU to one NIT and two NCAA Tournaments. After the 1995 NCAA East Regional upset of Big East Champion Villanova, Capel was named the CAA Coach of the Year and was a finalist for the National Coach of the Year. (ODU Archives.)

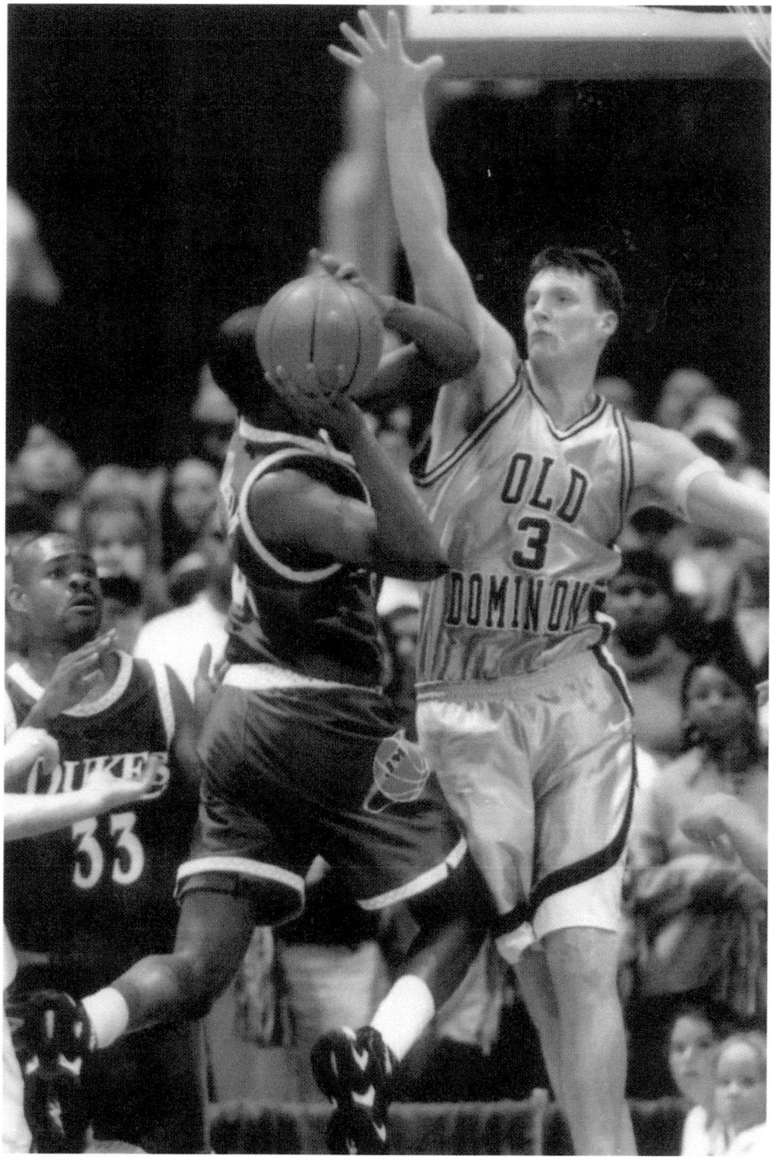


**Bowdler Goes High for a Block.** In a game during the 1997–1998 season against James Madison, Cal Bowdler goes high to block a shot against an unidentified James Madison guard. A 6-foot-10-inch forward from Rappahannock High in Sharps, Virginia, Bowdler was an understudy to Odell Hodge. During his junior and senior seasons, Bowdler led the CAA in rebounding and blocked shots. In a 1999 NIT win against Seton Hall, Bowdler went over the 1,000 career point mark, hauling down a career high of 20 rebounds. His play during his senior campaign earned him First Team All-CAA honors. Cal finished his career as a Monarch with 1,017 points, 783 rebounds, and 219 blocks. He was selected by the Atlanta Hawks in the first round of the 1999 NBA draft, where he played for three years. (ODU Archives.)

**Reggie Bassette, 1995–1999.** In this image, Bassette goes high for a rebound as Odell Hodge looks on. Reggie was a member of Capel's most highly touted freshmen class, which included Mark Poag, Skipper Youngblood, Michael Byers, and Cal Bowdler. This 6-foot-9-inch native of Richmond, Virginia, was a three-year starter for the Monarchs at the center position. A steady and balanced competitor, Bassette garnered 658 rebounds and blocked 199 shots in four years at Old Dominion. (ODU Archives.)

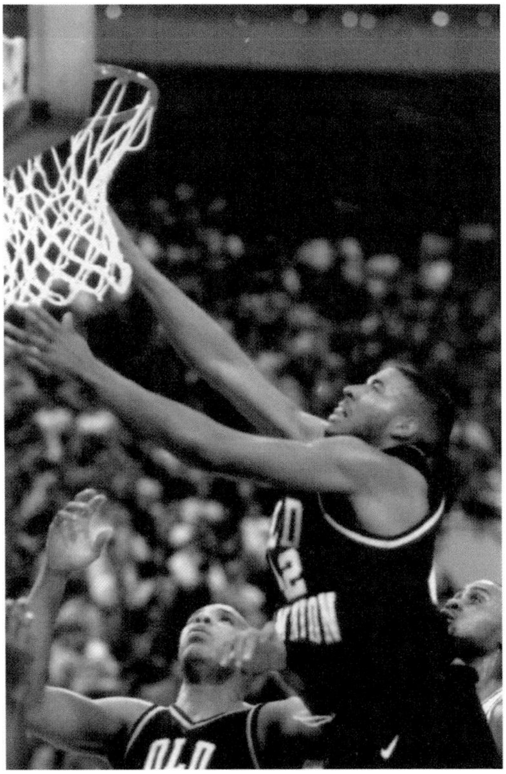

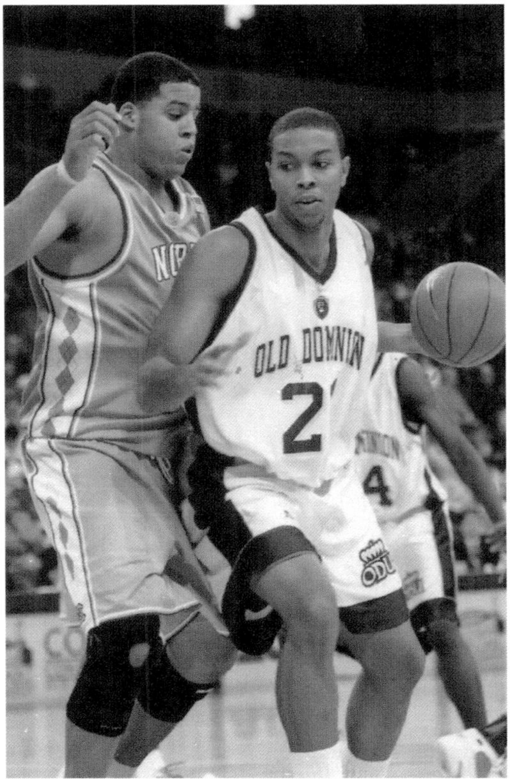


**Marsh Drives against North Carolina's May.** In the first regular season game at the Ted Constant Center on November 24, 2002, Ricardo Marsh attempts to drive against North Carolina's Shawn May. This 6-foot-8-inch power forward from Mebane, North Carolina, was a hard worker on both the offensive and defensive ends, leading the Monarchs in scoring both his junior and senior campaigns. Playing for both Capel and Taylor, Marsh would complete his Monarch career with 1,350 points and 690 rebounds. (ODU Archives.)

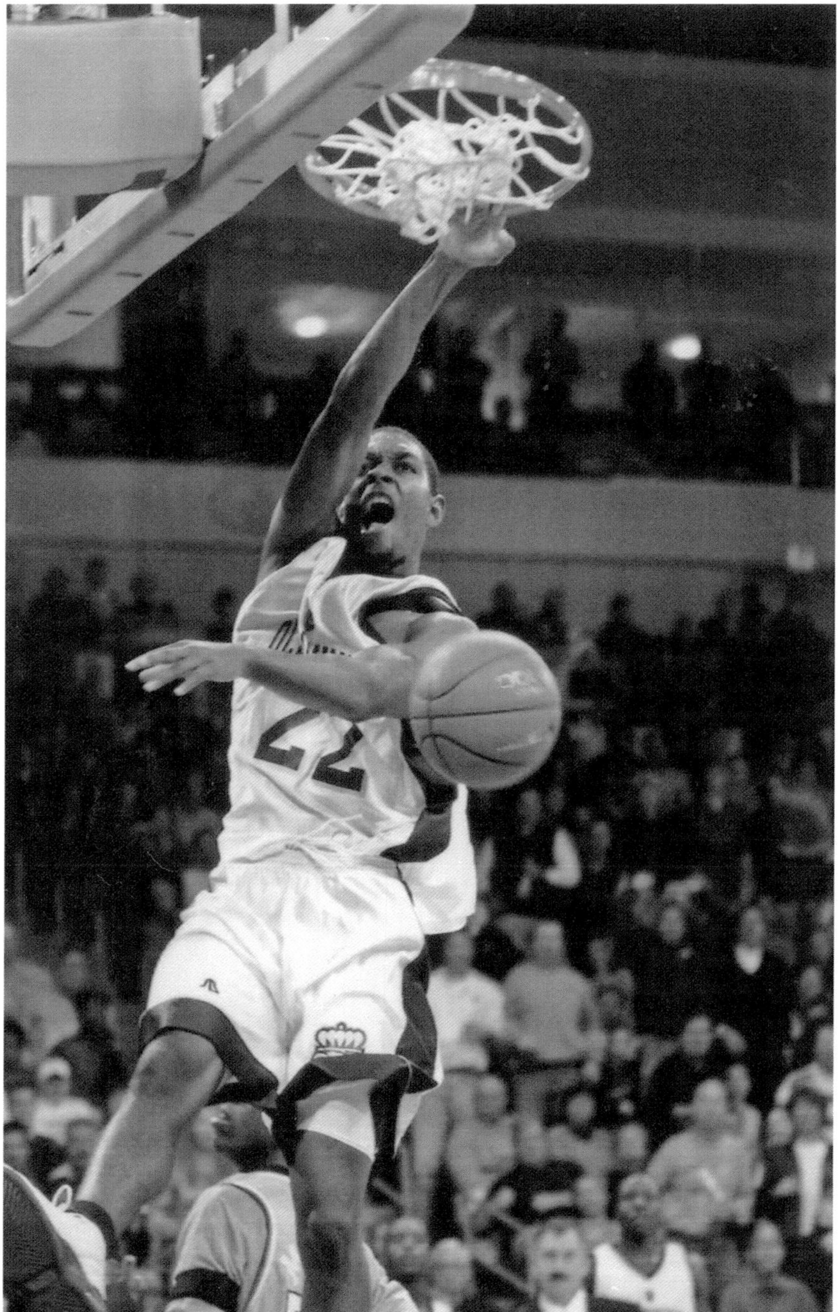

**RASHEED WRIGHT SLAMS ONE HOME.** Another player who played for both Capel and Taylor was this 6-foot-5-inch guard/forward from Greenville, North Carolina. Wright was the team leader on the court. Selected as a cocaptain his junior and senior seasons, Wright was a solid offensive player and a defensive specialist. In 2002–2003, Wright earned a spot on the CAA All-Defensive team. Over his four-year Monarch career, he stole 131 balls to go along with his 1,185 points. (ODU Archives.)

9

# A New Era Begins

## The Blaine Taylor Years

When Jeff Capel resigned, Dr. Jim Jarrett cited three factors that he believed were important in the selection of a new coach: first was to find someone who could galvanize the Monarch fans; second was to find someone who would run a clean and competitive program; and third was to hire someone who would recruit players who would excel both on the court and in the classroom.

After reviewing resumes, several impressive candidates emerged. Those interviewed included Winthrop coach Greg Marshall; North Carolina assistant Phil Ford; Stanford assistant Blaine Taylor; and former ODU star Kenny Gattison. Thirty-eight days after the process began, Blaine Taylor was introduced as the Monarch's 12th coach.

Taylor, 43, came to ODU after three years as Stanford's top assistant under Mike Montgomery. In his college days, Taylor had played point guard and served as graduate assistant for Montgomery at Montana. From 1991 to 1998, as head coach at Montana, he posted a 142-65 record. The Monarchs had their man, and now he had a daunting task of reviving a once-proud program.

Taylor inherited a team in 2001–2002 that had finished 13-18 the previous year. Returning were starters senior Pierre Green and juniors Rasheed Wright and Ricardo Marsh. Rounding out the starting five were sophomore center, 6-foot-11-inch Clay McGowen, and Kiah Thomas, a 6-foot-4-inch freshman guard from Norfolk. The Monarchs, in what would be their last year at the ODU Fieldhouse, posted a 13-16 record under Taylor.

The 2002–2003 team featured Monarch veterans Wright, Marsh, and Thomas; junior guards Troy Nance and John Waller; and a highly touted freshmen class of Alex Loughton, a 6-foot-9-inch center from Australia, Isaiah Hunter, a 6-foot-1-inch guard from Charlotte, North Carolina; and John Morris, 6-foot-2-inch guard from Pennsylvania. The highlight of the season was the opening of the Ted Constant Convocation Center, the new 8,600-seat, on-campus facility. On November 24, 2002, a sold-out crowd watched ninth-ranked North Carolina defeat the Monarchs 67-59. The Monarchs could only muster a 12-15 record in 2002–2003, but ODU's freshmen gave the fans a glimpse into a bright future.

The 2003–2004 campaign brought Taylor his first winning season as head coach. Returning starters Waller and Loughton were joined by sophomore guard Hunter and three newcomers: 6-foot-7-inch forward Arnaud Dahi; 5-foot-11-inch point guard Drew Williamson; and often-used substitute, 6-foot-7-inch forward Valdas Vasylius. With wins against Virginia Tech, George Washington, and 11 conference opponents, the Monarchs finished with a record of 17-12, the first winning season in four years.

Optimism surrounded the Monarchs as the 2004–2005 season included the return of juniors Loughton and Hunter; sophomores Dahi, Williamson, and Vasylius; and a 6-foot-1-inch newcomer from Florida, guard Brandon Johnson. The season culminated with a school record 28 wins, a CAA championship won by defeating VCU 73-66 in overtime, and an NCAA bid. ODU met eventual Final Four participant Michigan State in Worchester, Massachusetts, losing a hotly contested game 89-81.

After 28 wins in 2004–2005, expectations were high for the 2005–2006 season. Returning were seniors Loughton and Hunter; juniors Williamson, Dahi, and Vasylius; sophomores 6-foot-4-inch forward Brian Henderson, 6-foot-2-inch guard Abdi Lidonde, and 7-foot-3-inch center Sam Harris. The lone Monarch newcomer was 6-foot-6-inch forward Jonathan Adams from Georgia.

The season included 13 victories in the CAA, with wins over VCU, UNC Wilmington, and NCAA finalist George Mason. Out-of-conference victories included wins against Georgia, DePaul, Virginia Tech, and Marist. In the NIT, ODU defeated Colorado 79-61, Manhattan 70-68, and in the quarterfinals defeated Hofstra on their way to a game with University of Michigan in the NIT semifinals at Madison Square Garden. The Monarchs lost to Michigan 66-43, ending the season with a record of 24-10. That season included wins over teams from the SEC, Atlantic 10, ACC, Big East, Conference USA, and the Big 12.

Old Dominion returned seniors Williamson, Dahi, and Vasylius for the 2006–2007 campaign. Henderson, Johnson, Lidonde, Harris, and Adams were again counted on to provide depth. Freshman recruits included 6-foot-2-inch guard Marsharee Neely from Greensboro, North Carolina, and Gerald Lee, a 6-foot-9-inch forward from Finland.

During November and December, Old Dominion won seven out-of-conference games, including a 75-62 win over eighth-ranked Georgetown on the Hoyas' home court. Conference wins included a pair against George Mason, fresh off their NCAA Final Four run, and two decisive victories against Drexel. From January 24 to February 24, the Monarchs would go on an 11-game winning streak, which would include important wins over VCU, Drexel, Hofstra, and a road win against Toledo in ESPN's Bracket Buster game. Their 12th win was a CRA quarter-final victory against Towson. The streak came to an end the next evening as the Monarchs lost to George Mason in the semi-finals.

After losing in the semi-finals of the CAA Tournament, the Monarchs earned an at-large bid to the NCAA Tournament. The season ended with a loss to Butler in the Midwest Regionals in Buffalo, New York.

No one can gaze in a crystal ball and predict future wins and losses for the Monarchs, but as former coach Paul Webb said in his forward, "It is without question that Old Dominion's basketball future looks brighter than ever."

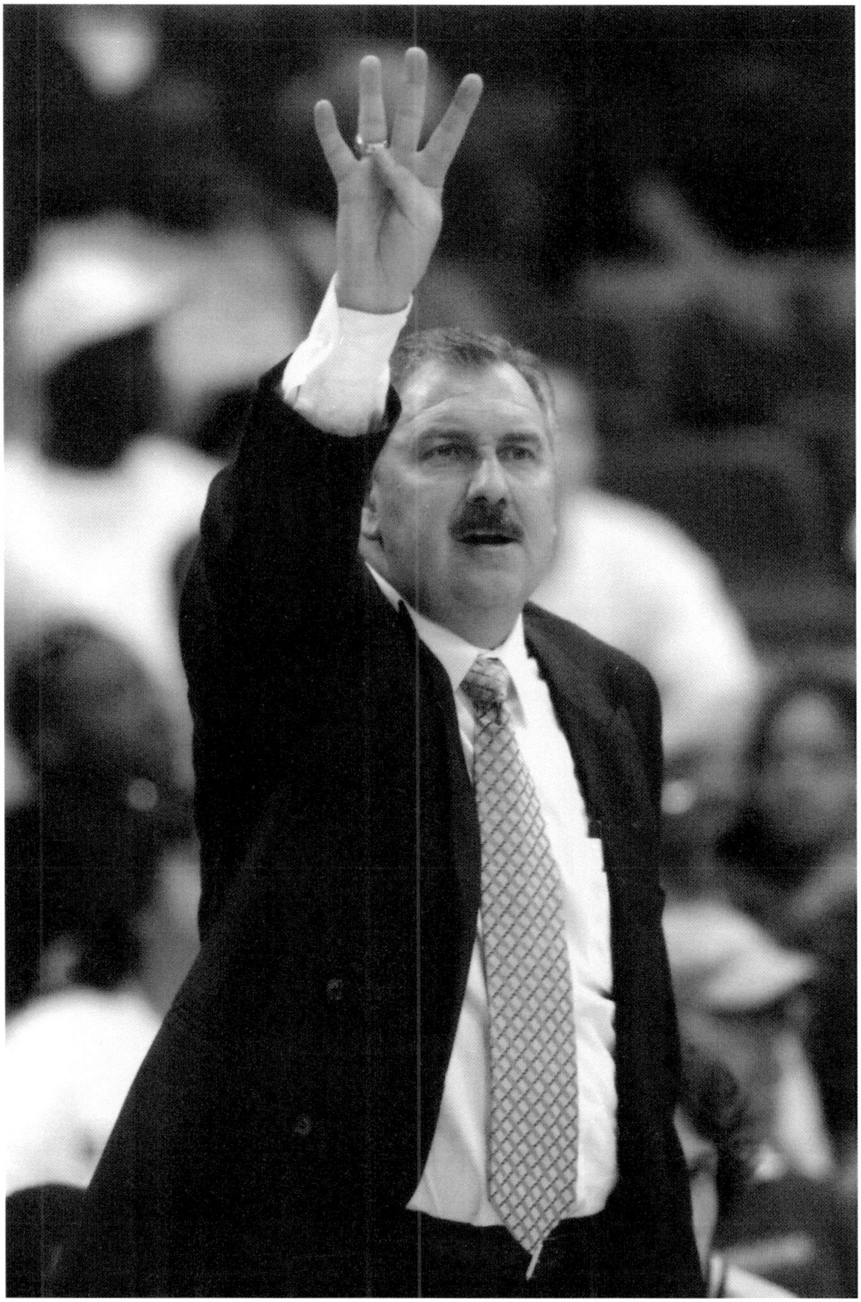

**Coach Blaine Taylor.** Taylor is a graduate of the University of Montana, where he played point guard and later became coach for the Grizzlies. During his eight years at Montana, Taylor posted a 142-66 record, which included five seasons with 20 or more wins. Reuniting with Mike Montgomery, his college coach, at Stanford, he would serve three years as an assistant. Since taking over the Monarchs in 2001, Taylor has brought the program back to prominence on the CAA and national scene. In his first six years, he took the Monarchs to two NCAA Tournaments and the NIT final four. (ODU Archives.)

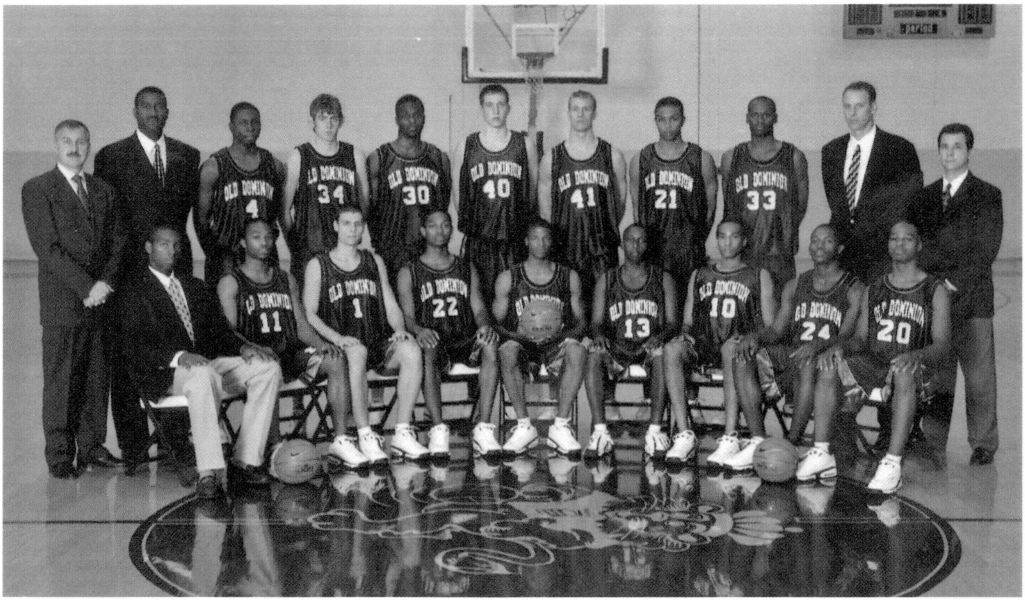

**Blaine Taylor's First Team, 2001–2002.** This Monarch team went 13-16 under Taylor. Pictured from left to right are (first row, seated) manager Bob Mills, Marcus Drewry, Andreas Themistocleous, Rasheed Wright, Pierre Green, Troy Nance, John Waller, Kiah Thomas, and Samir Hickson; (second row, standing) head coach Blaine Taylor, assistant coach Kenny Gattison, T. J. Waldon, Alan Treese, Charles Donnington, Clay McGowen, Joe Principe, Ricardo Marsh, James Smith, assistant coach Larry Kristkowiak, and assistant coach Jim Corrigan. (ODU Archives.)

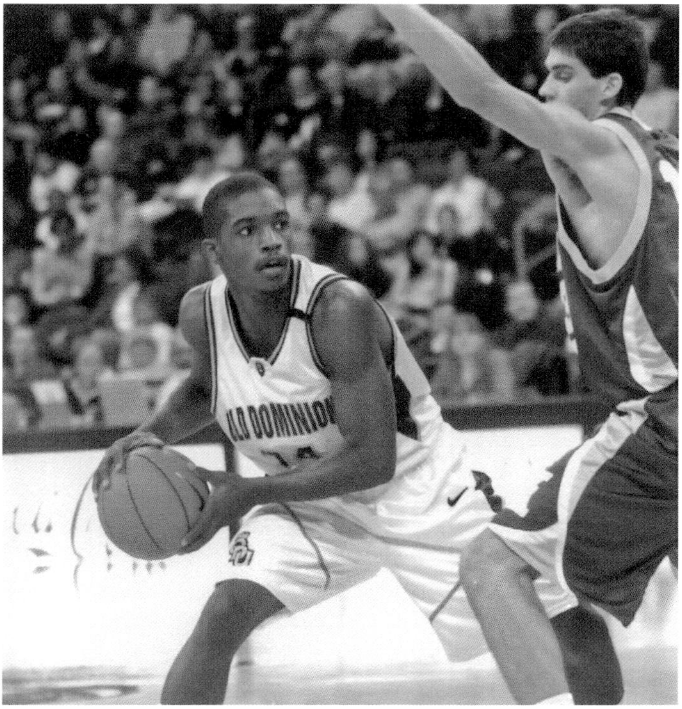

**Kiah Thomas, 2001–2005.** Coach Taylor's first scholarship at Old Dominion went to Granby High's Kiah Thomas. This 6-foot-4-inch guard started for the Monarchs his freshman and senior seasons. Thomas displayed his shooting skill in the 2004–2005 CAA Championship when he scored 14 points in an overtime win over rival VCU. (ODU Archives.)

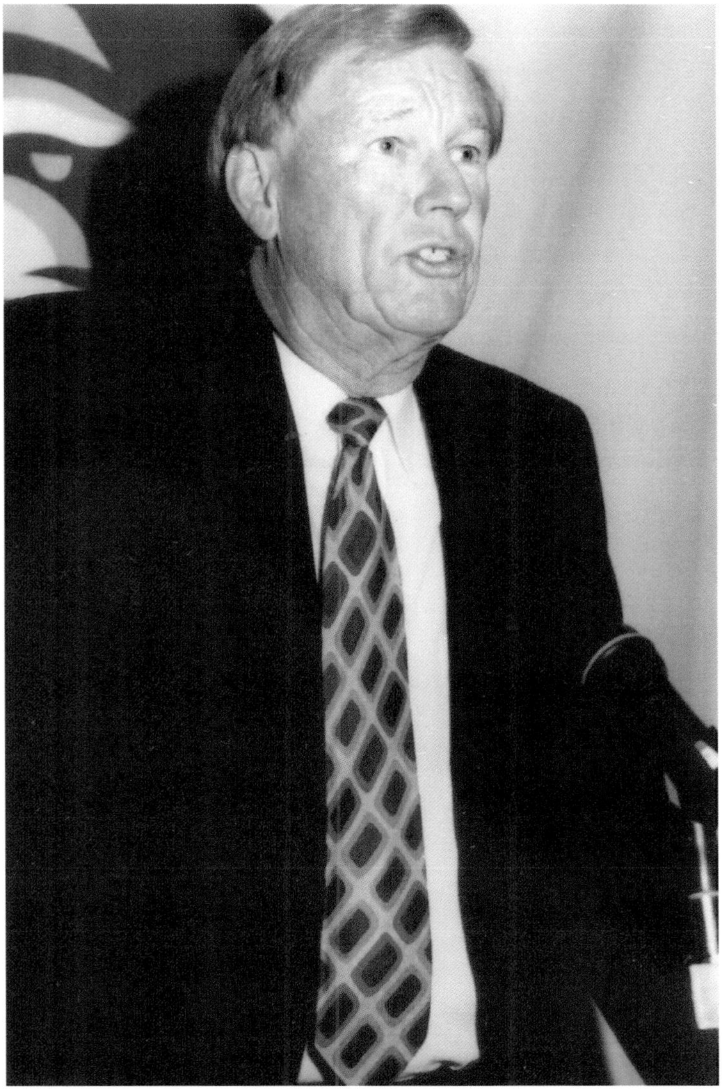

**FACE OF OLD DOMINION ATHLETICS.** In 1970, Dr. Jim Jarrett became the new athletic director. Jarrett replaced longtime coach and Athletic Director Bud Metheny, who stepped down from both positions. Dr. Jarrett has led Old Dominion from a NCAA Division II power to a healthy and well-respected NCAA Division I program. He was one of the first athletic directors in the nation to award scholarships to female student athletes. Under his leadership, the school's athletic programs have captured 32 national championships, and Old Dominion has built several state-of-the-art athletic venues, including the Bud Metheny Baseball Complex; a new sailing center; the athletic administration and basketball practice facilities; the ODU soccer building; a new indoor tennis facility; and the Monarchs' beautiful 8,600-seat basketball venue, the Ted Constant Convocation Center. Jarrett is currently overseeing the addition of football, women's crew, women's softball, and women's volleyball to the athletic programs in the near future. Dr. Jarrett was recently presented with the NCAA 2006 Lifetime Achievement Award presented by the NCAA Division I-AAA Athletic Director's Association. (ODU Archives.)

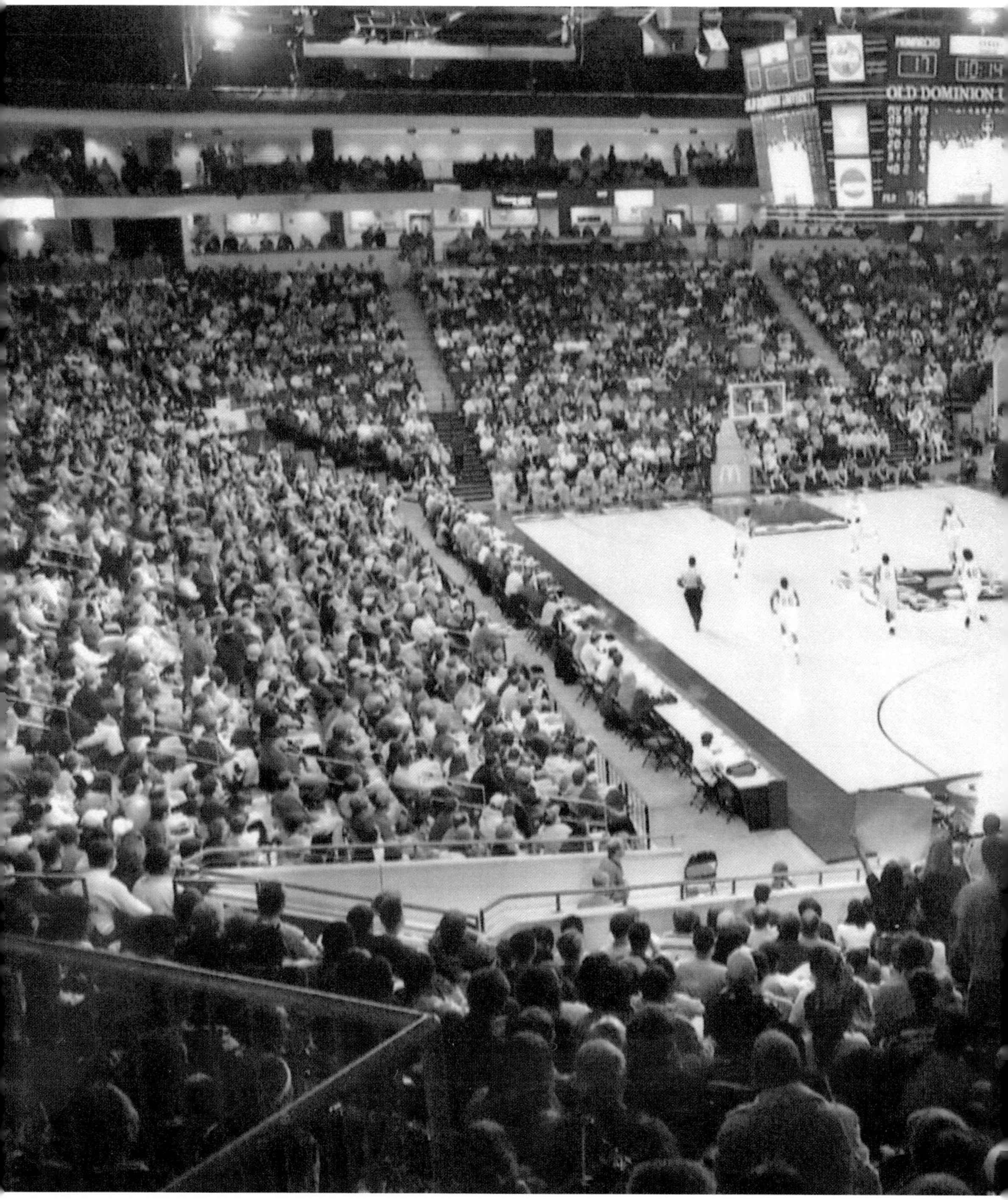


**TED CONSTANT CONVOCATION CENTER.** This photograph was taken on February 12, 2005, at a sold-out "Ted" during the Monarchs 82-76 victory against VCU. The Ted Constant Convocation Center first opened its doors to basketball in October 2002. This beautiful, multimillion dollar, on-campus facility seats 8,600 for basketball games and nearly 10,000 for concerts. There are 16

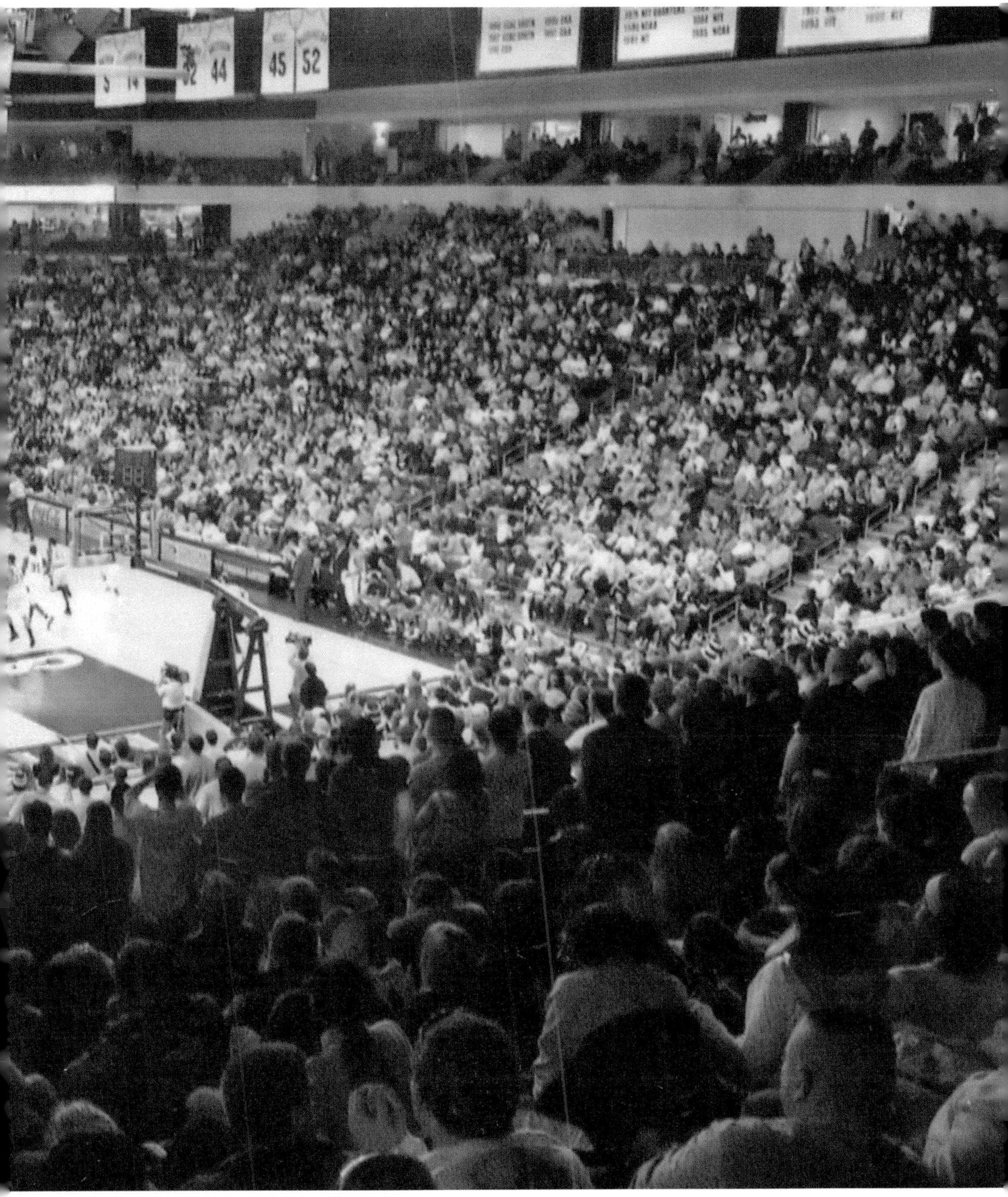


suites and a larger super box for entertaining groups at the game. The facility is equipped with state-of-the-art video and audio equipment, including a jumbo video scoreboard. It has truly become a home-court advantage when the Monarchs play in the Ted. (ODU Archives.)

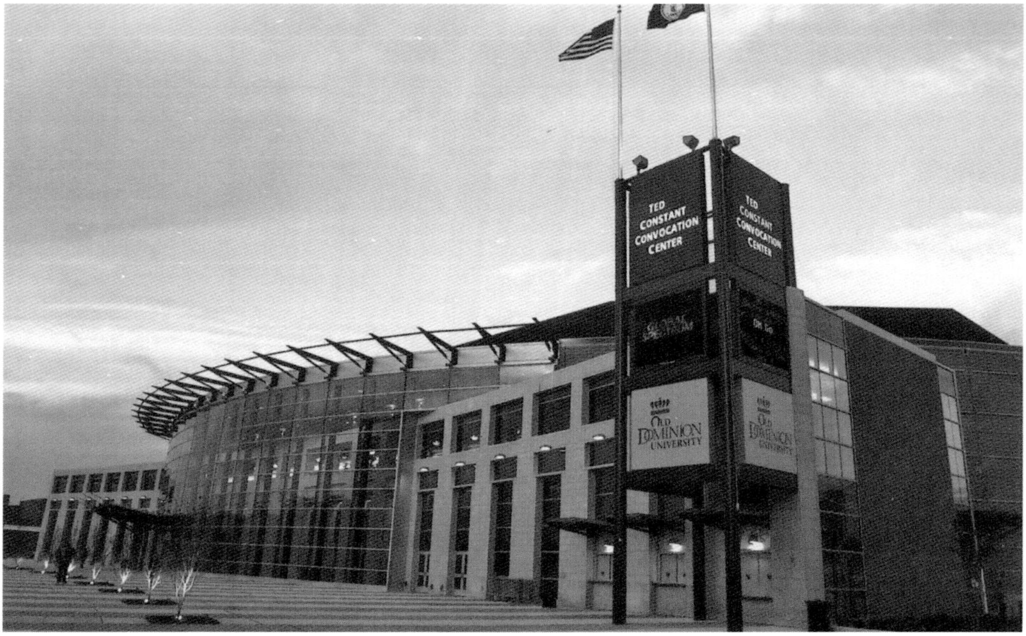

**TWILIGHT AT THE TED.** This image shows the Ted Constant Convocation Center only hours before a big game against a CAA opponent. The center, located on Hampton Boulevard, is the cornerstone of the University Village. Located directly behind the arena, the Village includes student apartments, retail shops, and restaurants, and there are plans for a hotel and movie theater. (ODU Archives.)

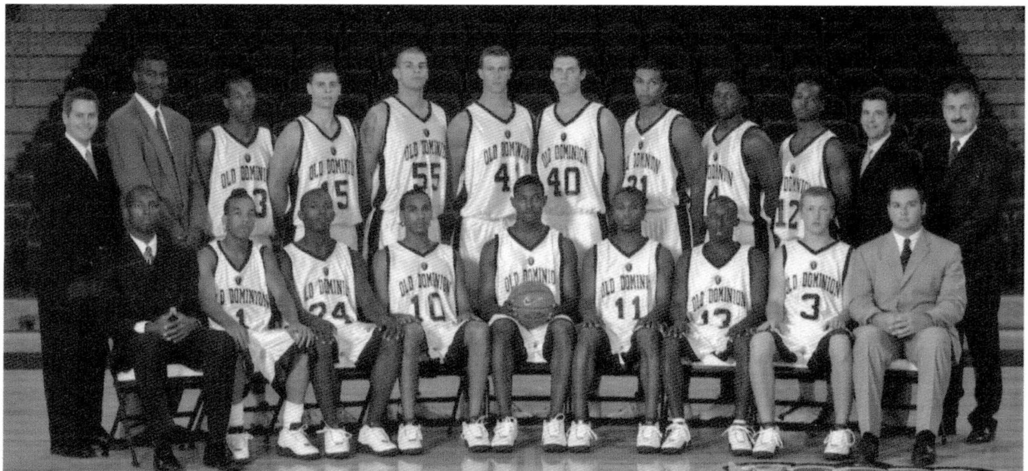

**OLD DOMINION MONARCHS, 2002–2003.** This Monarch squad compiled a record of 12-15. Pictured from left to right are (first row) manager Rob Mills, Isaiah Hunter, Kiah Thomas, John Waller, Rasheed Wright, Marcus Drewry, Troy Nance, John Morris, and manager David Morehead; (second row) assistant coach Rob Wilkes, assistant coach Kenny Gattison, Cole Pugh, Andreas Themistocleous, Janko Mrksic, Joe Principe, Alex Loughton, Ricardo Marsh, T. J. Waldon, Samir Hickson, assistant coach Jim Corrigan, and head coach Blaine Taylor. (ODU Archives.)

**BIG BLUE AND A FRIEND, 1978.** In 1970, Big Blue the official mascot for Old Dominion University was born. When he was delivered, ODU's mascot had light-blue fur. In this 1977 photograph, Big Blue poses with seven-year-old Tina Moore. Over the years, this scene has been repeated countless times to the delight of thousands of young children. (ODU Archives.)

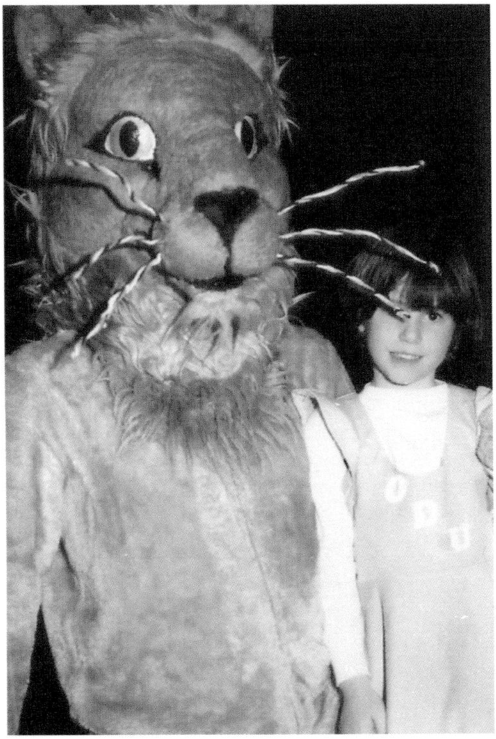

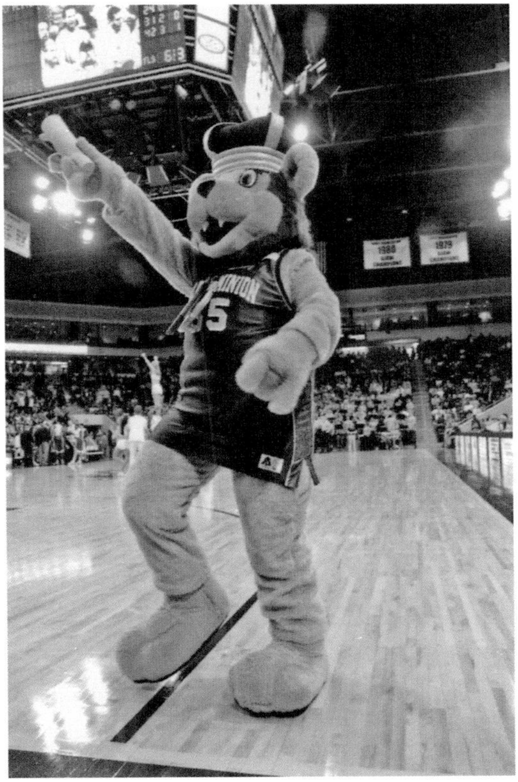

**BIG BLUE TRANSFORMATION.** Over the past 37 years, Big Blue has gone through an extreme makeover. Gone is the original mascot costume that was dyed light blue; it was replaced by a newer and more elaborate costume accented by a royal crown. Whether he's performing in dance routines, leading students in a cheer, or shooting T-shirts into the stands, Big Blue always adds excitement and atmosphere to the game. (ODU Archives.)

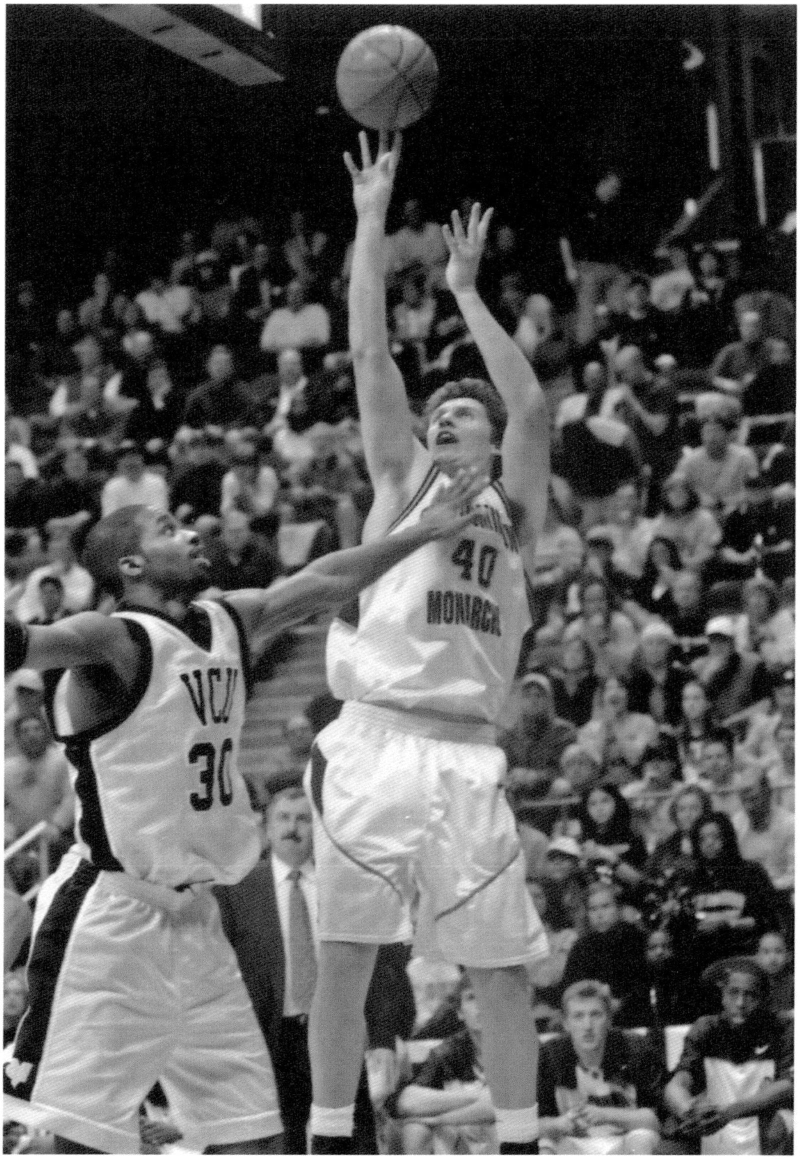


**ALEX LOUGHTON, ALL-AMERICAN.** From 2002 to 2006, this 6-foot-9-inch forward from Perth, Australia, was the face of Old Dominion basketball. Loughton was a versatile player who excelled both on the court and in the classroom. Alex was characterized by ODU coach Blaine Taylor as "an extremely smart and unselfish player with an unusual array of solid skills for a big man." A CAA All-Rookie selection in 2002–2003, he was selected to the CAA All-Conference teams the next three years. In 2004–2005, Loughton was selected as the CAA Player of the Year and Tournament MVP, as he helped lead the Monarchs to a 28-6 record and NCAA Tournament bid. A gifted student athlete, Alex was selected in 2005–2006 as an ESPN/COSIDA's Third Team Academic All-American and to the NCAA National Scholar Squad for three straight years. Loughton completed his career with 1,646 career points, 952 career rebounds, and 159 career steals. (ODU Archives.)

**MAN FROM DOWN UNDER.** In a November 29, 2003, game against 13th-ranked St. Joseph's University, sophomore forward Alex Loughton provided ODU fans a glimpse of the future. Loughton had 24 points, 5 assists, and 15 rebounds to lead the Monarchs in their upset bid. It took a half-court shot at the buzzer to secure a win for the Hawks. (ODU Archives.)

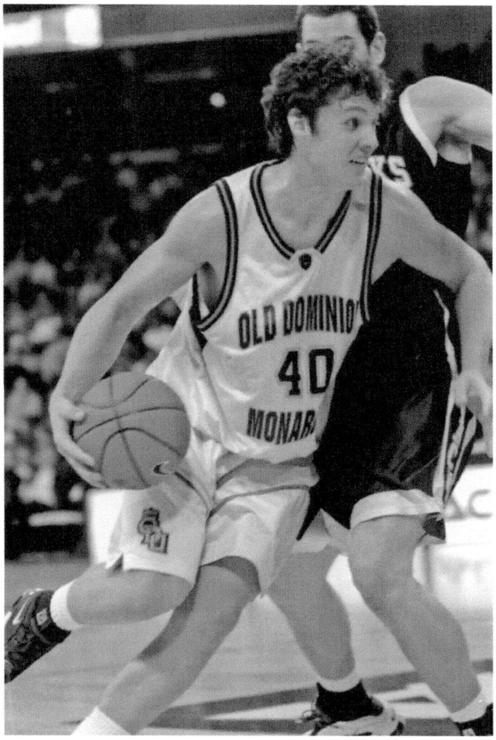


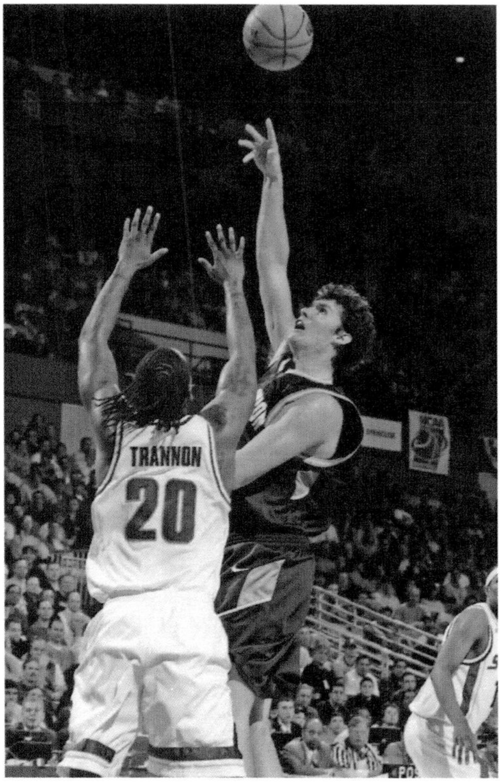


**A STELLAR PERFORMANCE.** Alex Loughton shoots a hook against Michigan State defender Matt Trannon in a 2004–2005 NCAA regional game in Worchester, Massachusetts. Loughton would have 22 points, 11 rebounds, and 6 assists—all game highs—in a losing cause to the Spartans. His performance on the national stage caught the eye of professional scouts from the NBA and international leagues. (ODU Archives.)

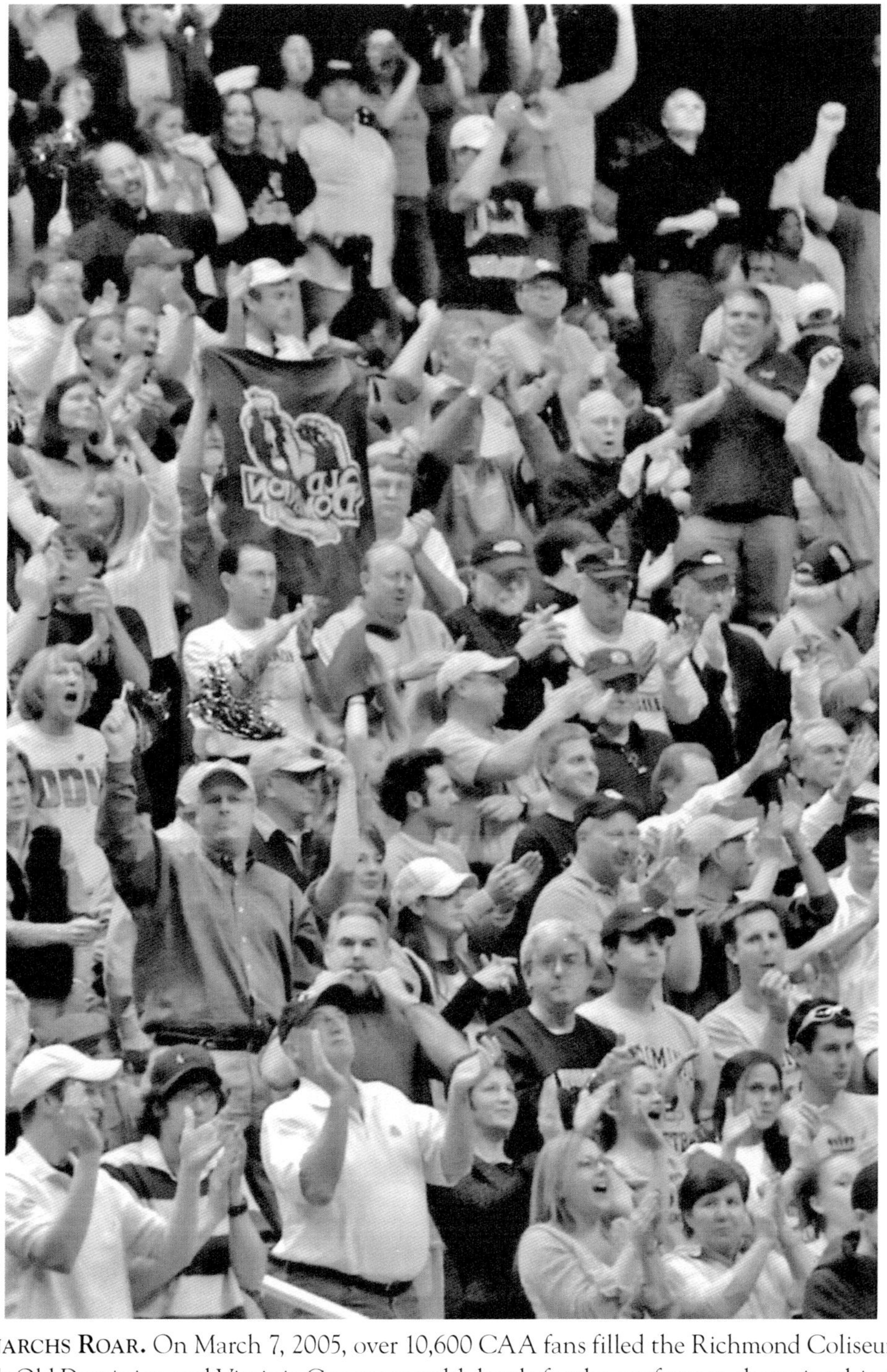

**MONARCHS ROAR.** On March 7, 2005, over 10,600 CAA fans filled the Richmond Coliseum to watch Old Dominion and Virginia Commonwealth battle for the conference championship. The Monarchs prevailed in overtime with a hard-fought 73-66 victory. In this photograph, some of the ODU contingent voice and show their approval. Old Dominion fan support for away games is one of the best in the CAA. (ODU Archives.)

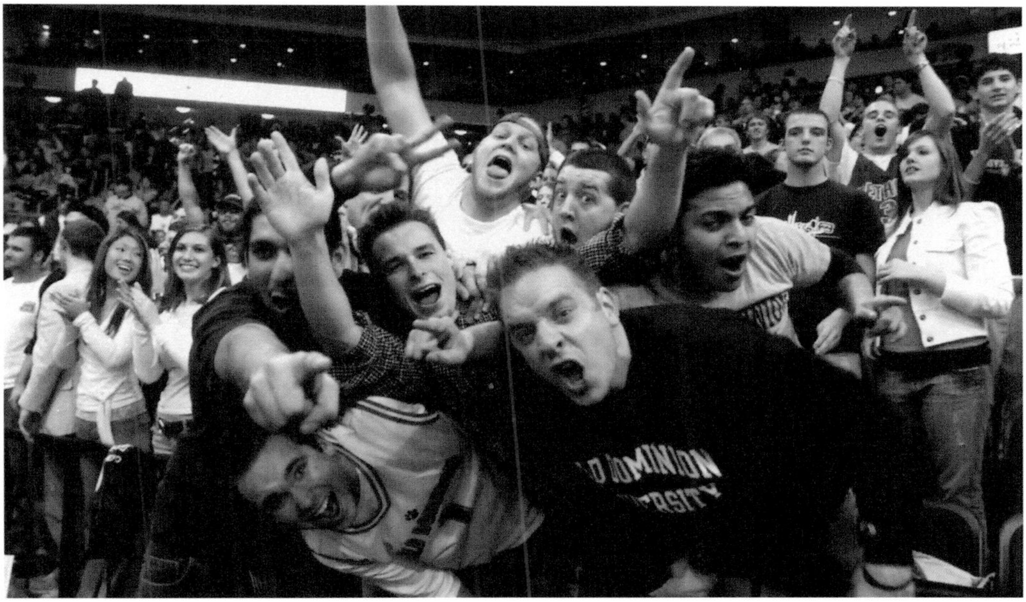


**MONARCH MANIACS.** Monarch Maniacs make the ODU basketball atmosphere at home games electric. The students at Old Dominion games provide high energy as they stand, scream, taunt the opposing teams and create both the pageantry and tradition of college basketball. (ODU Archives.)

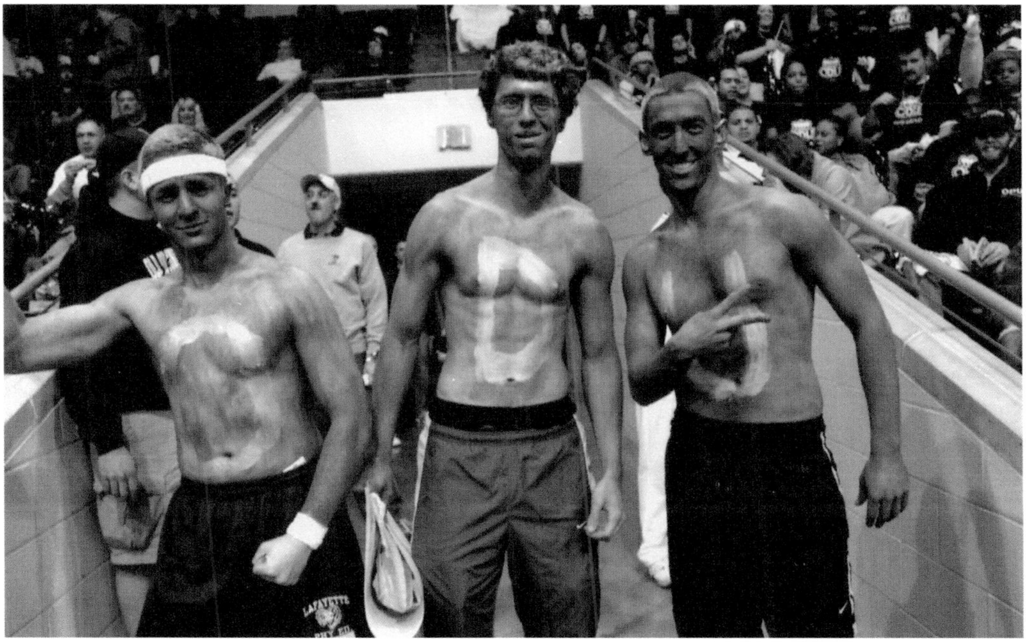

**O-D-U.** These three Old Dominion students show their passion and Monarch spirit at a 2005 game against Virginia Commonwealth University. With their painted bodies they join other spirited Monarch Maniacs with the slogan T-shirts, appropriately blue wigs, and crazy hats that adorn the student section. (ODU Archives.)

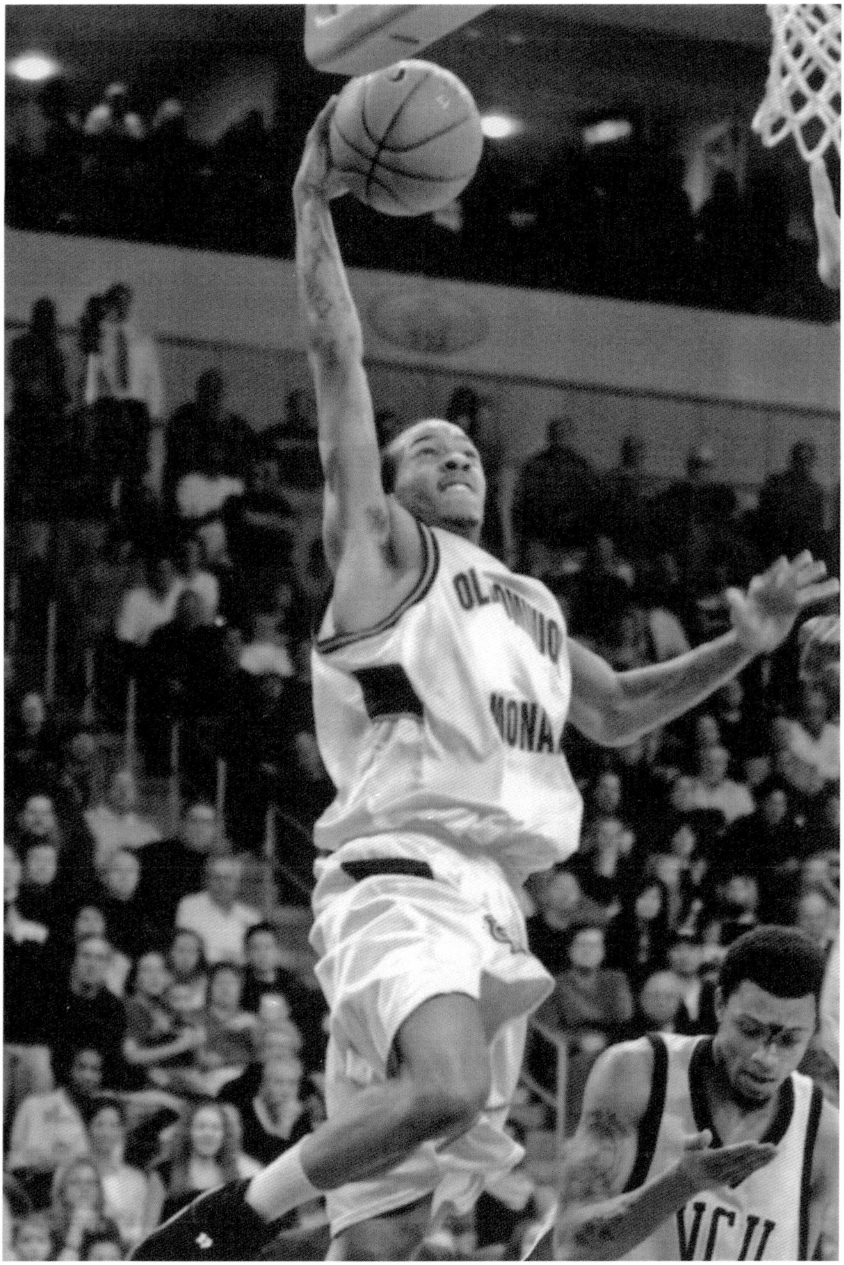

**Isaiah Hunter, 2002–2006.** A native of Charlotte, North Carolina, this 6-foot-3-inch guard played key roles for the Monarchs from 2002 to 2006. Hunter had a very quick first step and was very adept at seeing an opening to the basket. Monarch fans will never forget his breakaway dunk with less than a minute to play in Old Dominion's overtime defeat of VCU in the 2004–2005 CAA Championship game. The shot made ESPN's *Sports Center* that evening. Isaiah would score a career-high 29 points to lead the Monarchs to a 61-51 victory over Hofstra, and the team would gain a berth in the 2005–2006 final four of the National Invitation Tournament. Hunter would complete his Monarch career with 1,425 points. (ODU Archives.)

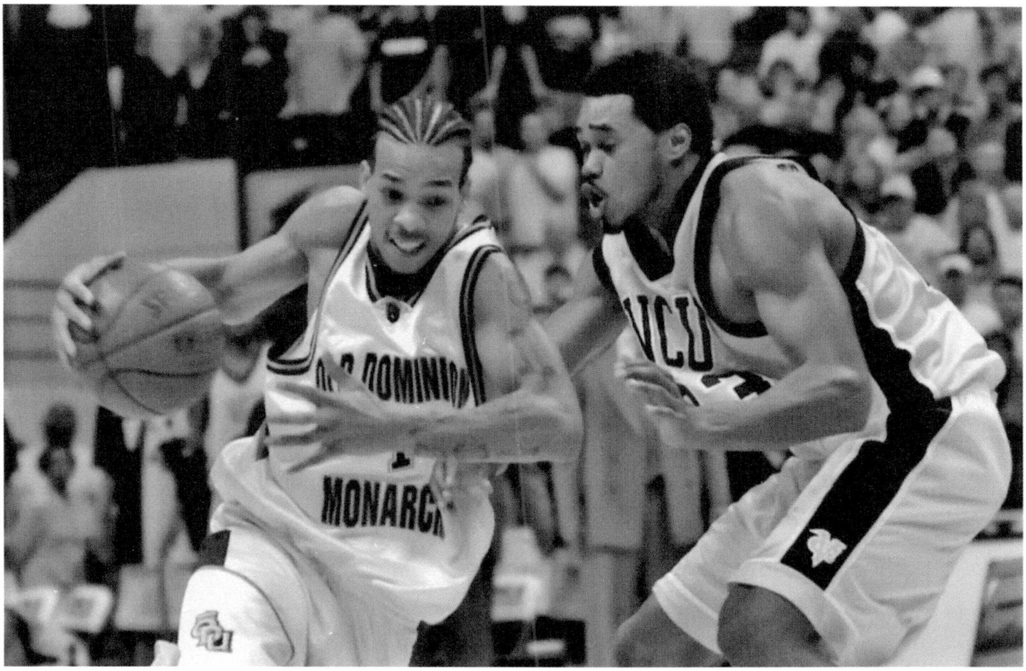


**HUNTER DRIVES FOR TWO.** Monarch guard Isaiah Hunter drives past a defender to score two of his 13 points in the March 7, 2005, overtime win against VCU. The game was played before 10,650 raucous fans in a sold-out Richmond Coliseum. Hunter would score eight points in overtime to help lead the Monarchs to a 73-66 victory in the finals of the CAA Championship. (ODU Archives.)

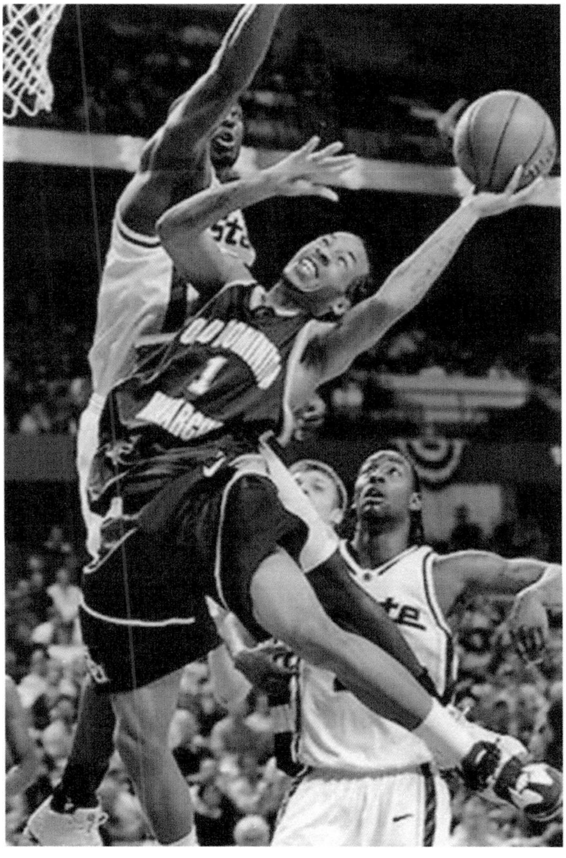

**ACROBATIC SHOT.** Meeting Michigan State in the 2004–2005 NCAA first round at Worchester, Massachusetts, Isaiah Hunter appears to be hanging in air as he scores two of his 13 points against a Michigan State defender. The Monarchs lost 89-81 to the Spartans, who would advance to the 2005 Final Four in St. Louis. (ODU Archives.)

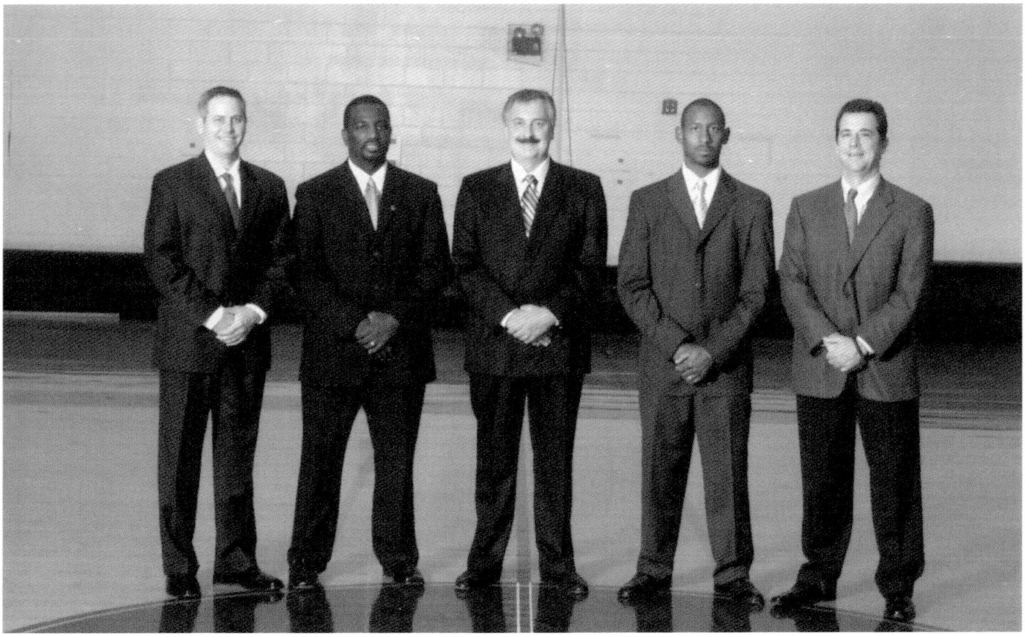

**OLD DOMINION UNIVERSITY BASKETBALL STAFF, 2006–2007.** Pictured from left to right are John Richardson, director of basketball operations; Rob Wilkes, assistant coach; Blaine Taylor, head coach; Jim Corrigan, assistant coach; and Travis DeCuire, assistant coach. (ODU Archives.)

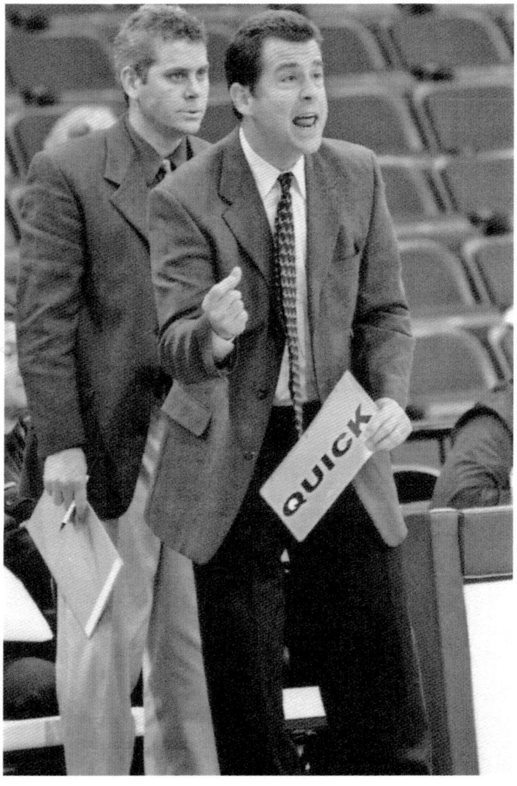


**JIM CORRIGAN, ASSISTANT COACH.** Jim Corrigan holds a sign directing the ODU offense. A 1980 graduate of Duke University, where he played guard for the Blue Devils, Jim has been an assistant coach on the collegiate level for 20 years, having also worked as an assistant at William and Mary from 1982 to 1994. Corrigan just completed his 13th season at Old Dominion, serving on the staffs of Jeff Capel and Taylor. (ODU Archives.)

**ROB WILKES, ASSISTANT COACH.** A 1993 graduate of Stetson University, Wilkes was a four-year member of the basketball team coached by his father and longtime Stetson coach Glenn Wilkes. Before joining the ODU staff in 2002–2003, Rob had stints as an assistant at Florida State, Georgia Southern, and Lyn University in Boca Raton, Florida. (ODU Archives.)

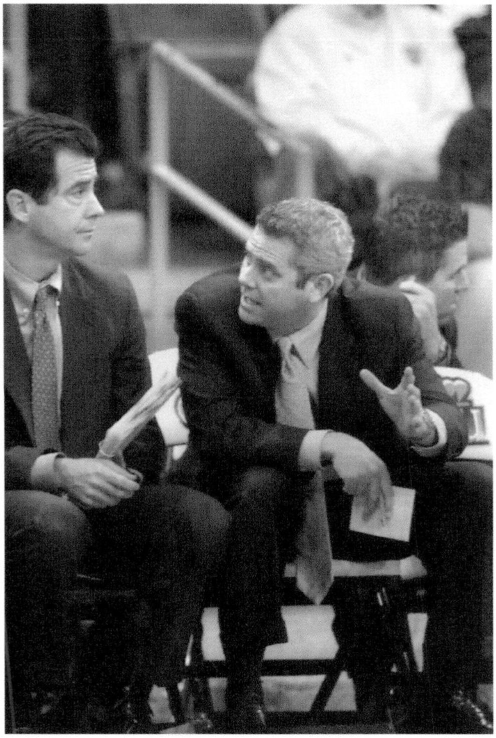

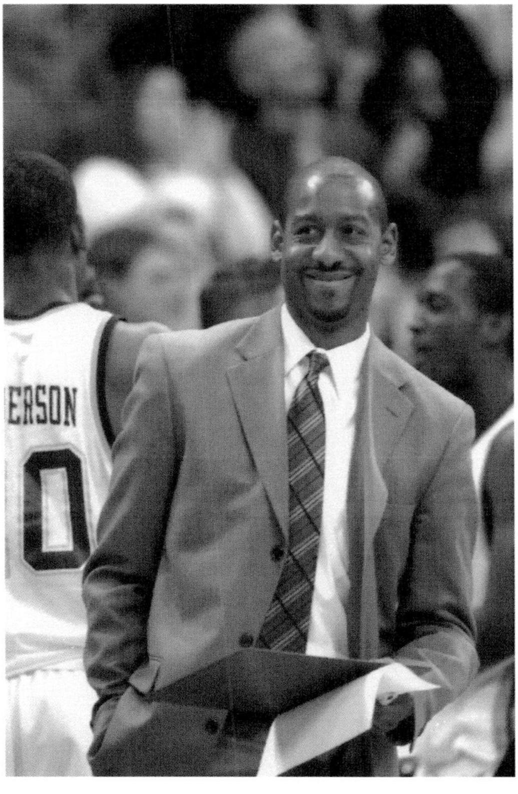


**TRAVIS DECUIRE, ASSISTANT COACH.** A member of Blaine's staff since 2003–2004, DeCuire came to Old Dominion after coaching successfully at the high school and junior college levels. A point guard who played at Montana under Taylor from 1991 to 1994, Travis was named Montana's MVP and to All-Big Sky Conference teams in 1993 and 1994. (ODU Archives.)

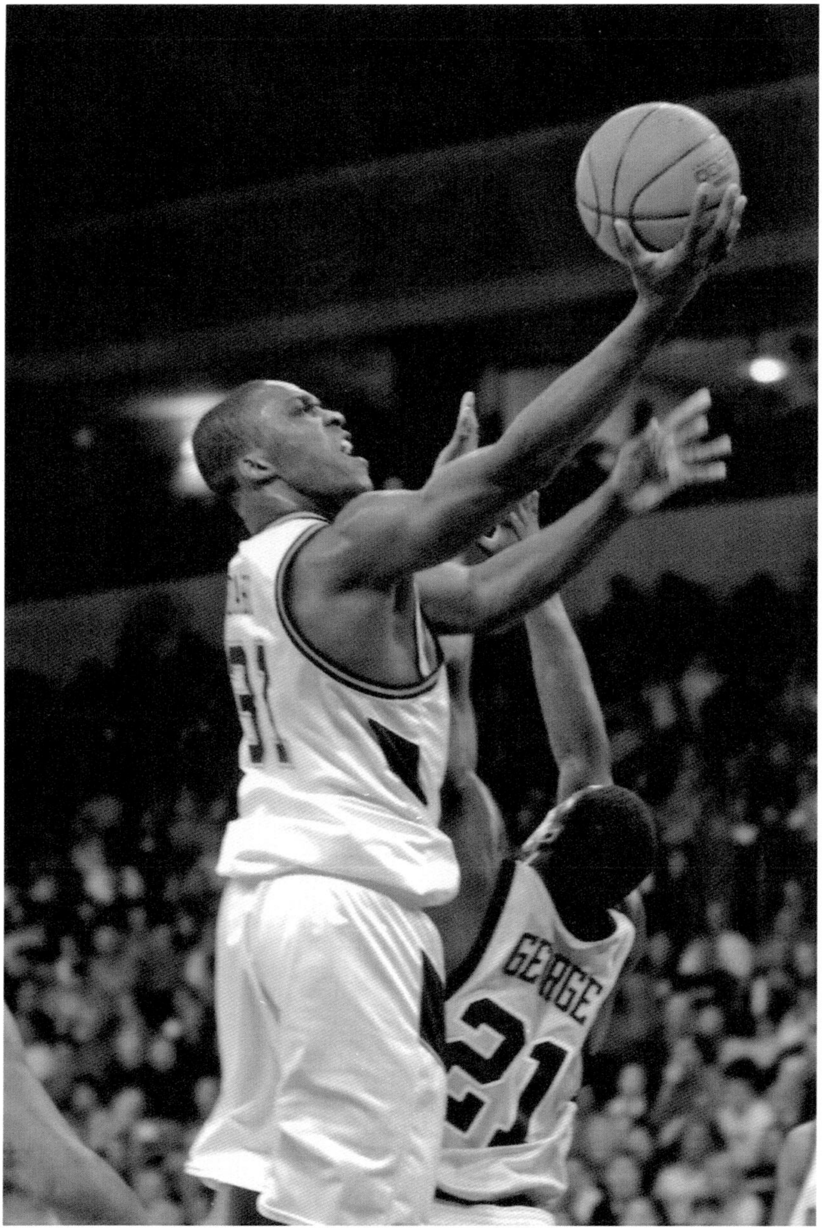


**ARNAUD DAHI, 2004–2007.** Born and raised in the Ivory Coast, this 6-foot-7-inch, 235-pound forward was considered a top 100 national recruit for the Monarchs. Dahi, a four-year starter for the Monarchs, was a gifted and powerful forward who was an excellent leaper. Arnaud led the team in blocked shots his first three seasons. A severe knee injury in the semifinals of the NIT severely hampered Dahi during the 2006–2007 season. It was late in the season when he returned to his prior form. Monarch fans had enormous respect for Arnaud, who had to go through two long off-season surgeries and rehabilitation bouts as the result of a severe shoulder and knee injuries. Dahi finished his career as a member of the Monarch 1,000 Point Club, collecting over 600 rebounds, 100 steals, and 135 blocks. (ODU Archives.)

**DAHI SLAMS ONE HOME.** Arnaud Dahi dunks for two of his 406 points during the 2005–2006 season. Arnaud, who played bigger than 6 feet 7 inches, possessed great leaping ability and an explosive first step. (ODU Archives.)

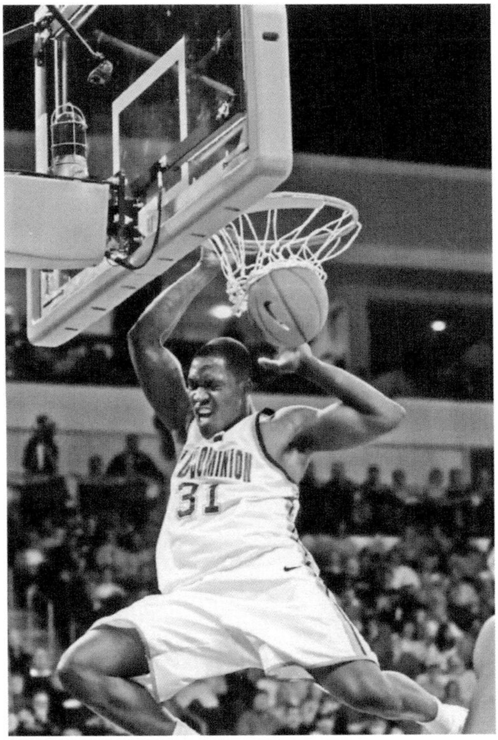

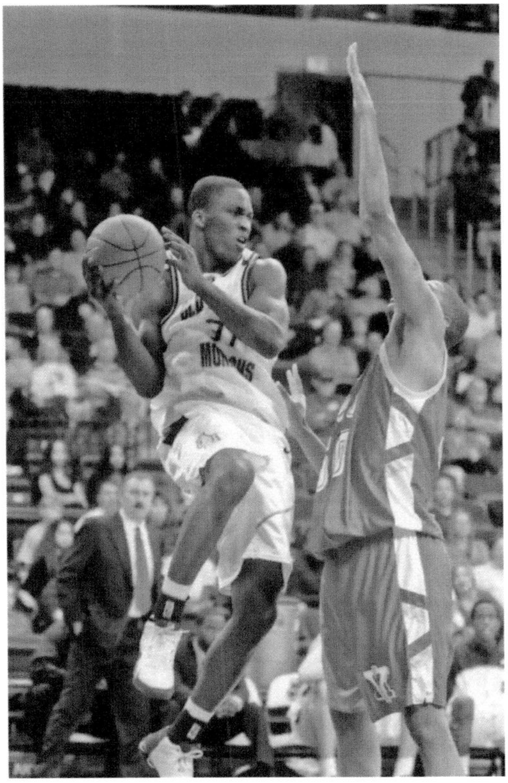

**MONSTER OF A GAME.** In a 2004–2005 game against Virginia Military Institute, sophomore Arnaud Dahi goes up over the outstretched arm of Tim Allmond. In only 21 minutes, Dahi scored 18 points, had 11 rebounds, 4 blocks, and 4 assists. The Monarchs would go on to easily defeat the Keydets by a score of 86-38. (ODU Archives.)

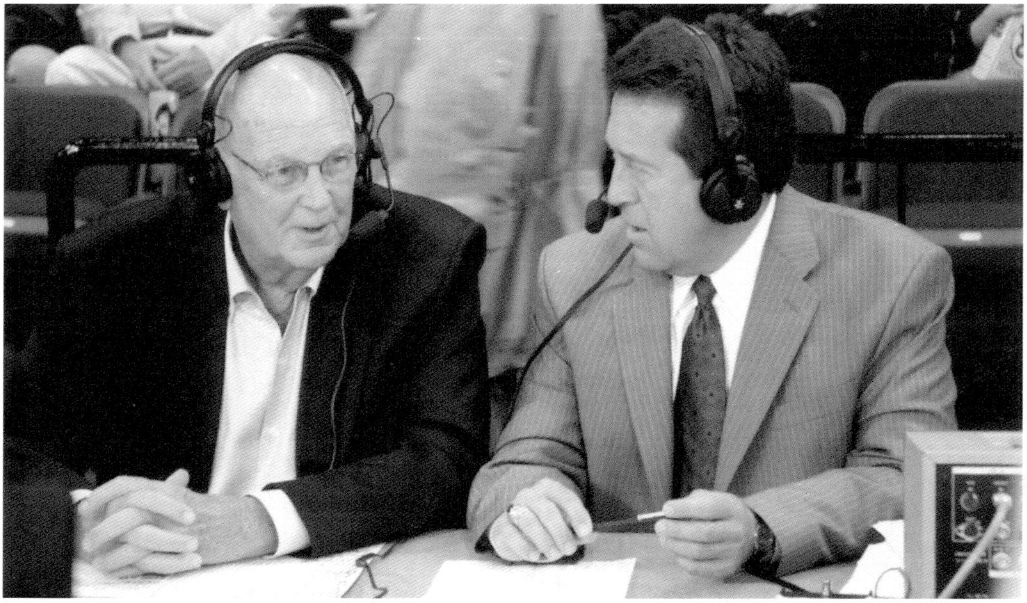

**Castleberry and the Ole' Lefthander.** Norfolk native coach Lefty Driesell (left) provides color commentary, as he and John Castleberry, "The Voice of the Monarchs," discuss a Monarch victory. As well as doing play-by-play for Old Dominion University basketball and the Norfolk Tides AAA franchise, John frequently broadcasts for CBS Radio Sports, Comcast Sports, and Westwood One. (ODU Archives.)

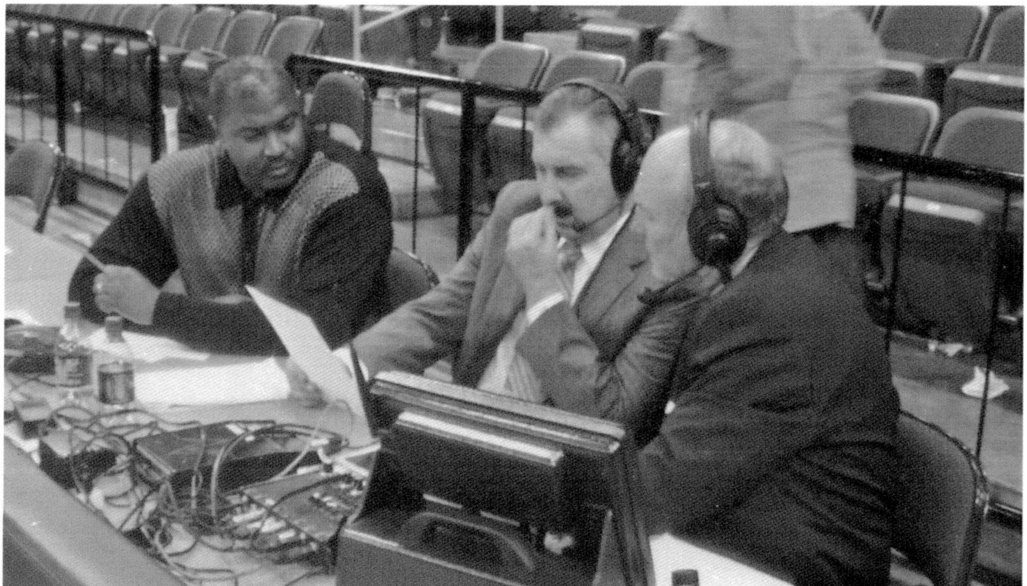

**Rick and Billy.** Rick Kiefner (right) and Billy Mann (left) discuss the game results with Coach Taylor (center) after an Old Dominion University win. Kiefner, class of 1969, and Mann, class of 1982, provide the color commentary on ESPN 1310 radio broadcasts at all Monarch home games and selected away contests. (ODU Archives.)

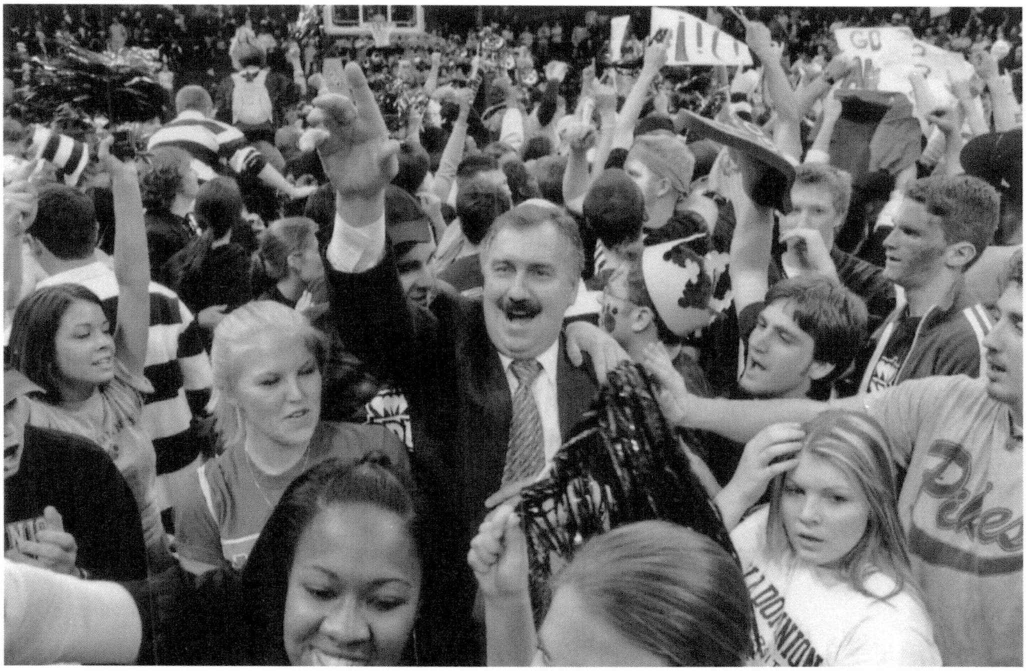

**Jubilant Celebration.** Coach Taylor and players are swarmed by hundreds of elated students on the floor of Richmond Coliseum after capturing the 2004–2005 CAA Championship. This was the Monarchs' first CAA crown under Taylor and his first step in bringing the basketball program back to prominence. (ODU Archives.)

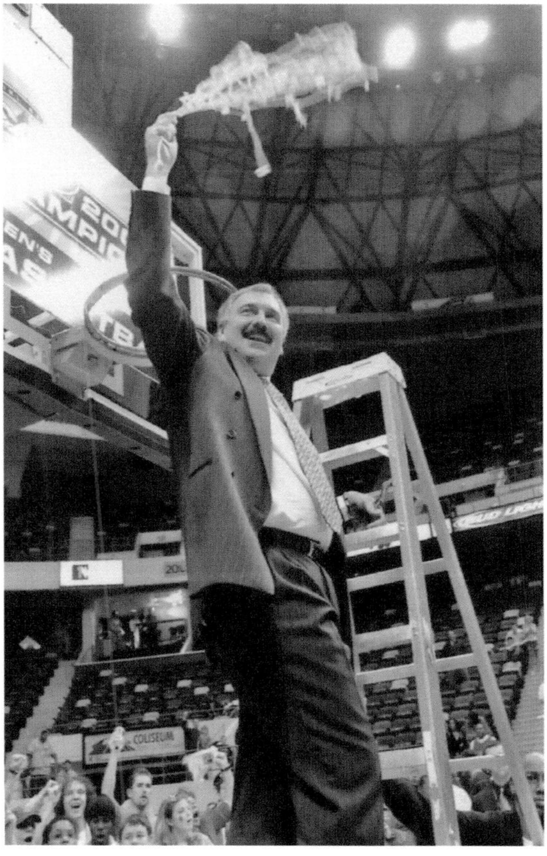

**A Wave in Victory.** A jubilant Blaine Taylor waves the net to Monarch fans after a 73-66 overtime victory over VCU in the 2004–2005 CAA Championship held at the Richmond Coliseum. The win assured the 28-5 Monarchs a bid to the NCAA Tournament. The Monarchs would lose a hard-fought game 89-81 to Michigan State. (ODU Archives.)

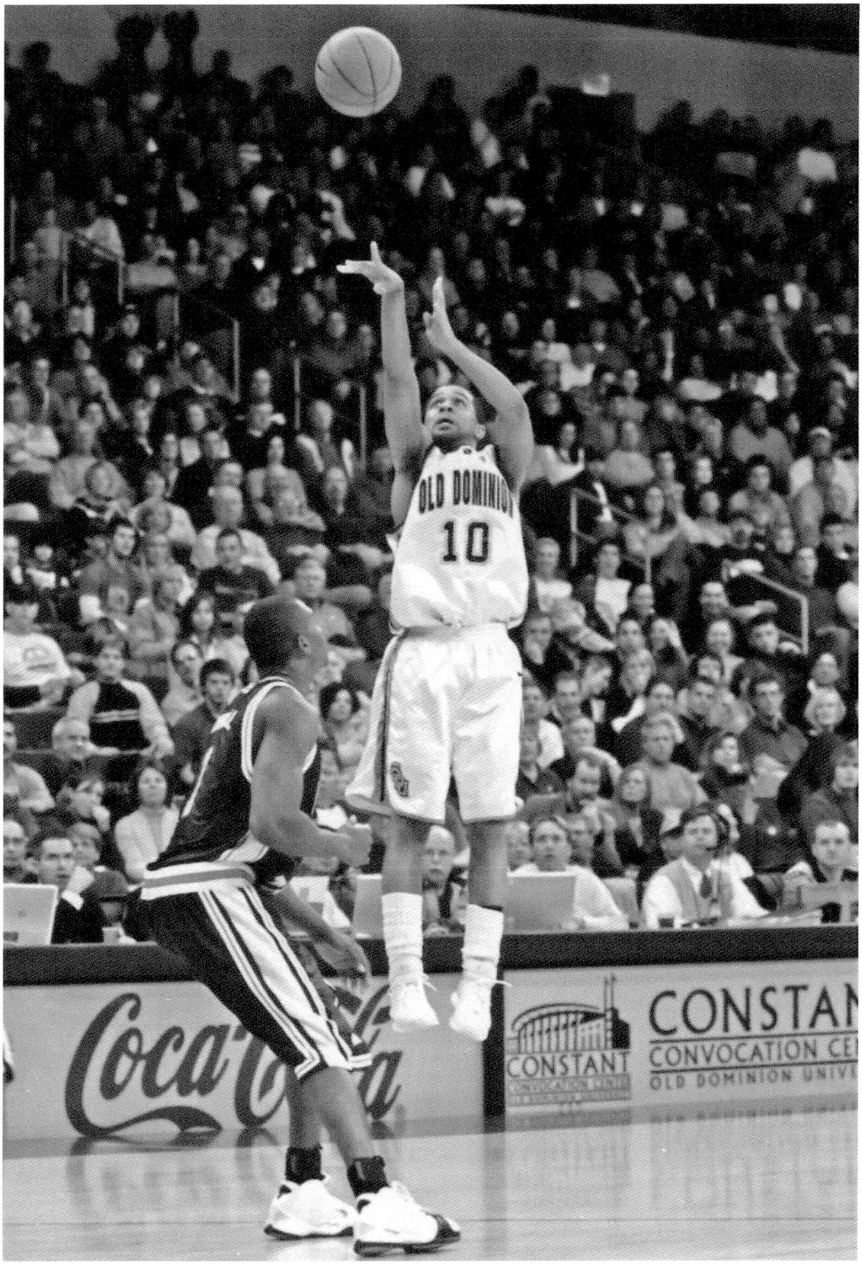


**Drew Williamson, 2004–2007.** For four years, this Burlington, North Carolina, native started at point guard for the Monarchs. Coming to Old Dominion as the 2003 North Carolina High School Male Athlete of the Year, Drew immediately made an impact on the court. He had all the tools and intangibles needed to lead the team. A tough, scrappy, and tenacious player with great court vision, Williamson made those around him better. Williamson regularly hit key shots to preserve Monarch victories. One of only two Monarch players in history with 500 assists and 200 steals, in 2007, he garnered Third Team All-CAA honors. Drew will go down as one of Old Dominion's finest guards. (ODU Archives.)

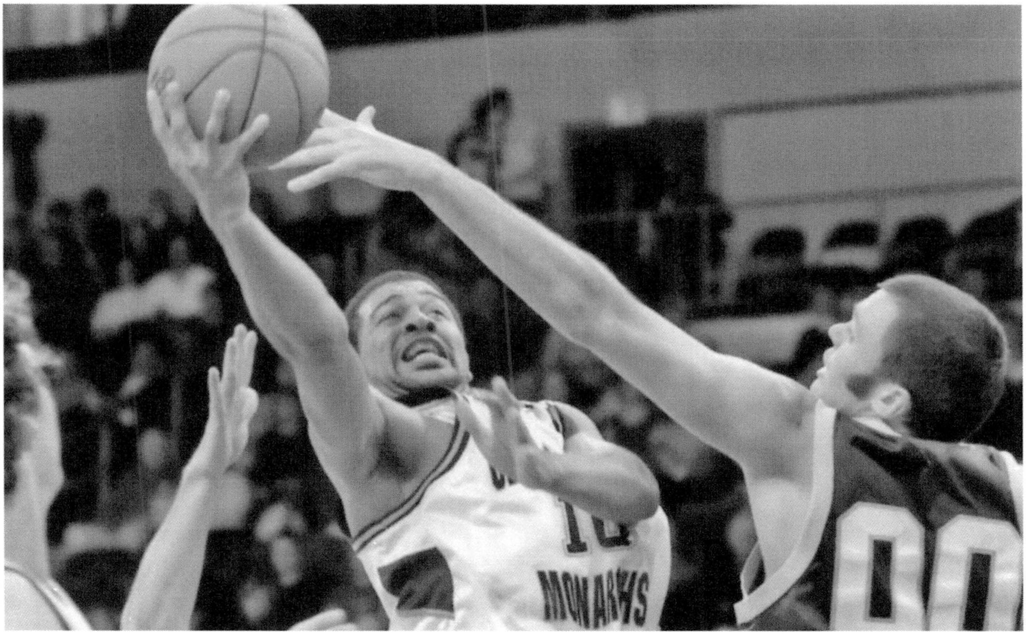


**DREW ATTEMPTS A LAYUP.** Drew Williamson attempts a layup in traffic against two defenders. As point guard, Drew was always looking for the open man, but was also never afraid to take the shot behind the three-point line or take the ball to the hole in traffic for one of his trademark layups. (ODU Archives.)

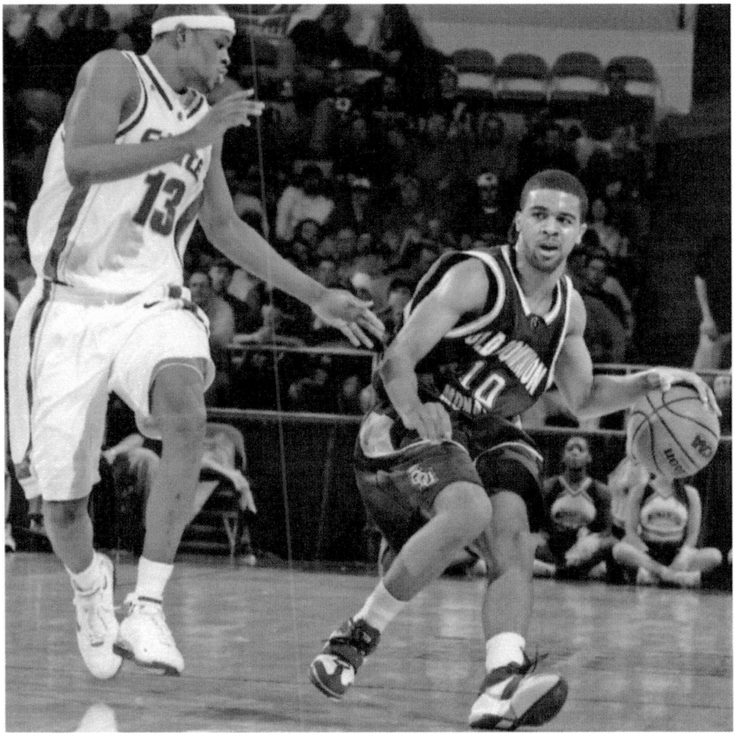


**DREW APPLIES THE BREAKS.** In the 2004–2005 NCAA Regional at Worcester, Massachusetts, Drew Williamson appears to be putting on the breaks against a Michigan State defender. Williamson, a sophomore, would score six points and dish off four assists against MSU. The Monarchs played with confidence and skill but lost in the last few minutes to the bigger, quicker, and stronger Spartans by a score of 89-81. (ODU Archives.)

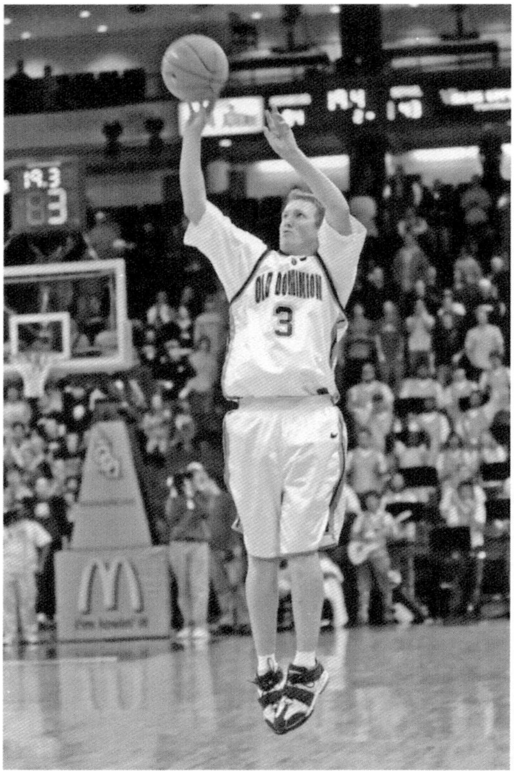

**JOHN MORRIS, 2002–2007.** When recruited by Old Dominion, this 6-foot-2-inch guard from Camp Hill, Pennsylvania, was one of only four players in the state to score over 2,000 points. A smart, tough, and heady player, Morris would often come into the game and hit a couple of three pointers in critical situations. A leader in the locker room and classroom, John graduated with a master's degree in business management. (ODU Archives.)

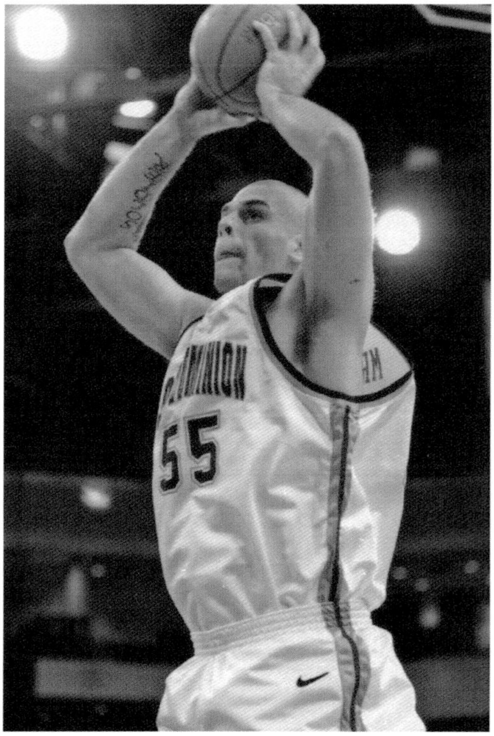

**JANKO, JANKO, JANKO.** Janko Mrksic a 6-foot-10-inch center from Ontario, Canada, helped to lead his Canadian Junior National Team to the finals of the world championship. Well liked by both players and fans, Mrksic rarely saw time on the court as a Monarch. However, whenever he entered a game, he was greeted with cheers of "Janko, Janko, Janko," by the "Jankonites," his own cheering squad at home games. (ODU Archives.)

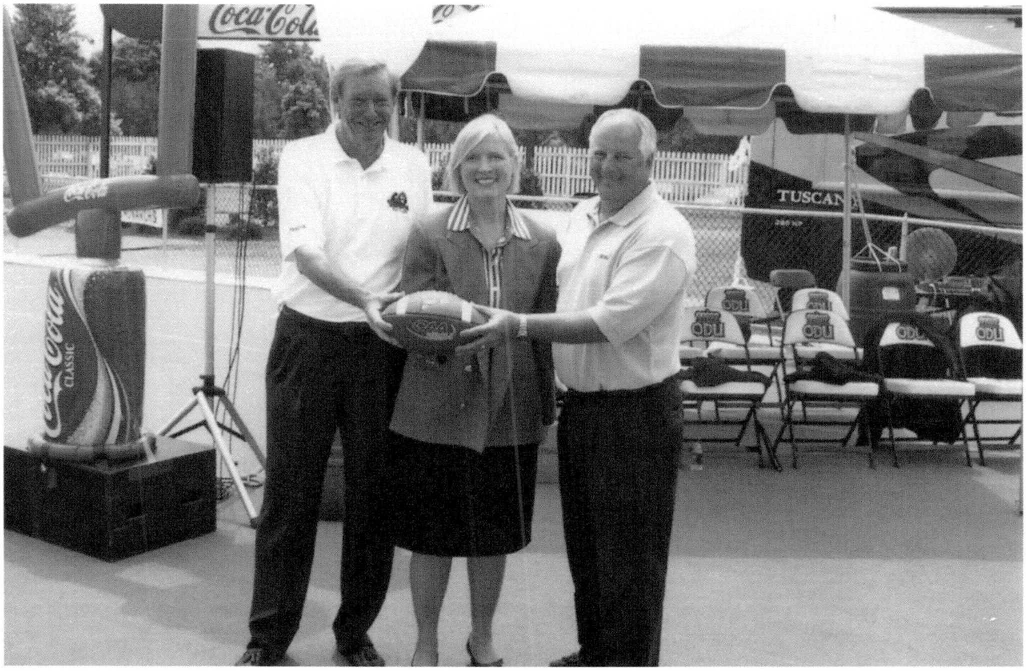


**Moving the University Forward.** Dr. Roseann Runte became the school's seventh president in 2001. Since coming to Old Dominion, Dr. Runte's leadership has been on display in both the academic and athletic programs. In this 2006 photograph, she is surrounded by Athletic Director Dr. Jim Jarrett (left) and CAA Commissioner Tom Yeager (right) as they announce the launching of football in fall 2009. (ODU Archives.)

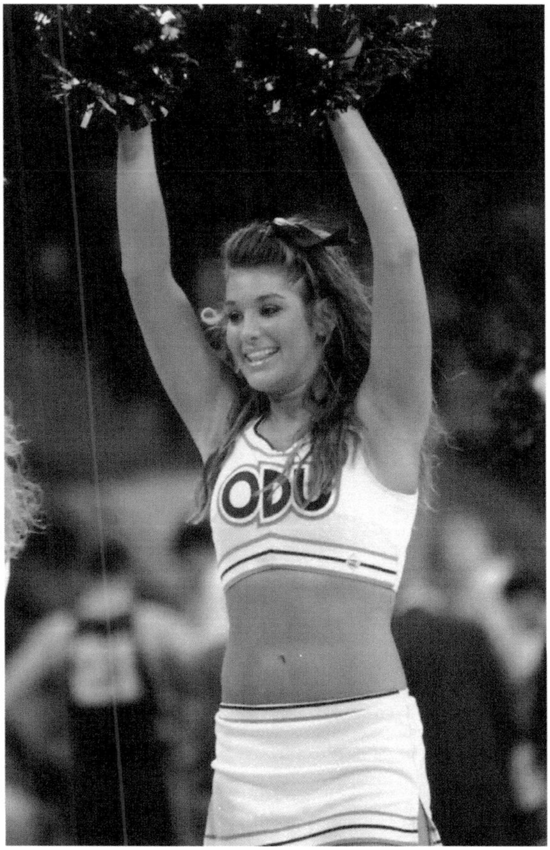


**Cheering for ODU.** Old Dominion cheerleader Briana Klink leads cheers at a 2006 Monarch basketball game. The cheerleading and dance squads at Old Dominion are a vital component in creating school spirit as they perform at all men's and women's home basketball games. Their hard work, determination, and dedication are evident at every game as they generate significant enthusiasm and vocal support. (ODU Archives.)

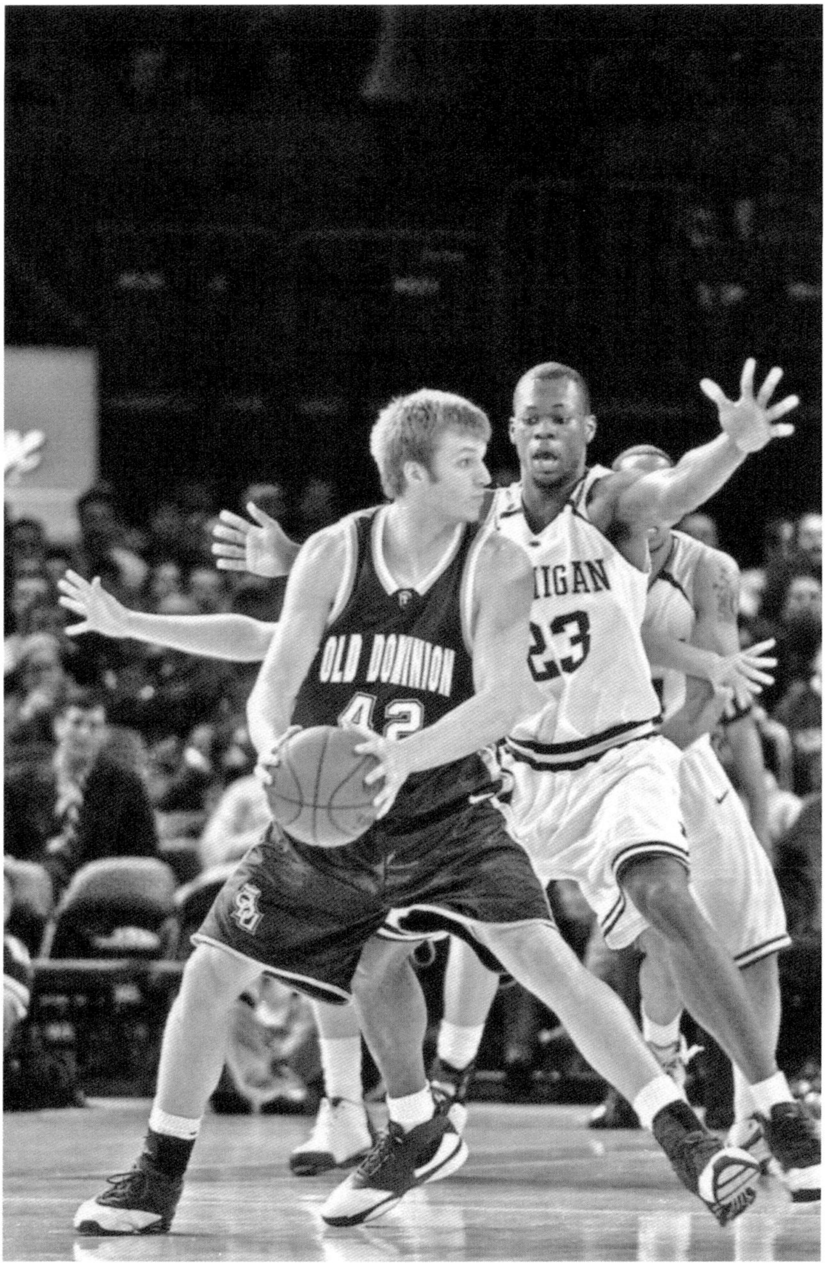


**Valdas Vasylius, 2004–2007.** Valdas Vasylius looks to make a pass in a 2006 NIT semi-final game against Michigan State. From 2004 to 2007, the 6-foot-7-inch forward from Klaipeda, Lithuania, was an important part of Old Dominion's success. Recruited out of Norfolk Collegiate, Vasylius was a strong, tough, and powerful left-handed player who was a threat both inside and outside for the Monarchs. With an ACL injury to Arnaud Dahi at the end of the 2005–2006 season, Valdas was called on to lead. He responded by averaging over 16 points a game and earning several double-doubles on the court. For his play in 2006–2007, Vasylius was selected First Team All-CAA. (ODU Archives.)

**VASYLIUS TAKES IT UP HARD.** Never one to avoid contact around the basket, Vasylius goes for two against the Manhattan Jaspers in a second-round NIT game on March 15, 2006. The Monarchs, playing before a home crowd, defeated the Jaspers 70-66 in a close game, advancing in the NIT. (ODU Archives.)

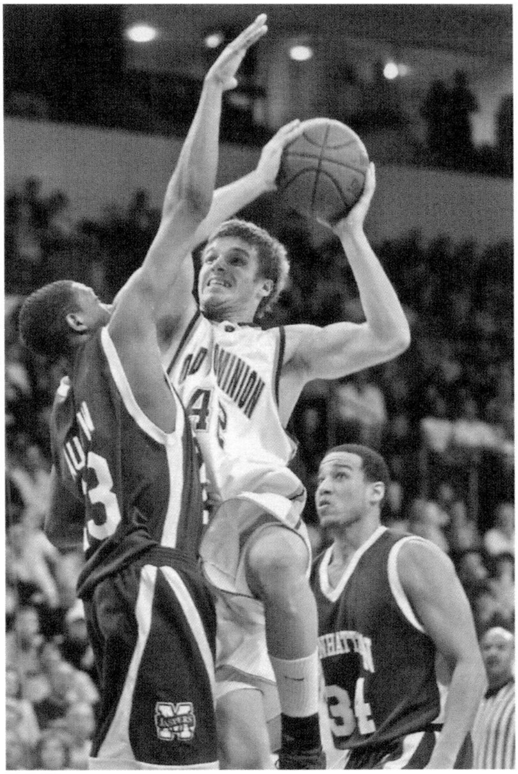


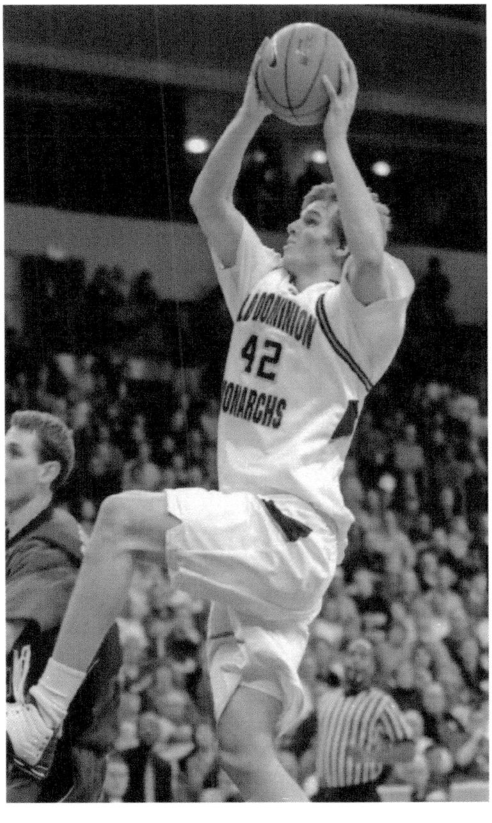


**VAL GOES FOR TWO.** Valdas Vasylius was the leading scorer for the Monarchs his senior season. In consecutive games against Virginia Commonwealth, Hofstra, and Toledo, Vasylius had three double-doubles for Old Dominion. In the Hofstra game, he scored a career-high 31 points and grabbed 12 rebounds for the Monarchs. (ODU Archives.)

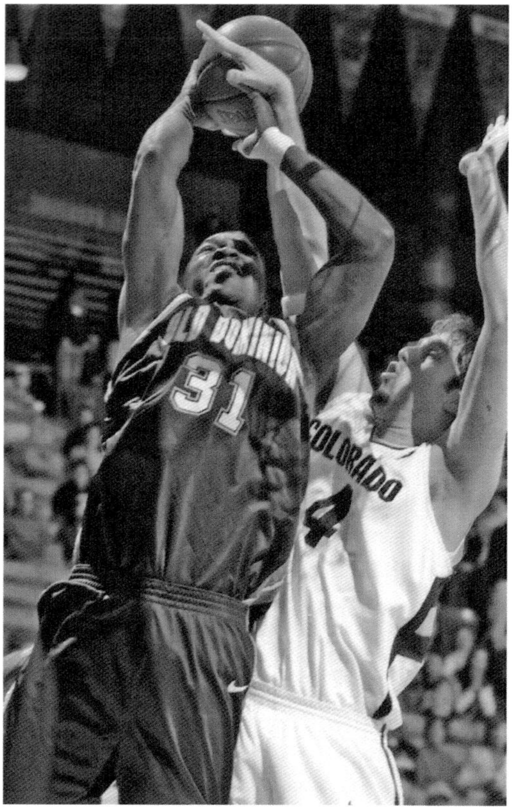


**DAHI BUFFALOES COLORADO.** Sent out west to meet Colorado in its first NIT matchup in 2006, the Monarchs slaughtered the Buffaloes 79-61. Arnaud Dahi scored 16 points and hauled down a game-high 10 rebounds for Old Dominion. Heavily favored Colorado, a member of the Big 12 Conference, was going for its 15th home win, a school record. The Monarchs win over Colorado set up a second-round game against Manhattan in Norfolk. (ODU Archives.)

**2006 NIT FINAL FOUR COACHES.** Smiling for the media in New York's famed Madison Square Garden are from left to right Dave Odom, South Carolina; Rick Pitino, University of Louisville; Blaine Taylor, Old Dominion University; and Tommy Amaker, University of Michigan. South Carolina would defeat Michigan in the finals to capture the 2006 National Invitational Tournament. (ODU Archives.)

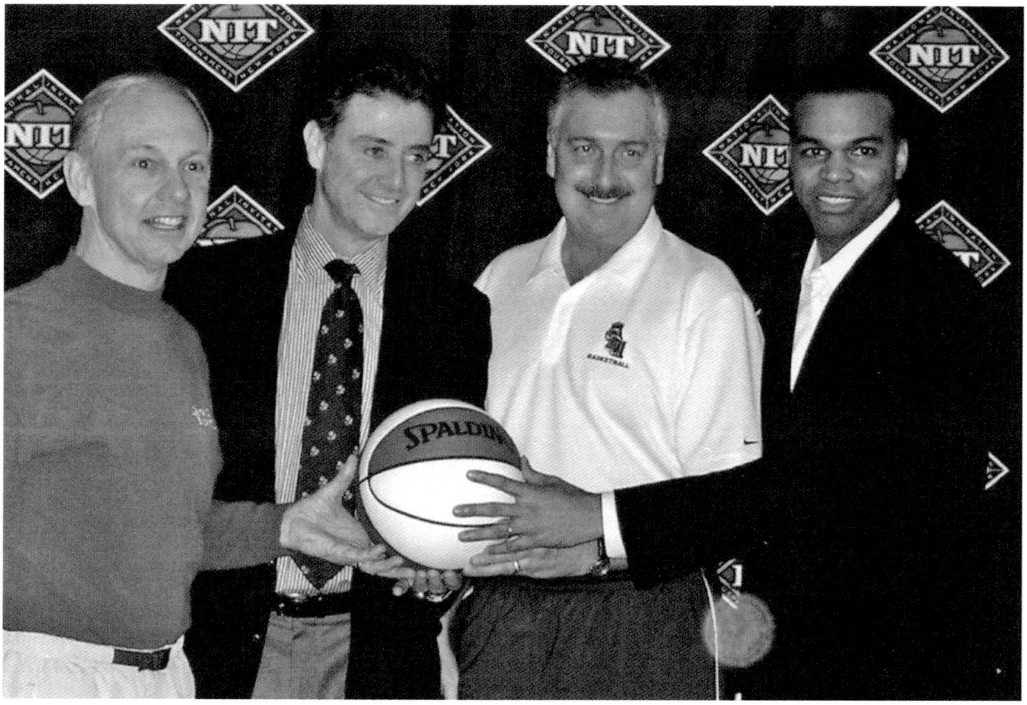

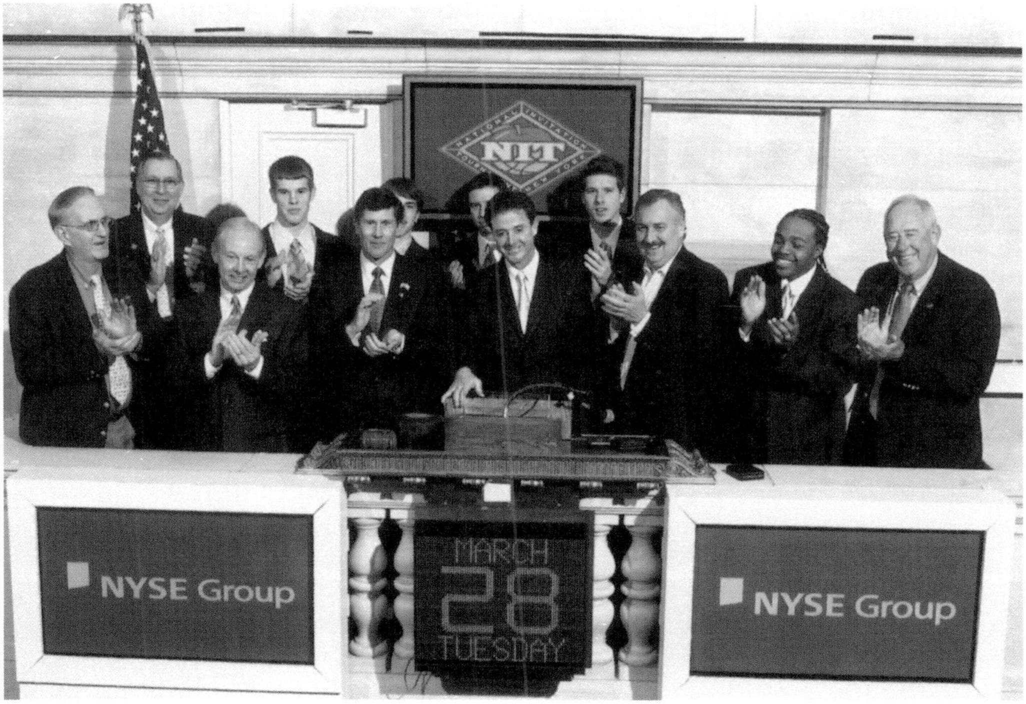


**MONARCH STOCK IS UP.** NIT and New York Stock Exchange officials surround Monarch coach Blaine Taylor, Rick Pitino from the University of Louisville, and Dave Odom from South Carolina. The coaches were there to ring the bell to start the March 28, 2006, biding on the floor of the exchange. The NYSE welcomed coaches and players to celebrate their success. (ODU Archive)

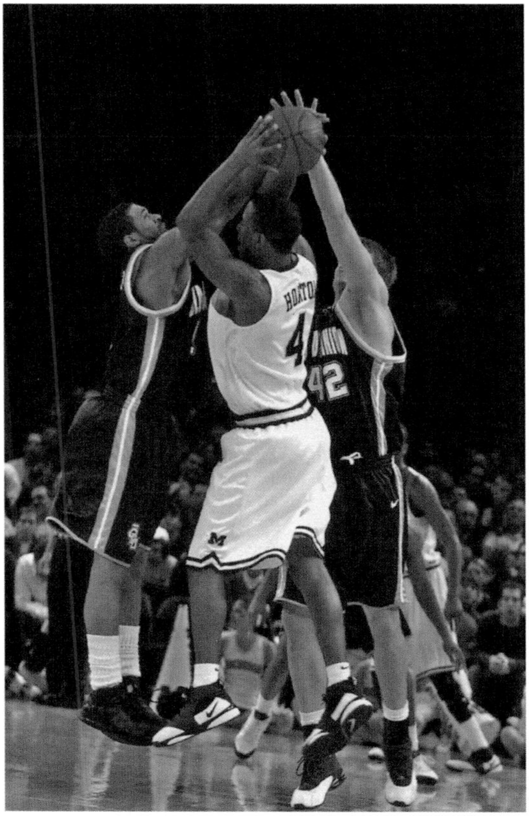

**TEAMING UP FOR A BLOCK ATTEMPT.** Drew Williamson and Valdas Vasylius attempt a block against a Michigan player in the semi-finals of the NIT. The Monarchs were ice cold, hitting only 28 percent of their field goals and losing to the Wolverines 66-43. To make matters worse, leading Monarch scorer Arnaud Dahi went down with a severe knee injury. (ODU Archives.)

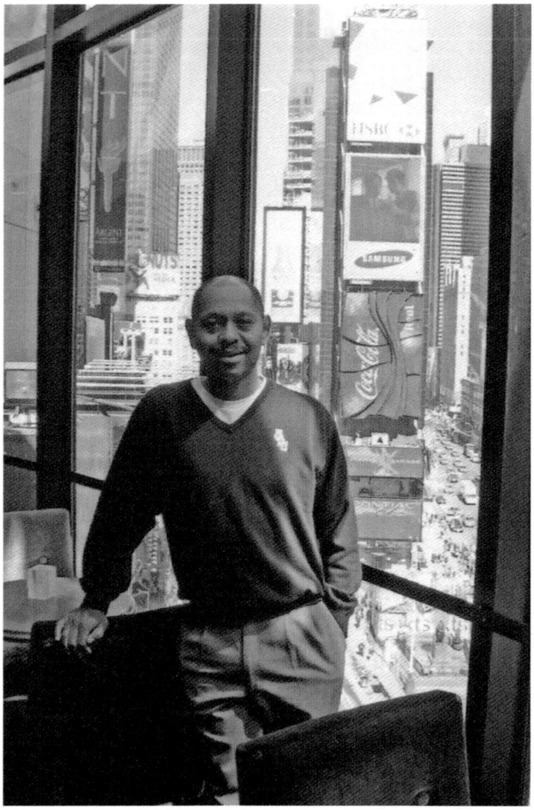

**Old Dominion's Sports Information Director.** No one knows the history of Old Dominion sports better than Carol Hudson. Here Hudson poses in a restaurant in Madison Square Garden during the 2005–2006 NIT. Since 1973, he has been a regular fixture at Old Dominion sporting events. A student manager for the 1975 Division II NCAA Champions, Hudson has been Old Dominion's SID for over 25 years. (ODU Archives.)

**Taking a Breather.** Drew Williamson and a teammate take a rest for several minutes before returning to the January 29, 2007, game against Winthrop. Williamson would have 12 points, 6 assists, and 5 rebounds to go along with 23 by Brian Henderson. The Eagles would defeat the Monarchs 71-63 in a close affair. (CSTG.)

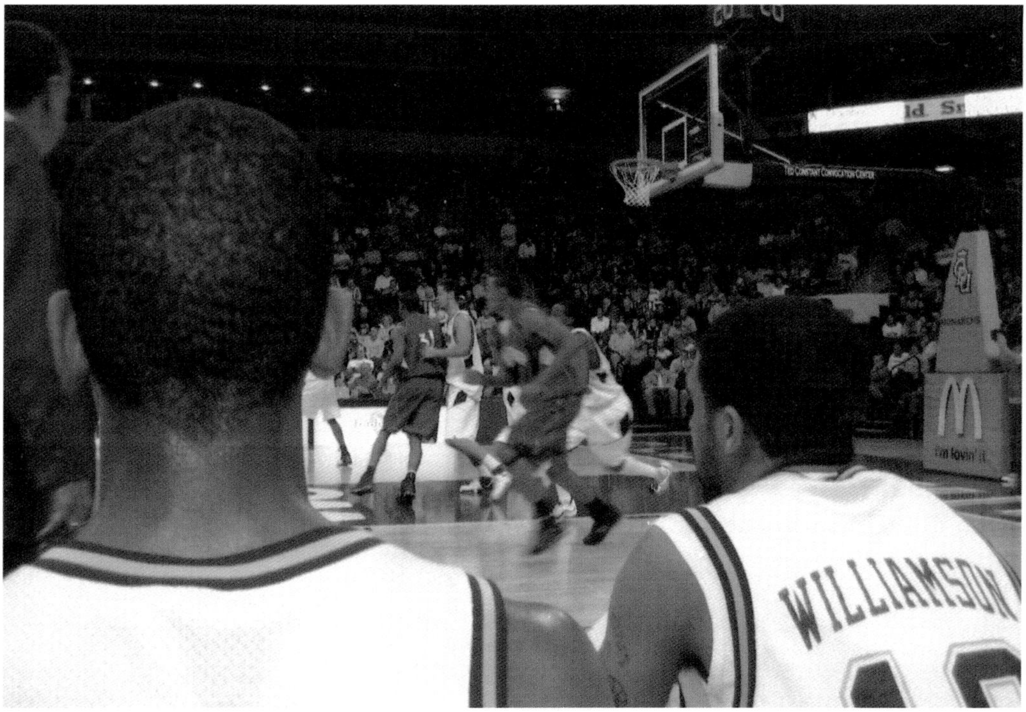

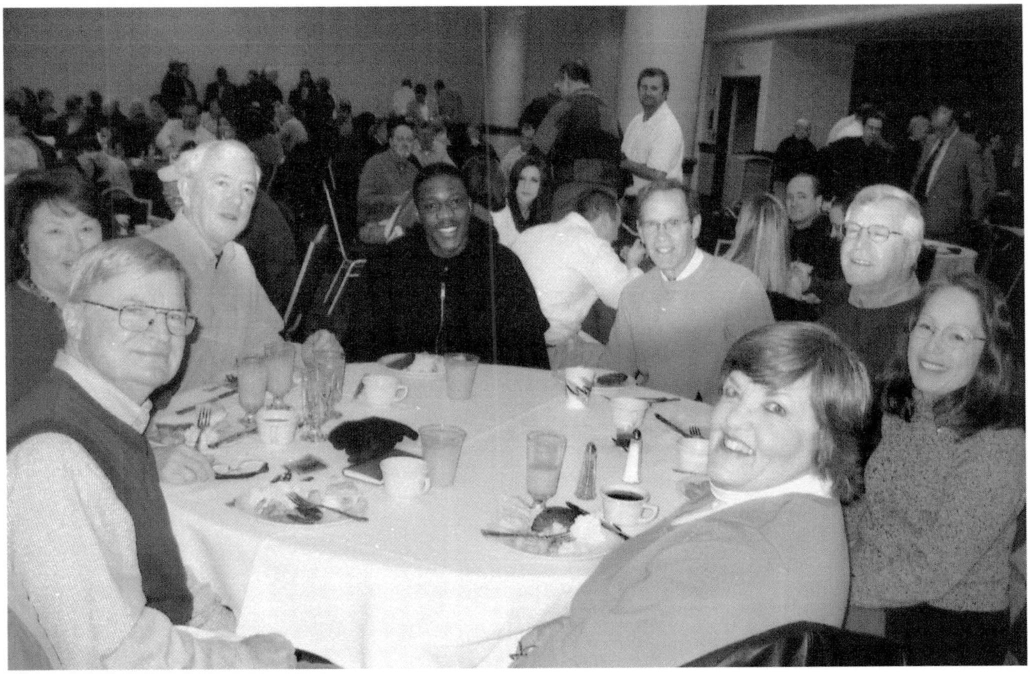

**Hoops Club Breakfast.** On February 5, 2007, Old Dominion hosted a breakfast to honor the seniors. Since coming to ODU, Taylor has instituted the breakfasts to introduce his players to the Monarch faithful. From left to right are Jerry Brown, Pat Keilty, Fred Keilty, Arnaud Dahi, Hervey Trimeyer, Pete Keilty, Bev Keilty, and Barbara Brown. (CSTG.)

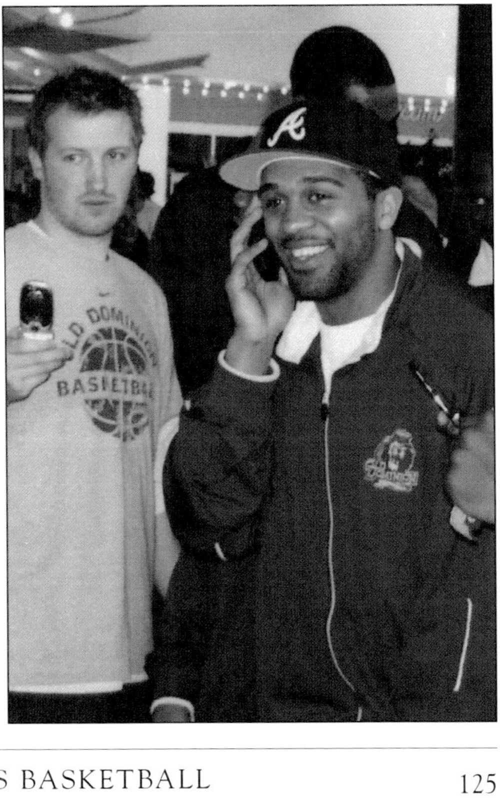

**NCAA Pairing Party.** Monarch seniors John Morris (left) and Drew Williamson (right) call family and friends only minutes after Old Dominion's name flashed on the screen during the 2007 CBS Selection Sunday broadcast. Players and fans met at the House of Blues Café, located on campus in Webb Center, to see if Old Dominion would get a bid and whom they would meet. (ODU Archives.)

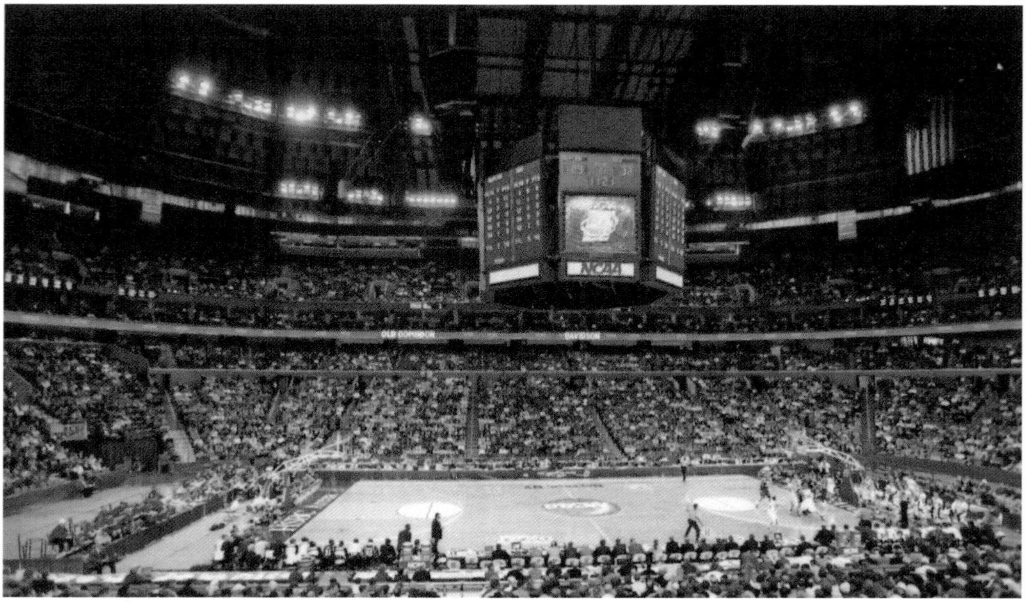

**HSBC ARENA, MARCH 15, 2007.** Old Dominion University faced the Butler Bulldogs in the NCAA Mid-West Regional before 18,649 in a sold-out HSBC Arena in Buffalo, New York. The Monarchs were stymied by the Bulldogs defense and were defeated 57-46 in a first-round NCAA matchup. After ODU's game in the afternoon, fellow CAA rival Virginia Commonwealth University would meet Duke in an evening contest. (ODU Archives)

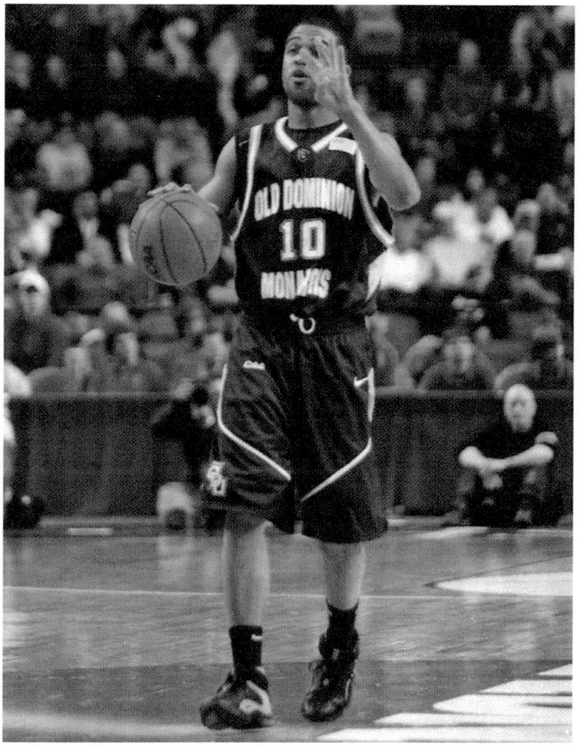

**DREW CALLS A PLAY.** Old Dominion point guard Drew Williamson signals a play in a game against Butler in the first round of the NCAA Tournament. The game would be the last for Williamson as a Monarch. Drew, a senior, along with Valdas Vasylius, Arnaud Dahi, and John Morris, were part of the winningest class in Old Dominion's history. Over their career they garnered an impressive 93 victories. (Tom Wolf/ODU Archives)

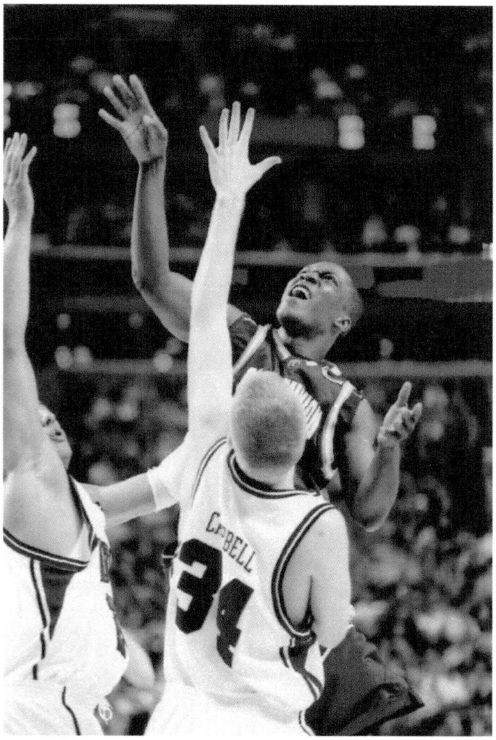


**DAHI PUTS UP A SHOT.** Monarch forward Arnaud Dahi puts up a shot over two Butler defenders in a 2007 NCAA first-round tournament game. After defeating the Monarchs, the Bulldogs would defeat the University of Maryland and advanced to the Sweet Sixteen. Dahi would finish the game, his last as a Monarch, with 10 points. The 6-foot-7-inch forward completed his career as a Monarch with 1,323 points. (Tom Wolf/ODU Archives.)

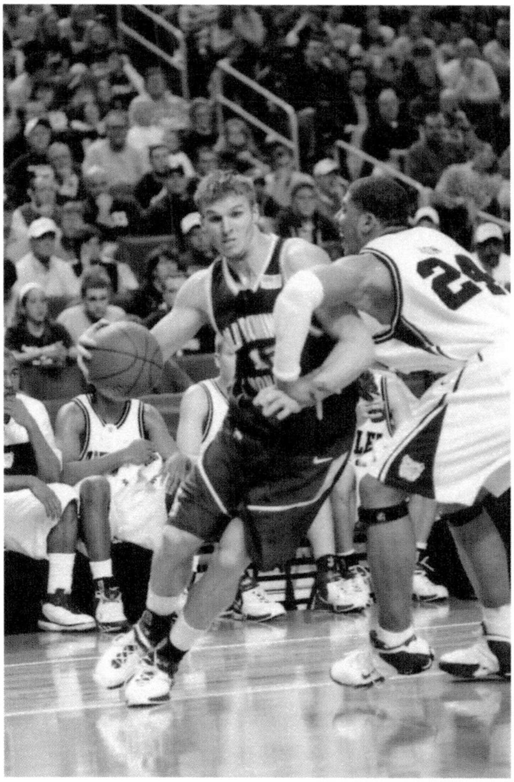


**VAL ATTEMPTS TO DRIVE.** Old Dominion University forward Valdas Vyslius looks for a lane to the basket in a game against Butler University in the 2007 NCAA Tournament. The Monarchs, who led at halftime, could not find their range in the second half and were defeated 57-46. Vasylius, the team's leading scorer for the season, would score only 10 points in the game. For his career Vasylius would end up with 1,345 points. (Tom Wolf/ODU Archives.)

Find Your Place in History.

www.arcadiapublishing.com

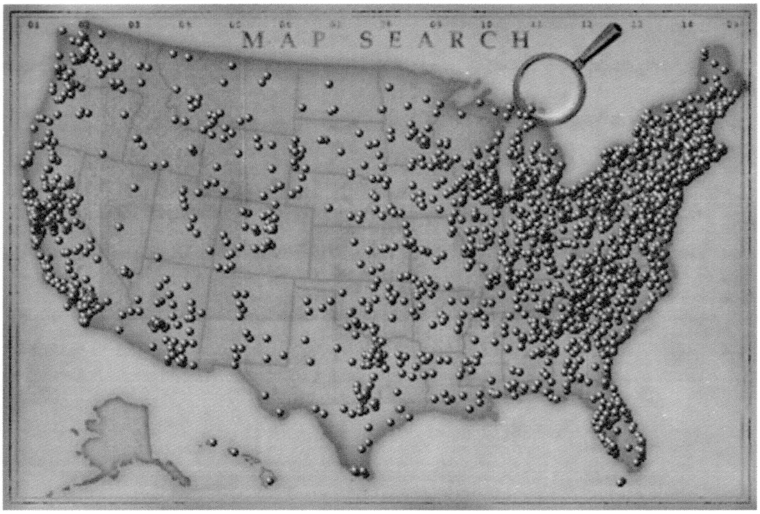


Discover books about the town where you grew up, the cities where your friends and families live, the town where your parents met, or even that retirement spot you've been dreaming about. Our Web site provides history lovers with exclusive deals, advanced notification about new titles, e-mail alerts of author events, and much more.

MADE IN THE USA

Arcadia Publishing, the leading local history publisher in the United States, is committed to making history accessible and meaningful through publishing books that celebrate and preserve the heritage of America's people and places. Consistent with our mission to preserve history on a local level, this book was printed in South Carolina on American-made paper and manufactured entirely in the United States.

This book carries the accredited Forest Stewardship Council (FSC) label and is printed on 100 percent FSC-certified paper. Products carrying the FSC label are independently certified to assure consumers that they come from forests that are managed to meet the social, economic, and ecological needs of present and future generations.

FSC
Mixed Sources
Product group from well-managed forests and other controlled sources

Cert no. SW-COC-001530
www.fsc.org